THE KING OF SPRING

THE KING OF SPRING

The Life and Times of Peter O'Connor

Mark Quinn

The Liffey Press

Published by
The Liffey Press Ltd
Ashbrook House, 10 Main Street
Raheny, Dublin 5, Ireland
www.theliffeypress.com

© 2004 Mark Quinn

A catalogue record of this book is
available from the British Library.

ISBN 1-904148-52-2

Photographic still from Twentieth Century Fox film
Golden West © 1932 Twentieth Century Fox. All rights reserved.

Photograph of builders of the *Nellie Bywater* taken from the book
Schoonerman by Captain Richard England, published by Hollis & Carter.
Reprinted by permission of The Random House Group Ltd.

Printed in the Republic of Ireland by Colour Books Ltd.

CONTENTS

This book is dedicated to Tom, Rosemary and Rachel.

Prologue

IN AUGUST 2001 A SPECIAL ONE-OFF sports event was held in Waterford Athletic Stadium to celebrate the centenary of Peter O'Connor's world record long jump in 1901. A hundred years before, O'Connor had launched himself into athletic history by jumping 24' 11¾". The new record created shockwaves across the English-speaking world. No one had ever come so close to breaking the 25-foot barrier, an aspiration mirrored in the attempt to run a four-minute mile in the 1950s. Since the early 1880s, Irish jumpers had proved themselves the dominant force in the world of long jumping. With a few exceptions, Irishmen had held the world record for the best part of 20 years. Now once again an Irishman was redefining the boundaries of human accomplishment, throwing down the gauntlet to a stunned world of athletics.

Exactly 100 years later, to the day, Danny McGrath, a veteran Irish athlete, was a guest at the unveiling of a plaque marking O'Connor's achievement in the jumping pit at Waterford Athletic Stadium. Although it was a fine summer's day, with just a light breeze, only a few hundred people turned out for the event. It was a far cry from the heady days in 1901 when O'Connor drew crowds in their thousands to watch him jump. Back in the early years of the twentieth century Irish athletics was in its heyday and Irish athletes figured amongst the best in the world, proving themselves especially adept at jumping and throwing events. Sports coverage in the press was extensive and there was even a weekly newspaper, *Sport*, entirely dedicated to the comprehensive reporting of athletics, GAA, racing and cycling news.

Danny made his way to the long jumping pit, nimbly negotiating the clusters of dignitaries and onlookers on the track. On his way he stopped briefly to greet and share a few words with some of Peter O'Connor's grandchildren and great-grandchildren. It was then, just before the ceremony commenced, that I was introduced to Danny. I told him I was researching the life of Peter O'Connor and wondered if he had ever met him or remembered anecdotes about him. With the news that there might be a book in the offing, a glint came into his eye and Danny took me by the arm and quietly whispered, "I'll tell you something. Peter O'Connor was a great man; there's hardly a man alive in Ireland today who'd be a patch on him. He really deserves much more than this. If people today only had met him, they'd know." With that Danny ambled off to perform his duty in witnessing the unveiling of the plaque to his old friend. A quarter of an hour later a host of young aspiring athletes took to the track for the day's sports, a few casting sheepish, lingering glances at O'Connor's record of 24' 11¾", etched on the plaque by the jumping pit.

A few weeks later I went to visit Danny at his home in Cappoquin in County Waterford, to see if I could find out a little bit more about the man whose life I was gradually trying to piece together. Because Peter O'Connor had died in 1957, there were not very many people who had clear recollections of him apart from a few descendants. Meeting Danny was a golden opportunity to talk to someone who had known Peter well and had even travelled to the Olympic Games with him. In the late 1930s and early 1940s, Danny was one of Ireland's brightest medal prospects and was on a selection panel for the 1940 Tokyo Olympics. He was just coming into his own as an athlete when war broke out in Europe. One memorable day in 1941, when he was at his athletic peak, Danny won four Munster titles: the 220 yards, 440 yards, high jump and discus. By the time hostilities ceased in 1945, Danny's best years as an athlete were over and with them any realistic aspirations of representing Ireland at Olympic Games. Nonetheless, in 1948 when the opportunity arose to travel to the new-hope London Games, he jumped at the chance. One of his companions on the trip was Peter O'Connor, then aged 76. This was to be Peter O'Connor's last attendance at an Olympic event. Since competing in Athens in 1906, he had been to every successive Olympic Festival and, despite his venerable age, his love of travel and athletics was as strong as ever.

When Danny had finished telling me about his trip to the 1948 London Games, how they had travelled, what they had talked about, and his impressions of London after the Blitz, we set off from Cappoquin for Ardmore, one of the most scenic spots in County Waterford and the site of one of Ireland's finest round towers and monastic sites. There a close friend of Danny's, Con Power, was on holiday with his family. Con's father, Denis, had been part of the original "invasion team" that the GAA sent to America in 1888 to drum up support for Gaelic football and hurling, as well as to generate funds for the Association back home. Though Con had never met Peter O'Connor, he had many colourful stories to relate regarding the man and his legacy.

Before we went back in time to discuss Peter O'Connor's era, Danny and Con began to recount stories about O'Callaghan and Tisdall, Ireland's gold medal heroes at the 1932 Los Angeles Olympics. Peter O'Connor had travelled to Los Angeles as an official of the National Athletic and Cycling Association of Ireland (NACA) and was one of the judges of the long jump contest. In recalling O'Callaghan, Con said he had never seen a man so self-contained or sure of himself. He looked as if nothing could faze him. O'Callaghan had been the first Irish athlete to win a gold medal after the formation of the Irish Free State in 1922. This was in the shot-put event at the Amsterdam Games in 1928. Four years later he retained his Olympic title in Los Angeles and might have added a third in a row had Ireland been able to send a team to Berlin in 1936. O'Callaghan was the first Irishman to have the Irish tricolour raised at an Olympic Games. Danny, who had been listening attentively, pointed out, however, that O'Callaghan's win in 1928 was not the first time an Irish *flag* had graced the Olympic stage. That moment belonged to Peter O'Connor.

Almost a quarter of a century before, at the Intercalated Games in Athens in 1906, three Irishmen made an international protest, the first overtly political act of a modern Olympics. Having moved swiftly and clandestinely to the centre of the ancient Olympic marble stadium, a tall thin Irishman scaled a 20-foot pole and then unfurled a large green flag. A crowd of almost 60,000 looked on, first in bemusement, then with apprehension as Greek soldiers and officials rushed to the scene. The efforts to bring down the daredevil scaling the heights were hampered by a duo of Irishmen, Con Leahy and John Daly, who were standing guard at the base of the pole, causing a stand off with the Greek military. Like everyone else, the Greek soldiers, known as *evzones* (who belonged to an elite infantry regiment and wore traditional kilt-like uniforms), were taken completely unawares. Throughout the Games there was a significant military presence in the stadium to ensure no crowd trouble since the Greek and British royal families were in attendance daily. There had been some signs of social unrest, culminating in a riot outside a hotel in which participants from the Games were staying. The last thing the highly trained *evzones* probably expected was trouble from the participants themselves. Yet there, plain for all to see, precariously perched at the top of a pole, a renegade Irishman called Peter O'Connor vigorously waved a large green flag. He stayed up there for several minutes to make sure everyone in the stadium could see the flag's green hue and perhaps make out the gold lettering that was immaculately embroidered in Irish, beneath the symbol of a Celtic harp: *Erin go Bragh*, Ireland forever.

The Irishmen's actions were a direct snub to Crown Prince George of Greece, who had insisted that a Union Jack be raised should one of the three Irish athletes win a medal at the Games. As the Union Jack was raised to signify O'Connor's silver in the long jump, the Irishmen had moved into action, hijacking the occasion to show the assembled world media where their true allegiances lay. It was a bold act of defiance calculated to cause maximum embarrassment to the British royal family. In time it would become Peter O'Connor's calling card, the exploit that guaranteed him a footnote in the annals of early Olympic history.

Peter O'Connor's name has gradually slipped from the national consciousness, and even the circumstances surrounding this significant episode have become blurred. Yet Peter O'Connor's plight is not unusual. He was but one of a number of Irish athletes competing in the early twentieth century who left an awesome legacy for successive generations to emulate but whose stories have been long since forgotten.

Ever since I began researching the life of Peter O'Connor, I became drawn into a world that I never knew existed. I was amazed to discover that for a brief scintillating golden era in the late nineteenth and early twentieth century, Ireland produced a large number of world and Olympic champions. Delving into Olympic and Irish athletic historical records, the incredible success story of Irishmen in track and field in that period came to light. Contemporaries of O'Connor such as Tom Kiely, John Flanagan, Martin Sheridan, Con and Pat Leahy, had few if any equals in domestic or international competition. Many of these now forgotten sporting heroes left Ireland for America and represented the "western democracy" in the early Olympics. Reluctant to represent the United Kingdom, athletes such as Sheridan and Flanagan were high-profile members of an extensive Irish sporting diaspora who represented various countries under different flags. O'Connor was one of the star athletes who chose to stay in Ireland, although the Athens episode clearly demonstrated his nationalist ideals.

As Danny talked enthusiastically about Peter O'Connor, it became clear that he regarded the Irish long jumper as amongst the best athletes that Ireland has produced. O'Connor was cut from the same cloth as the likes of Bob Tisdall, Pat O'Callaghan and Ronnie Delaney, to name but three. Yet his generation of athletes had competed before the advent of radio and television. Consequently, there were no visual records to cement the collective memory of the Irish people.

When I began researching the life of Peter O'Connor, I was amazed to discover that very little was known about him. Not even his family were sure when or where he was born. In the course of his life, he built up a well-known solicitor's practice and was to all intents and purposes the epitome of middle-class respectability, and it was this image of the man which persisted long after he had died. Those who remember him today often do so because the solicitor's office still bears his name in Waterford. More often than not, it is presumed that O'Connor came from a well-to-do, affluent family and had a comfortable start in life, as well as a comprehensive education. Such presumptions could not be further from the truth, as O'Connor's life story is far more complex than appears at first glance. The finely dressed, well-spoken man of later years, whose home was a fine Georgian house in the affluent Newtown area of Waterford, had to earn his position in society the hard way. There was no soft landing for the young Peter O'Connor. Coming from relatively humble origins and with only a basic primary education, O'Connor was very much a self-made man, his ambition in life fuelled by a desire to prove himself to the world. What follows is an attempt to piece together his extraordinary life story, spanning eight decades, and the forgotten world in which he moved, a time when Irish giants of athletics held the world in thrall.

1

Birth and Background

U P TO RECENTLY THERE HAD always been a certain amount of confusion as to the precise place and year of Peter O'Connor's birth. It was well known that his family had been in the Wicklow area for generations, yet the registration of his birth could not be found in local records. The story behind how he came to be born in England mirrors that of countless Irish men and women who were born across the water as a result of their parents' migration to find steady work. Unlike many Irish migratory labourers of the nineteenth century, Edward O'Connor was a skilled artisan who could command a good price for his shipwrighting skills. Edward was one of a select number of shipwrights engaged to construct the first maritime vessel built by a new shipyard in Millom in Cumberland. The vessel was a schooner that would become known as the *Nellie Bywater* and was the last fully rigged schooner to be built in the British Isles.[1]

On 24 October 1872, Mary O'Connor gave birth to her third child, a boy. In attendance was her delighted husband Edward who had been waiting expectantly for his family's latest addition. The birth was without complications and both mother and son were deemed healthy. Two days later the proud parents had their son baptised in the church of Our Lady and St James in Millom. The baby boy was named Peter after Mary's father, Peter O'Brien. Six weeks later in December his birth was registered in the district of Bootle in Cumberland, as it was then known.

At the beginning of the nineteenth century, Millom had been a small nondescript town of sandstone and slate cottages, situated at the estuary of the Duddon river on the northwest coast of England. In 1850, the discovery of iron ore deposits near the shores of Hodbarrow point, in the vicinity of the small port, led to the opening of a mine. Now strategically placed near a valuable natural resource, the town quickly expanded and became a thriving, bustling seaport. When an iron works and a railway connection followed the opening of the mine, it was not long before some of Millom's leading citizens felt a shipyard was a commercial necessity to ensure the economic growth of the town. A famous Welsh shipbuilder, William Thomas, came to Millom and opened up shop on the shores of the Duddon; his first project, the construction of a schooner of 99 registered tons, an ambitious undertaking for a shipyard with no track record. To ensure the project would get off on a sure footing, Thomas engaged the services of Hugh Jones, an experienced shipwright, to act as foreman. The schooner would be built to Jones's design and the best craftsmen employed.[2] Since there was no existing shipbuilding tradition in Millom, Jones sent out word on the grapevine that there was the promise of several months of well-paid work for experienced shipwrights. A short hop away on the other side of the Irish channel, Edward O'Connor must have got wind of the job. In the summer of 1872, Edward travelled to Millom with his pregnant wife and young family in tow and settled into lodgings in Wellington Street. On 24 October of that year Peter O'Connor was born in Wellington Street, Millom, in the small district of Bootle in the county of Cumberland, in the reign of Queen Victoria and within the jurisdiction of the British Empire. As work on the schooner was winding down and the final preparations were being put in place for *Nellie Bywater*'s launch, Edward crossed the Irish Sea once again and brought his family back home to Wicklow.

Wicklow town's location on the east coast of Ireland at the mouth of the River Vartry, some 30 miles south of Dublin, makes it a natural port of call for ships. The Celts called the area *Inbhear Deas*, "the beautiful inlet", but the settlement situated at the estuary of the River Vartry takes its name from the Danish *Wigginge Lough*, meaning the "Lake of the Ships".[3] The Vikings were the first to recognise the importance of the site as a strategic outpost and established a trading station there in the eighth century, effectively founding the town. Reluctant to venture inland, the Vikings clung close to the eastern seaboard, Wicklow forming a vital link in a chain of settlements connecting Dublin, Arklow and Waterford. By the early nineteenth century, Wicklow town was ostensibly a fishing village with a limited amount of trade and commerce, a small but convenient safe haven for ships seeking shelter when storms battered the Wicklow coastline. The town's fortunes and that of the entire county took a dramatic turn in the 1830s when valuable hidden natural resources were discovered in various pockets of the county, most notably lead deposits in Avoca. During the next half century, Wicklow town established itself as an important port of call on the east coast, gradually expanding and improving its harbour, and in 1865 harbour works were completed, providing adequate berthing facilities for an increased number of ships.[4]

Wicklow town must have been an exciting place for Peter O'Connor to grow up in the 1870s. As a busy port and trading outpost, there would have been a constant to-ing and fro-ing of boats and visitors to the coastal town. No doubt many of the ships' captains and assorted hands would have had tales of adventure and exotic places to regale to young lads such as Peter. Though the town was the second biggest population centre in the county of Wicklow after Arklow, numbering some 3,404 in 1864, it had a small and relatively close-knit community. Somewhat incongruously placed at the end of High Street, Wicklow Gaol stood as a reminder of the county's troubled past. Though there had been little if any civil disturbance in Wicklow since Robert Emmet's Rising of 1803, the United Irishmen's five-year struggle against the English authorities would have been fresh in the collective memory of most Wicklow townsfolk. While growing up, O'Connor's strong sense of national identity was no doubt nourished by tales of the '98 rising in the county and the subsequent imprisonment and execution of several of its leaders. Both sets of his grandparents had lived through the troubled years of Famine in the 1840s and witnessed many transportations to the colonies from Wicklow port. O'Connor's nationalist outlook must inevitably have been shaped by their experiences of those difficult times.

Though chance had dictated that Peter O'Connor would be born in England, his family had been rooted in Wicklow for generations, living off the land as well as from the sea. Since the late 1690s, the Connor family, as they had been called then, farmed and lived on some 40 acres of land known as the "Commons" in the Dunbur area just south of the town, on a rising headland promontory.[5] Their land bordered the sea and stretched from the old black castle on the outskirts of the town almost to Wicklow Head, giving spectacular views of Bray Head and the Irish Sea. By the mid-nineteenth century the Connors had been at Dunbur for six generations, and were firmly rooted in the Wicklow landscape. Because their land was somewhat exposed to the elements, the family homestead was surrounded by an orchard. The uneven, sloping land was for the most part given over to pasture and dairy farming. A relatively small stake, it could only realistically support one family. Therefore, for successive generations, one son would take on the family farm while the other brothers either looked for work in Wicklow town or became sailors. There were undoubted dangers involved in making a living from the sea, particularly for those who were fisherman or merchant seamen, but a dependence on the land also carried its own risks, particularly when trying to survive on a small holding.

Peter O'Connor's immediate family was more involved in seafaring and the maritime world than farming. Both his father Edward and grandfather Arthur were shipwrights, skilled tradesmen involved in the building and maintenance of maritime vessels, though in his youth Arthur had probably worked with his brothers on the family farm at Dunbur.[6]

It took a seven-year apprenticeship to become a fully fledged shipwright and develop the necessary skills in timber construction to keep merchant ships watertight and seaworthy. Owing to the highly specialised nature of their work and the perennial dangers facing ships at sea, reliable shipwrights were very much in demand. Arthur Connor's decision to become a shipwright in the 1830s proved an opportune and lucrative one. After the numerous great conflicts of the late eighteenth and early nineteenth centuries, American independence and the end of the Napoleonic wars, a sustained period of peace and relative calm dawned. Consequently, worldwide trade prospered, leading to an insatiable demand for ships of all types. By 1837, Irish shipwrights earned on average four shillings a day, at least five times that of a labourer at that time.[7]

An active and busy man about town, Arthur married a local girl, Esther Murphy, in the mid-1830s and the young couple settled in Coates Lane, a narrow slipway just off High Street and adjacent to the commercial heart of Wicklow town. There in a small, two-room, slate-roofed cottage the newlyweds settled down to rear a family. Arthur and Esther were practising Protestants and their prized possession was said to be a King Edward VI Bible that was kept safe at home under lock and key. In the course of time Esther bore him three children, Bride, Edward and Michael. The eldest son Edward continued the family tradition of shipbuilding and trained under the watchful eye of his father. The two appear to have been close, their working and family lives intertwined.

Arthur and Esther seem to have been tolerant parents and they gave their son Edward their blessing when he decided to marry a local Catholic girl, Mary O'Brien, in 1869. Indeed, in spite of the prevailing attitudes in Ireland at the time towards mixed-religion marriages, there was little or no obstruction to the match. Wicklow being such a small town, the Connors knew the O'Brien family very well and the two families moved in the same social circles. Mary's father, Peter O'Brien, was a sea captain of some repute and her mother, Martha Judd, came from a family of well-known skinners with a respectable background.

Edward Connor and Mary O'Brien were married in Wicklow Catholic Church where Edward promised to bring up his children in the Catholic faith. After their marriage, the family became known as O'Connor rather than Connor. Their first son, Arthur, was born in 1869, followed two years later by a girl, Mary Patricia. With a growing family, Edward was anxious to find some way to increase his income, particularly during dry spells when there were few ships in port, and this is the likely reason why he went to Millom for such a prolonged period in 1872 to help in the construction of *Nellie Bywater*.

On their return from Millom, Edward, Mary and their two sons, Arthur and Peter, moved into a house on Kilmantin Hill, which they shared with Mary's parents Peter O'Brien and Martha Judd. Mary Patricia, their daughter, had sadly died during their stay in England. Here the young Peter O'Connor spent the first eight years of his life, living just around the corner from the imposing shadow of Wicklow Gaol. The young Peter seems to have become very much the favourite of his maternal grandparents.

Peter O'Brien had spent much of his life on the high seas and was a tough strong man, whose hands were marked by years of toil, handling the sheets of the many vessels he had sailed on. For someone from such a rough-and-tumble seafaring background, it must have turned many heads when the former sea captain married Martha Judd. Hailing from Kent in the 1500s, Martha's antecedents were minor aristocrats involved in farming, the most famous of whom was Andrew Judd.[8] The family's association with Wicklow began in the late seventeenth century when Ambrose Judd, the great grandson of Andrew Judd, became a follower of Charles Fox, the founder of the Quaker religion, and moved to Ireland to escape persecution and to spread the word of the radical movement. For two generations the Judds were farming Quakers, who retained the skills of the skinner and tanner, until Ambrose's grandchildren married outside of their religion and eventually their descendents embraced Protestantism. Most likely the Judds would have remained members of the Church of Ireland had it not been for a tragic hunting accident in 1812 when John Judd accidentally shot and killed his son. Stricken by remorse, in an attempt to make amends to his Catholic wife, he converted to Catholicism, and their future children, amongst them Martha Judd, were subsequently brought up as Catholics.

Peter O'Brien and Martha Judd seem to have had a bigger input into Peter O'Connor's upbringing than Arthur and Esther Connor. His closeness to his maternal grandparents was probably due to the fact he was brought up as a Catholic, whereas his paternal side was Protestant. Martha Judd would also play an important role in helping the young O'Connor settle on a course in life through her family connections. Likewise Grandpa O'Brien, who was a staunch teetotaller and firm supporter of the Temperance Movement, would help shape O'Connor's destiny through his championing of an abstemious lifestyle. Throughout his life Peter O'Connor kept a silver temperance medal given to him by Peter O'Brien and, having promised from an early age never to touch a "drop", his only vice would be the pipe, continuing the family tradition.

After returning from Millom, Edward continued to ply his trade for the next seven years in Wicklow town and up and down the Irish coast as occasion demanded. With the arrival of two new infants, Esther in 1874 and Martha in 1876, it became less feasible for him to travel farther afield and leave Mary to manage the growing family alone; six more sisters were to follow in the coming years: Julie (born 1878, died 1879), Elizabeth, Gertrude, Agnes, Edith and Evelyn. Following a fall-off in demand for skilled shipwrights and a general decline in the fortunes of the shipping industry, Edward had to rethink his position in life. Times were changing and it was becoming clear that the future of shipping lay not in traditional wooden-built vessels but in steam-powered boats. With the beginning of construction of a breakwater and steamship pier at Wicklow port in 1880,[9] the writing was on the wall and there was no escaping the fact that the glorious era of the merchant sailing ship was coming to an end. Seeing the lie of the land, Edward cast his mind around for alternative employment. Fortunately for him and his family, a golden opportunity was about to present itself.

From the early 1870s the Wicklow Town Commissioners had undertaken to build a waterworks, a reservoir that would provide fresh drinking water for the rapidly expanding town. By 1880, this dream finally became a reality and the project was completed at

Ashtown Lane, a secluded spot on high ground, situated inland on the fringes of Wicklow town. A small but sturdy lodge house was built at the entrance of the reservoir to house a supervisor. The job of overseeing the waterworks was just the opportunity Edward was looking for and promised a fixed monthly salary and rent-free lodgings. Running the waterworks required a skilled technician not unlike a shipwright, someone adept at repairing leaks and carrying out or supervising essential maintenance. The town had waited a long time for its own waterworks and a pair of safe hands was required to ensure it was kept in good running order. Most likely there were only a few suitable candidates for the post. In light of his experience as a shipwright, good public standing and possibly aided by his Protestant background, Edward O'Connor succeeded in becoming the waterworks' first overseer. The presence of his father-in-law, Peter O'Brien, on the board of the Town Commissioners may also have helped swing things in his favour.

Soon after the waterworks were officially opened, the O'Connor family left the hive of activity that was Wicklow town for their new home in Ashtown Lane. Having spent most of his early childhood in the shadow of Wicklow Gaol, just off one of the town's main thoroughfares, now at the age of eight Peter O'Connor was about to enter a completely different world.

ରଃ

EVEN TODAY, THE OLD WATERWORKS in Ashtown, now home to an angling club, is situated at one of the outermost fringes of Wicklow town. Though the town has expanded in many directions, Ashtown Lane remains relatively untouched and one suspects little has changed since the time Peter O'Connor first roamed the surrounding fields and woods. The old reservoir is situated on elevated ground, surrounded by sloping, rolling fields, now for the most part given over to pasture. Still much removed from the hustle and bustle of urban life, only the sound of birds and the rustling of grass penetrates the silence and serenity of the old waterworks. From the reservoir itself there is a commanding view of the distant town, with the steeple of St Patrick's church rising above the surrounding woods. The long and winding road that leads up to the reservoir is still encroached upon by thickset hedges and overhanging trees. At the entrance to the old water-works, directly to the right, in near perfect condition, stands the lodge house where Peter O'Connor spent his adolescent years. Small and sturdy, the overseer's slated house was placed close to the road, near a little stream that wends its way downhill in the direction of the town. Now boarded up, the house is somewhat dwarfed by large trees that have grown up since the waterworks were abandoned. It is hard to believe that, at one time, this small dwelling housed the entire O'Connor family of eleven. Indeed, the small gate lodge, specially built for the overseer, could not have been intended for such a large family.

Despite the squeeze, the young Peter must have been de-lighted with his family's changed circumstances. His new home was a world apart from the busy port, creaking ships and the clat-ter of carts, as well as the forbidding presence of Wicklow Gaol. Now immersed in the healthy environs of the Wicklow country-side, he, his brother Arthur and his seven sisters had the run of the country. This seems to have been a particularly easygoing and carefree period in O'Connor's life.

The move to Ashtown also signified an important new step in the life of the young Peter O'Connor. There for the first time he discovered a new passion that would in time change his life:

> Having inherited a natural gift of suppleness and spring . . . I became imbued with the ambition, when a small lad, to reach, by doing a hop, step and jump from the doorstep of my home, a grass margin over an intervening gravel space. My first at-tempt was many feet short, but I was determined to succeed, and so it became a habit of mine almost every morning to take this exercise for several years, and I ultimately succeeded in not only reaching the grass margin but went many feet be-yond it.[10]

The gravel path that the young O'Connor set out to traverse still exists today, as does the grass verge now buried beneath long grass and nettles, and it is easy to imagine a small lad propelling himself from the doorstep of the small grey dwelling house. One wonders what inspired O'Connor to make those few tentative jumps and then persevere for so many years until he had cleared the grass verge.

Left to his own devices, he seems to have begun to jump of his own accord. Yet it is also possible that the young O'Connor took his cue from the many spectacular jumping and athletic feats immortalised in old Celtic tales such as the epic romance *The Pursuit of Diarmuid and Gráinne* and the exploits of Fionn MacCumhail's warrior band, the Fianna. In order to join the Fianna, young warriors had to undergo numerous trials of strength and agility and only those who were fleet of foot, capable of jumping their own height and accomplishing other athletic feats unscathed were accepted.[11] Though the Irish language and culture were in decline by the early 1880s, the art of storytelling still endured and O'Connor would certainly have known many of the stories and sagas of old. Any interest he had in Irish language or culture was more than likely encouraged by his primary school teacher who was a known supporter of the Irish language.

Shortly after moving to Ashtown, Peter O'Connor began to attend Wicklow Boys National School in Wicklow town, situated in the old abandoned parish church on St Patrick's Hill. Each day he and his brother Arthur would make the trek down from Ashtown. The man responsible for O'Connor's primary education was Eugene Moriarty, a Kerryman, who arrived in the school in 1877. Moriarty had studied at Dublin's Marlborough Street Training College from 1863 to 1865 and achieved the distinction of being classified a Class 1 teacher. Despite his status, however, inspectors from the Department of Education, sent out to monitor the school's progress, on one occasion contended that "neither in skill, power or control or energy is he of the highest merit". Moriarty's chief defect, according to the inspector, was that he was "quite too easy going".[12] Unlike many teachers of the time, he seems to have been reluctant to use the rod as a source of "inspiration" for his students. Moriarty's relaxed approach was not without its merits, however, as a later report from the inspectors of the schools attested to in 1882 (although much of the credit was given to Canon Dillon, the local parish priest):

> It is with much pleasure we have to point to the marks obtained by the pupils at the recent examination at the Wicklow Male National school as it evidences not alone the attention to their studies and industry of the pupils but the great care which the teachers have exercised over the boys and the warm interest which they have taken in the advancement of the school. We believe the credit of the system of marks and general attention to school duties is almost entirely due to the Reverend Canon Dillon who by a system of prizes for highest marks, by his encouragement and the marked interest which he has taken in these matters has produced the happiest results amongst the young people and through them on their parents. As a proof of the good effect of this system . . . the inspector after complimenting Canon Dillon on the high state of efficiency of the school told him that the answering of the school was 90% on the subjects examined which is far in excess of the average.[13]

By the time Peter O'Connor reached 14½ years of age, he had arrived at the first critical juncture in his life. The seven years that he had spent under the tutelage of Mr Moriarty were at an end. His primary education was complete and it was already time to move on, to go out and make his way in the world. When the National Education system was formed in the 1830s it ushered in a new era of state funding for primary schools which were supposed to be non-denominational. The language of instruction in the schools was English, which was also the principal subject. In practice, each church set up parish schools controlled by the relevant priest or minister, as was the case in Wicklow where Canon Dillon presided over the school. Since the vast majority of students left school aged 10 or 11, many were barely literate and had only a fundamental grasp of arithmetic. Thus O'Connor was quite

fortunate to have been educated until the age of 14½, even if that
education was incomplete.

   Initially elated at the notion that he would not have to attend
school any more, it did not take long for the young Peter
O'Connor to realise that his new-found liberty was not without its
constraints. Indeed many doors and entire worlds would remain
closed to someone of his background and limited education. The
big question now was what to do with his life. It was in many respects the same question that faced several generations of Irish
males after finishing primary education in the late nineteenth century. Though state aid for secondary schools had been forthcoming in 1879, Wicklow was not one of the areas designated for a
secondary school. If O'Connor's parents wanted to give their sons
a further education, it would have to come at a great price. The
two boys would have to commute to Bray on a daily basis by train
or become borders at an all-boys fee-paying secondary school.
With nine children and their old age still to provide for, this was
an expense that the O'Connor family could ill afford:

> I was deemed a clever boy, and in due course went through
> the different standard books from the first to the sixth (second
> stage). After I had passed my examination in the latter my
> parents were complimented by the principal teacher on the
> great progress I had made, and [were told by him that] it would
> be only a waste of time for me to remain in school any longer,
> as I could not be taught more. At the early age therefore, of 14½
> years I left school, much to my own delight (I had no sense
> then), and imagined I was sufficiently educated to hold my own
> against the most learned in the world. Oh, what a mockery. I
> only too soon discovered what my "finished education" was. I
> certainly knew how to read, write and spell fairly well,
> but those accomplishments with a confused, jumbled-up
> knowledge of geography, grammar and arithmetic, represented
> the sum total of my education!! As for history, [English or Irish]
> literary knowledge, mathematics and the languages I knew no
> more about them than a new-born babe. . . . Unfortunately my
> parents could not afford to send me to college or to send me by
> rail daily to attend good secondary schools in Bray or Dublin.

So equipped as I was, I started out in the world to try and earn
a living with my pen. For years I was a drudge at the bottom
of the ladder, while younger boys were promoted over my
head, as a result of their superior education.[14]

O'Connor's limited formal education meant that many callings in
life, such as medicine, law and the civil service, were closed to
him. Whichever direction he went, no matter what profession he
chose, he would have to start at the bottom rung and gradually
climb his way up. Since the opportunities in his native town were
few, he would have to look farther afield for gainful employment
and future prospects. Like many of his generation who left school
with their education incomplete, he eventually drifted into the life
of a clerk, a scribbler and pen-pusher condemned to dusty offices
and drudgery. Later in life he would look back on his National
School experience with anger tinged with regret, apportioning the
blame for his mediocre start in life squarely at the door of the British government. He had grown up at a time when the remnants of
an oral and bilingual tradition, though diminishing, were still apparent, and it is quite likely that he spent his early life listening to
and speaking both Irish and English. Caught at a linguistic crossroads when the transition from Irish to English was nearing completion, he would have considerable difficulty as a young man
learning correct English pronunciation:

It was the policy of the British government always to try to
prevent higher education for the "ignorant Irish", and its establishment of mis-named "National" Schools has suited their
purpose admirably. . . . My pronunciation, my grammar and
my general ignorance brought many a hot flush of shame to
my cheeks, and even now in manhood and with the advantage
of self-study for several years after I left my native town, and
of going to night schools whenever the chance presented itself,
some of the ill effects of my inferior education still remain. It is
hard, cruelly hard, to eradicate bad pronunciation and grammar in speaking when acquired at school. Thank God I have at
last prospered in life but I may thank my own self-study,
ambition and perseverance for it. Such is my experience of

education in National Schools. [Wicklow boys] through the want of higher education lack ambition and are content to remain after leaving school, idling about their native town, in the sometimes vain hope of earning a decent living wage. As a result of the way he is handicapped in education, the Wicklow boy is unable to secure any of the numerous positions in the government service through competitive examinations.[15]

Douglas Hyde, the founder of the Gaelic League, was one of the fiercest critics of the English-speaking National Primary School system, maintaining that an incomplete and botched education did more harm than good and was equally responsible for the erosion of Irish language and customs:

> Bright-eyed, intelligent children . . . with all the traditional traits of a people cultured for fifteen hundred years . . . come out at the end with their natural vivacity gone, their intelligence almost completely sapped, their splendid command of their native language lost for ever, and a vocabulary of five or six hundred English words, badly pronounced and barbarously employed substituted for it . . . the unique stock in trade of an Irish speaker's mind, is gone for ever and replaced by nothing.[16]

Hyde's description evokes the sense of confusion and linguistic incompetence that would dog O'Connor's late adolescence and early manhood. There is no doubt that his future obsession with obtaining the best possible education for his children stems from this period in his life. Equally, the gradual realisation that his generation had been badly neglected by a disinterested British government would help to shape his political and nationalist ideals.

After leaving school, O'Connor would spend the next couple of years discovering just how little he really knew, despite the generous compliment of his former teacher Mr Moriarty that he had nothing left to learn. The craft of shipwright that had sustained his family for two generations had all but died out, so he would have to choose a different path. Peter O'Connor seems to have spent the next couple of years in Wicklow town waiting for an opportunity to come his way. With plenty of time on his hands and little constructive to do, O'Connor began playing Gaelic football and competing in jumping events when the opportunity presented itself. By 1888 he was beginning to show some athletic promise, although he still viewed sport as nothing more than a mild diversion:

> At the age of 16 years I could generally beat youths of my own age and young men much older, in jumping events which, to pass the time, were frequently indulged in before the start of football and ploughing matches in the County Wicklow or in a field where we played football. I had no opportunity of competing at open sports and never gave any real thought to pursuing athletics as a pastime.[17]

At the time, competitive athletics in Ireland were very much in their infancy, and in the 1880s the majority of athletic events took place in Dublin and involved for the most part university students or gentlemen. Though the GAA had been formed in 1884, its influence in Wicklow was not particularly strong and it would be many years before it made significant inroads into the county. It would be another six years before O'Connor took to the athletics field. Much more critical at this time was working out what to do with his life. It had been almost two years since he had left school and he still had no discernible path to follow.

The balance of probabilities suggests that at this time the young man was taken in hand by his cousins, the Judd family. There is every reason to believe that this is so. O'Connor was 17 when his grandmother Martha Judd died in 1889 at the age of 85. Since her marriage to Peter O'Brien, she had lived all her life in Wicklow town on Kilmantin Hill, beside her cousin John Judd, a retired skinner, and his wife Anne. As such, she remained in close contact with the extended Judd family. Since Peter left school Martha would have seen her grandson loitering around Wicklow with few prospects of making a good start in life, or furthering his education. As the years slowly slipped by and the young boy stood on the threshold of manhood, she may have asked her nephew Michael Judd to take his young cousin under his wing and give him a leg up in the world. Michael Judd, who was at the time operating a successful skinners' business in Dublin in Hendrick Street, was twelve years Peter's senior. Though he did not employ his cousin immediately, it is thought that with time, when O'Connor had gained the basic necessary skills, he was employed as a clerk at the Hendrick Street storerooms. By taking him into his business, Michael Judd gave O'Connor the chance to leave Wicklow behind and finally begin some sort of career. Once outside of Wicklow, he would have the chance to complete his education, to fill in the gaps that had been left by his lack of a secondary education. He would study calligraphy, take elocution lessons and learn shorthand to give him a chance to make something of himself, and enable him to aspire beyond his present station in life, both intellectually and materially.

Before old Edward Connor of Dunbur, Peter O'Connor's grand-uncle, died intestate in 1892, he may well have wondered what would happen to the land his family had farmed continuously since 1698. As a widower with no children, it was left to his brother Arthur, the retired shipwright, to sort out his estate. Arthur himself at 88 was faced with an unenviable task. Only two of his grandchildren could realistically continue the family tradition but he knew the younger generation were not interested in being farmers. By 1890 the eldest of his grandsons, Arthur, was considering a career in the civil service and intended to emigrate to America. His other grandson, Peter, likewise did not want to be tied to the land and hoped to leave Wicklow to obtain further education and eventually enter the legal profession. The two brothers' reluctance to become tied to the land and a relatively small holding was quite symptomatic of the times. Ever since the Famine, there existed a general unwillingness amongst many young men to become farmers, particularly when family holdings were relatively small. There was also a certain stigma associated with working the land. Much like the Irish language, the land had become associated with poverty, a hard life and few prospects of social advancement. This psychological shift was underlined by many Irish emigrants to the US in Victorian times, who preferred the squalor and poverty of urban life in cities such as Boston and New York to the rural American West. For most other ethnic groups, acquiring land in America not only promised independence and a return to a healthy lifestyle but was fundamental to the concept of the American dream. In the aftermath of the Great Famine, however, Irish attitudes to the land were more complex.

Before Arthur could complete the administration of the estate, he died in 1893. Shortly following his death, the old farmhouse suffered a catastrophic fire in which almost all the furniture and possessions in the cottage were lost. The old Connor homestead was reduced to an uninhabitable ruin, and the land at Dunbur deserted.[18] The land that had supported the Connor family since the late 1690s was later sold and a 200-year tradition came to an end. Peter O'Connor does not seem to have had anything to do with Dunbur after his grand-uncle's death. Most likely he was too busy trying to get his own career off the ground.

O'Connor's family background was quite an unusual one for the times as his father was Protestant and his mother Catholic. Equally surprising is the fact that six of O'Connor's sisters entered convents after attending the Dominican Convent in Wicklow town. Esther was the only sister to get married, after emigrating to the United States. In this day and age it may be surprising that so many girls from one family would enter religious life. Yet in late Victorian Ireland this was by no means uncommon. Considering the size of the family, it was extremely unlikely that Edward and Mary could provide all their children with sufficient dowries, if and when they chose to marry. Since the Great Famine, attitudes towards marriage had changed and people were now much more reluctant to marry until their early thirties and only when the match had a sound financial basis.

Little is known of O'Connor's life from his late adolescence to his mid-twenties, but it is quite reasonable to assume that these were difficult, formative years. O'Connor would later intimate that these lost anonymous years filled him with the ambition and passion that so characterised his later life. When he finally emerged in Clifden several years later, however, he was a young man full of purpose, ambition and with a thirst to prove himself in the world. He had filled in many of the gaps left by the absence of a secondary education and now was about to embark on a new life as a clerk in a small solicitor's office in the West of Ireland.

2

The Clifden Years

WHEN PETER O'CONNOR TRAVELLED to Clifden for the first time and gazed upon Connemara's vast treeless and seemingly impenetrable expanse of bog and mountain, he might have been forgiven for thinking that he was travelling through a land that time had forgotten. Even today, Connemara is a bewitching, other-worldly place, a desert of moss, turf and discarded stone. The plantations of Norwegian spruce that now dot the Connemara landscape in awkward clumps were only being gradually introduced to Ireland in 1894 and few if any trees could survive in much of the region's boggy, acidic soil. Since Famine times, when the area had been depopulated, there were only a few pockets of urban life in the region, mostly coastal towns that made their living from the sea. O'Connor's destination, Clifden, was one of the most remote towns in Western Europe, though the nearby town of Cleggan, some five miles away, was further removed from western civilisation.

Today the town of Clifden retains much of the old-world charm and ambience it must have had when Peter O'Connor first arrived there in May 1894. No doubt after the long rocky journey from Galway through the barren Connemara wilderness, he was delighted to find a small town bustling with life. Then as now, Clifden's three main streets were linked, creating a small triangular urban centre, full of public houses, trading outposts and eateries. A short distance from the heart of the town, a hill leads down to the port, sheltered from the rough Atlantic seas by Clifden Bay.

Nowadays tourists come from all over the world to savour the immensity and vastness of the Connemara wilderness, its desolate beauty a magnet ever since *The Quiet Man*, starring the legendary John Wayne, graced cinema screens. In 1894, however, before the advent of tourism, Connemara's countless deserted cottages and Famine villages were testament to the hardship of life in this most beautiful but unforgiving of environments.

When Peter O'Connor decided to move to Clifden, the town's fortunes were in the ascendant. A railway line connecting Clifden to Galway city was in the final stages of completion. The new rail connection promised a vital social and economic lifeline for those living in one of Ireland's most remote towns. Cutting an unlikely path through Connemara's vast stretches of dense, waterlogged terrain, it was hoped the railway would also inject a new lease of life into the area. On its eventual completion in 1896, Clifden would become the most important urban centre in the region and the railway would operate until 1935 when the costs of maintaining the service proved too high.

O'Connor seems to have had little trouble adapting to life in Clifden or to his new position as a solicitor's clerk. Redmond Connolly, the man whom Peter O'Connor had come to Clifden to work for, was one of the town's most noted residents. His father, John, had been one of the first to come to Clifden in 1815 when the town was founded, opening a drapery and dry goods store. The Connolly family had stood their ground throughout the hard years of the Famine when many other settlers left and, after studying law, Redmond Connolly went on to establish a solicitor's practice in the town. Despite the remoteness of the practice's location, Connolly had achieved a certain amount of renown in the late 1880s through his role in defending two men accused of murder in nearby Letterfrack.[1] Now that Clifden was about to be connected by rail to Galway, Connolly probably decided to take on another clerk because the town had high expectations of an increase in business and traffic.

Some weeks after his arrival on a Sunday afternoon in July, Peter O'Connor was invited to go on an excursion by a group of young townsfolk to Kylemore Castle. One of Victorian Ireland's most striking gothic mansions, the castle stands beneath the slopes of Doughruagh and faces onto Lough Pollacappul. The castle was built in the 1860s by John Henry Mitchell, a wealthy Manchester businessman of Irish descent. Situated in one of the West of Ireland's most scenic spots, near Kylemore Pass on the road to Leenane, the castle, which is built into the face of a mountain, has a fairytale quality to it, looking onto a serene lake and close to a cluster of woods. In 1894 when O'Connor visited Kylemore Castle it still belonged to the Mitchell family, although an agent was by this time principally involved in administering the estate. Whether or not the Clifden party gained access to the castle grounds, its famous Victorian walled garden and Italian landscaped gardens is not known. It could be that the party merely admired the castle from the new Galway road that Mitchell had built across Lough Pollacappul. Some time later when Mitchell got into financial difficulties, the castle and his vast estate of 13,400 acres, his life's work and passion, was sold.

While having a picnic in the grounds of, or near, Kylemore, some of O'Connor's companions — national school teachers and keen sportsmen — decided to have a hop, step and jump competition. O'Connor, who was a comparative stranger to most of them, was instantly attracted and so amazed his companions by his jumping feats that "one of them, a National School teacher, said [he] had a colossal spring and that he had never seen a man accomplish such distances".[2] O'Connor was delighted to be able to make a good first impression with his new Clifden friends, especially since it had been years since he had competed against other people. Though he could not have known it at the time, the impromptu athletics contest at Kylemore that sunny July afternoon was a pivotal moment in his life. At the age of 22 he was about to discover that his particular gift marked him out from other men.

> I went on this excursion practically unknown, and, after my return, it was speedily broadcast throughout the town that I was a wonderful jumper, so I suddenly became, as it were, famous for reasons then unknown to me. I subsequently

discovered that there was keen rivalry and jealousy between footballers and athletes in Clifden and those in a village called Cleggan, some five miles away. In this latter village there were four brothers who were being educated in a College in Dublin, and on their return for Summer holidays, they won all the prizes in running and jumping at various athletic sports, giving athletes in Clifden no chance of winning any of the events, and Clifden had ceased to secure victory against Cleggan. Shortly after my exhibition of jumping at Kylemore Castle, a deputation comprising the leading shopkeepers of Clifden waited on my employer to give me a day off to attend the big gala day at Cleggan, held annually, comprising horse races, boat races and athletic sports. . . . At first I refused, stating that I had no athletic togs or shoes, and against trained athletes I could not hope to succeed, but they had been told so much about my jumping, they asked me not to let Clifden down; so I promised to take part and do my best.[3]

The annual fleadh at Cleggan in the summer of 1894 was Peter O'Connor's baptism into the world of competitive athletics. Taking place in Europe's most westerly town and hidden deep in the recesses of Connemara, the events of the day provided a social and sporting occasion of no small importance. People from miles around and the nearby island of Inisbofin flocked to the small fishing port to take part in the day's entertainments. Beneath the air of festivity, the stage was set for a highly charged local derby between Cleggan and Clifden, as the best men from the two small rival communities displayed their talents on the sports field. While it was common enough in those days for there to be healthy competition between neighbouring parishes, just what the source of the intense rivalry was between the two towns is hard to ascertain but it may well be that the people of Cleggan felt somewhat aggrieved that Clifden was about to be connected to Galway city by rail, effectively making it the most important town in west Connemara. In order to reassert the town's athletic supremacy over Clifden, Cleggan would rely on one trusty family of brothers who had proved all-conquering in previous years. The four college students probably expected an easy victory once again as Clifden's hopes rested solely on the shoulders of a tall, lithe and unassuming stranger who had only weeks before moved west to the town. Though O'Connor was an unknown entity, there was no reason to suspect that he might be a serious threat to the Cleggan champions. Nonetheless the brothers were unwilling to cede any advantage to their new opponent:

> On the day of the sports I asked a Clifden merchant to en-
> quire if one of the four Cleggan brothers would lend me a
> pair of spiked shoes in the jumping contests. I observed the
> indignant refusal to the request, and, being of an excitable
> disposition, it made me more determined to do all I could to
> conquer them. . . . [4]

O'Connor had been left in no doubt as to the extent of the rivalry between the two small communities and the point-blank refusal of his request set the stage for a highly charged and acrimonious battle. Local pride was at stake and no quarter would be given.

ⒸⒼ

THE ENSUING JUMPING CONTESTS had all the hallmarks of a classic encounter as the plucky small-town solicitor's clerk took on the well-heeled and experienced university students from the big city. It was the first of countless occasions when O'Connor would square off against this type of competition. Having been treated so discourteously by his opponents and forced to jump in his socks, O'Connor was determined not to take the insult lying down and showed for the first time the kind of mettle that would mark his later career. In spite of a lack of footwear and, much to the chagrin of the Cleggan brothers, he won all three jumping events. Somewhat akin to an unknown gunslinger, O'Connor had come to the rescue of Clifden, ending Cleggan's dominance on the sports field. In the aftermath of the shock defeat and the blow to local pride, one of brothers challenged O'Connor to a considerable wager:

One of the four brothers took his defeat so badly that he approached a Clifden merchant in my presence and offered to make a wager for a substantial amount that he would give me a handicap of 10 yards and a beating in a 100 yards race, for which I had not been entered. His challenge and the way it was made so angered me, that I told him I would, before the Summer was over, meet him and his brothers in athletic running events, and I hoped with equal success to defeat them as I had done in the three jumping events. After this contest, I realised for the first time that God had really endowed me with this wonderful gift of spring, so I purchased athletic togs and spiked shoes, and I then started to train regularly, assisted by many Clifden youths, and made rapid progress. Some six weeks after the Cleggan sports, I travelled to Leenane, two long touring cars with many Clifden merchants accompanying me, to take part in the athletic sports there. The four brothers from Cleggan attended, and I not alone won the same three jumping events, but also beat them and many others in the only running event in which I took part, namely, the 220 yards race. This was the second peculiar event in my life, which finally determined me to pursue athletics and develop my gift of spring.[5]

In the space of a few short weeks, O'Connor had gone from being a stranger in Clifden to local hero and found himself unexpectedly in the limelight.

Though the young Peter O'Connor probably did not know it at the time, Ireland had a long tradition of success in the long and high jump. The 1870s and 1880s had witnessed the beginning of a revival in traditional athletics, thanks to men such as Michael Cusack and Maurice Davin. The first Irishman to stake his claim to being one of the world's best long jumpers was Pat Davin, who set a world record on grass of 23' 2" at Monasterevin in 1883. Jumping contests and the importance of athletic prowess were features of Irish life long before the modern athletics revival. As a young man O'Connor had often competed at jumping contests that took place after harvests or ploughing competitions.

Such gatherings had been occurring in Ireland for countless generations and the origins of these impromptu trials of strength and agility can be traced back to the ancient Celtic Tailteann festivals that were held in Ireland from prehistoric times through to the twelfth century. The most important sources for this ancient sporting festival are found in Irish mythology. The Book of Leinster, a tenth-century manuscript, reported that the ancient Tailteann festival was believed to have originated in prehistoric times after the island of Ireland was invaded by a race known as the Tuatha Dé Danann. These new invaders were credited with mystical powers and great physical prowess. Lugh, one of the princes of the Tuatha Dé Danann, instituted the Aonach Tailteann, a festival of funeral games in memory of his foster mother Tailtiú. The Celtic Prince was also reputed to have brought the game of *ficheall* (chess), the bell, the horsewhip and the fair to Ireland. The Aonach or fair that Lugh founded was held each year during the fortnight preceding and the fortnight following the first day of August, harvest time. Lugh was one of the principal gods of Celtic Europe. Equated with the Roman God Mercury, his festival, Lúnasa, in August celebrated this period of the year.[6] The Aonach is thought to have taken place each year until the twelfth century when the sports festival was discontinued following the Anglo-Norman invasion. Thus the gatherings and contests that O'Connor attended from his earliest youth can be traced back to that prehistoric sporting tradition. Though the Tailteann Games had not taken place for some eight centuries, their memory lived on through the oral tradition. The mythological connection with the mysterious and magically endowed Tuatha Dé Danann may also have accounted for the belief that the Irish had a peculiar "springiness" that other races lacked. Over the course of the next two decades, O'Connor and other Irish jumpers would do much to strengthen that notion, lending the myth some credence.

Now that he had made his debut in competition, O'Connor soon discovered that the athletics scene was flourishing in Ireland. In the late nineteenth and early twentieth centuries, before the rise in popularity of team sports, athletics was by far the most popular sport in Ireland. Apart from the GAA, which had been formed in 1884 to promote and safeguard national games such as hurling,

Gaelic football and traditional track and field sports, another association, the IAAA, was also actively involved in organising athletics. The Irish Amateur Athletics Association was essentially the
Irish equivalent of the English Amateur Athletics Association and
was therefore perceived to be more representative of unionist
rather than nationalist interests. The existence of both the GAA
and the IAAA meant that, as O'Connor started out in his athletics
career, he could compete in sports organised by both associations.
Following a dispute in 1885, shortly after they were formed, the
GAA and IAAA managed to reach a satisfactory working arrangement that would last for two decades. The thinly veiled rivalry between the two organisations would initially prove to be in
the interests of athletes, as almost every week of the summer there
would be a GAA or IAAA sports event to attend or compete in. A
golden era in Irish sport was about to begin and Peter O'Connor
could not have chosen a better moment to accidentally stumble
upon the world of athletics.

In the summer of 1895 O'Connor began to compete regularly in
athletics events in the Connaught region. After their great success
at Cleggan the previous year, Clifden decided that it would host its
own sports event that September in conjunction with the annual
races, and O'Connor was made honorary secretary to the sports
committee. The highlight of O'Connor's first season competing in
amateur athletics came at a college sports held in Galway city. Because the railway line was still incomplete, O'Connor took the early
morning "long car" from Clifden to Galway city. Owing to a delay
when he arrived, he found that almost all the events had taken
place. Luckily the hop, step and jump (which is now known as the
triple jump) had yet to be contested so the journey had not been in
vain. O'Connor easily won the event and the distance he covered
amazed both the crowd and the official IAAA handicapper, E.J.
Walsh, who was overseeing the event. Walsh was so impressed
with O'Connor that he told him that he had an abnormal spring
and that, were he to dedicate himself to long jumping, there was no
man in the world who could beat him. He could scarcely believe
that O'Connor had never had any formal training in athletics and

relied purely on raw talent. Peter knew he was a good athlete but this was the first time anyone of note had ever told him that he had the potential to become one of the world's best. Walsh encouraged him to enter a day's sports at Ballinasloe to be held a few weeks later at which he would also be present.

When O'Connor turned up at Ballinasloe, he won the 100 and 200 yards, the high jump and the long jump from a grass take-off, covering a distance of 22' 6". Some days later Walsh published a report of the day's competition in *Sport*, singing the praises of O'Connor and predicting that with proper training from a board take-off and barring accidents, the Wicklowman would some day set a world record. Such was his belief in O'Connor's potential that Walsh contacted Tom Kiely, already a much celebrated athlete and formidable competitor. Though they had never met, Kiely wrote to O'Connor detailing the dimensions of a board take-off, how to train in order to achieve more speed and accuracy, and advising O'Connor to give up the hop, step and jump and the high jump and to concentrate on the long jump.

O'Connor must have been amazed by the extent to which his jumping had aroused the interest of so many distinguished sports personalities. Though he did indeed welcome Kiely's advice, he did not take it all on board. For the time being he had no intention of dedicating himself purely to the long jump, certainly not while he was carrying off prizes on a weekly basis in the sprints and other jumping events. Nonetheless, the attention he was now receiving in the local and national press was an extra incentive to keep improving. In the years to come, O'Connor would not forget the support and encouragement of E.J. Walsh, crediting a large part of his future successes to the man who effectively discovered him. Furthermore, the advice that Tom Kiely gave O'Connor at Walsh's instigation proved extremely useful and helped set him on the right path. How much O'Connor would achieve depended on his willingness to train and to travel to compete.

For the following two seasons O'Connor competed for the most part in Connaught — Clifden, nearby Leenane, Ballinasloe, Castlerea, Tuam, Loughrea and Galway. Owing to the difficulties and costs involved in travel, he did not or probably could not travel farther away for sports events. If he had any realistic ambitions to improve as an athlete, he would have to leave Clifden. After almost three years working as a clerk for Redmond Connolly, he now knew what was involved in the running of a solicitor's office and he probably felt it was time to move on to a larger town and bigger practice. He had come to Clifden in May 1894 with next to nothing, in the hope of beginning a career in the legal profession. Just over three years later he would leave the West, very much a new man instilled with a clear sense of direction and purpose.

3

Mullingar

IN THE AUTUMN OF 1897 Peter O'Connor left Clifden and the wilds of Connemara for the Midlands. The move was no doubt motivated by a desire to improve his career prospects. He now had a good working knowledge of the legal profession and Clifden was too small and remote to hold a young man of O'Connor's ambition for long. He probably had been keeping an eye out in the national and regional newspapers for news of vacant positions in solicitors' practices in larger towns. After a short spell at Daly's Solicitors in Galway city, in the summer of 1897, an excellent opportunity to move on to bigger and better things presented itself.

In a rare sporting excursion from the westerly province, O'Connor travelled to Mullingar in County Westmeath to compete at an inaugural athletic sports event. The long rail journey proved to be well worth it because, apart from winning the long and high jumping events with relative ease, he learned that the position of managing clerk in P.J. Nooney's Solicitors was vacant or soon to be so. Having proved himself on the athletics field, O'Connor was equally successful in obtaining the vacant position. He returned to Galway city, handed in his notice and soon was once again on the road, leaving the West for the flat Midlands. The promotion from ordinary clerk to managing clerk was a small yet distinct step up the social ladder, and O'Connor's slow but determined ascendancy through the echelons of the legal profession was underway.

When he arrived in Mullingar, it was a prosperous market town located in the heart of horse-breeding country. Relatively large, Mullingar offered its residents a very active social and cultural life, the highlight of the sporting calendar being the town's annual horse show. Polo and cricket were also particularly popular at the time, underlining the strong Unionist presence in the area. Neither the GAA nor athletics had made strong inroads here before O'Connor's arrival. Though the town's social calendar was filled with an array of diverse public entertainments, including four major fairs each year, until 1897 the town lacked an athletics meeting of note. There had been sporadic meetings since 1885, but the notion of an annual sports day really took hold only when athletics made its debut at the Newbrook racing grounds in 1897. The race course had come into being in the early 1890s when the commercial potential of developing a racing venue was recognised by local businessmen and the proprietor of the town, Lord Greville. The new Newbrook course was an instant success, summer race meetings proving especially successful from a social and financial perspective. Little by little Newbrook was developed, undergoing various renovations, and in 1896 a three-acre site was converted as venues for athletics, equine and agricultural events.[1] The following year, in September 1897, O'Connor competed in Newbrook's first athletics meeting and some weeks later made the permanent transfer to the Midlands.

ଔ

THE MOVE WAS TO HAVE AN IMMEDIATE and long-lasting impact on O'Connor's sporting life since he was now centrally based and had access to a far greater number of sporting events. Now relocated to the Midlands, O'Connor would quickly become a familiar figure at sports up and down the country.

However, he did not devote all his free time to athletics but looked for new ways to branch out and broaden his knowledge and abilities. A major social outlet during his time in Mullingar was the St Mary's Temperance Club whose members were required to abstain from alcoholic liquor for five years, attend two meetings monthly and wear the society's medal and ribbon on the first Sunday of each month.[2] As O'Connor was a Catholic and teetotaller, the society was a natural port of call, since he was newly arrived in the town and hoping to make some social inroads.

In 1898, the centenary year of the unsuccessful rebellion of the United Irishmen, St Mary's dramatic society decided to put on a play on the life of Robert Emmet, one of the United Irishmen who had orchestrated the 1803 rebellion after the failure of 1798. For his "treason", Emmet was sentenced to death by the British authorities and immediately became a martyr to Irish nationalists. His famous speech from the dock was great source material for nationalists anxious to commemorate 1798 and 1803. O'Connor became an en- thusiastic member of the dramatic society and was evidently con- sidered "quite a capable performer". Regardless of his ability as an actor, his career on the stage was destined to be short-lived. None of the costumes that had been sent down from Dublin could fit the tall, lithe Wicklowman, the predicament eventually proving an insuperable barrier to both actor and company.[3] Nonetheless, be- ing involved in theatre gave O'Connor the chance to meet and get to know local people and also provided an invaluable opportunity to gain some experience and confidence as a public speaker while simultaneously refining his speech and pronunciation. O'Connor was still anxious to eradicate the rough accent and faulty grammar that had dogged him since early manhood.

The move to Westmeath was not only advantageous from a career perspective but would also prove crucial in his develop- ment as an athlete. In the previous two seasons O'Connor had be- gun to consolidate his reputation as an accomplished long and high jumper, winning both events at many of the sports meetings he attended. Thus far he had not dedicated himself specifically to either discipline and was content to develop his all-round ability. In Connaught, he had met few jumpers who could severely test him. That would all change in Mullingar when O'Connor came up against his first great sporting nemesis, and as the 1898 season un- folded he found himself slowly embroiled in a public gladiatorial contest with political undertones.

എ

IN THE HISTORY OF IRISH ATHLETICS, few athletes have made a more startling impact than Walter Newburn. Born in Ballinrobe, County Mayo on 27 February 1874, Newburn was the son of an auctioneer and came from a Protestant Unionist background. He first came to the public's attention in 1896 when he won both the GAA and IAAA long jump titles with moderate jumps of 21' 6½" and 21' 7" respectively. Newburn missed the GAA Championships in 1897 but won the IAAA long jump title with the improved distance of 22' 5½", as well as the 100-yard sprint in a time of 10.4 seconds. Though creditable long jump performances, they gave no indication of the amazing form that Newburn would attain in 1898, when for a few short scintillating months, the Mayo man held the athletics world in thrall and became a national celebrity. By all accounts he cut a most remarkable figure on the Irish athletics scene. At well over six feet tall, he was very much a giant in his time, contemporary sporting pundits nicknaming him Niagara Newburn. Though it is not known precisely what his proportions were, there seem to have been few if any athletes who could match his physique in Ireland or England at the time and certainly none who specialised in sprinting and long jumping.

Walter Newburn was undoubtedly the sensation of the 1898 Irish amateur athletic season. Though he seemed more likely at first to make his mark as a sprinter, in 1898 he stunned the Irish athletics fraternity by his long-jumping exploits. After a respectable beginning to the season with a jump of 23' 4" on 21 May at Queen's College in Cork, less than a month later at the Dublin Postal Sports on 18 June Newburn registered a jump of 23' 9⅔" — an improvement of almost 6 inches. Though this sudden breakthrough amazed the likes of O'Connor, more was yet to come in the annual Ireland vs Scotland fixture that July in Ballsbridge. Flying high on the crest of his recent good form, Newburn established a new world record of 24' 0½". The following month at a sports in Monasterevin, Newburn beat Pat Davin's long-standing long jump record from a grass take-off by one inch with a jump of 23' 3". In less than three months, the relative newcomer from Ballinrobe rewrote the record books with a flurry of exceptional performances unprecedented in the world of long jumping. Overnight Newburn shot to international fame and was credited by an American athletic champion, Malcolm Ford, with accomplishing feats "so far in advance of anything which the most celebrated running broad jumpers of the world has ever done that it could scarcely be believed".[4]

Newburn's irresistible form and ensuing celebrity was a real eye-opener to Peter O'Connor. Though he had latterly begun jumping over 23 feet regularly and was considered one of Irish athletics' brightest prospects, the distances Newburn was accomplishing redefined the state of play and overshadowed O'Connor's recent improvements.

ೞ

TWO DAYS AFTER HIS HISTORIC WORLD record jump against Scotland, Newburn came to Mullingar to jump in the Newbrook Sports. So soon after his Ballsbridge success, the town was buzzing with the prospect of seeing the Mayo man in action. Such was Newburn's recent form, there was every reason to expect that he might further improve on his new world record.

Owing to the success of the previous year's sports, Mullingar had also been invited to stage the Five Miles Bicycle Championship of Leinster in 1898, a considerable honour for a sports event only in its second year of existence. The horse racing track at the Newbrook grounds was particularly well adapted to cyclists and considered one of the best in the country. As the grandstand was the principal source of revenue for the sports, it was patronised by the town's leading citizens and the local gentry and all events would finish in front of or in full view of the stand. O'Connor was on hand the day before the sports and the organisers asked him to select an area at Newbrook that would be suitable for long jumping. This he duly did and the ground was prepared for the following day's contest. Preparing a long-jumping area the day in advance of a sports could help to reduce the chance of competitors sustaining injuries, as turned soil significantly reduced the impact on landing.

Though all the elements were in place to ensure a memorable sports meeting, a combination of a comedy of errors and some

rather dubious judging cast a cloud over what should have been a
highly successful day. The first controversy erupted when one lap
too many was added to the five-mile cycle and the first-place fin-
isher found himself relegated to second place because his runner-
up had been in the lead at the end of the penultimate lap. Though
this honest, although embarrassing mistake could be put down to
inexperience, many eyebrows were raised at the judges' handling
of the 100 yards handicap sprint. Officials came under considerable scrutiny and their behaviour led to accusations of favourit-
ism. Many bystanders and competitors were amazed to find the
judges of the sprint standing well behind the finishing line in both
the heats and the final. It was later alleged, by an anonymous correspondent, that this oversight helped Newburn and the English
champion Cooper to overtake the other competitors:

> I have not the slightest doubt but that certain members of the
> committee managed to extend the distance of the 100 so as to
> give Cooper and Newburn the chance of catching the handicap
> men. If it was not a deliberate act, they were at least perfectly
> cognisant of the tapeholders having made a mistake during the
> run off of the heats and then had not the manliness to rectify it.[5]

The unfortunate victim of this dubious judging was none other
than Peter O'Connor, who was beaten at the tape by Cooper,
though at the 100 yards distance he was in the lead. O'Connor
was understandably irate, but worse was yet to come.

Following the disappointment of being hoodwinked in the 100
yards handicap, the long jump competition followed. Earlier that
day when Newburn had arrived on the grounds, he had inspected
the jumping area that O'Connor had chosen the night before. Expressing his disapproval of O'Connor's choice, the new world record holder demanded that the long jump take place in an area of
his own choosing. Though there was nothing wrong in such an
action *per se*, the area that Newburn selected was, according to
many observers, far from flat because there was a noticeable
downhill gradient. Because he was still very much the hero of the
hour, nobody seems to have been willing to contest the matter

with Newburn, and O'Connor for his part chose to keep silent. It would take two hours before the new jumping area was ready. When the competition did finally get underway, O'Connor sprained his ankle badly on his second jump and was forced to retire from the competition and watch from the sidelines.

As the contest progressed, Newburn repeated his world record breaking form of the previous days with a gargantuan leap of 24′ 6¾″. The Mullingar crowd went wild, thinking that they had witnessed a new world record on their very own Newbrook grounds. Newburn's jump was huge, an improvement of some 6½ inches on the world record he had set against Scotland two days previously. To all knowledgeable athletics fans present, however, it was clear that the distance jumped could not stand officially. Apart from the incline, there was also said to be a significant wind that may have favoured the jumper. Newburn's jump made him an instant local hero and one imagines that few present really cared whether the jump would be acknowledged as a valid new world record. For the organisers, the spectacular jump was probably a welcome antidote to the simmering controversy surrounding the 100 yards as well as the farcical finish to the Leinster Five Miles Bicycle Championship. Those controversies did not go away, however, although on the day they were eclipsed by Newburn's jump. Indeed, O'Connor was particularly disappointed at his shoddy treatment at the hands of partisan judges.

A few days after the Mullingar Sports, an exhibit appeared in the windows of Jack Gordon's drapery shop celebrating Newburn's jump of 24′ 6¾″. The display consisted of the take-off board used at the Newbrook grounds "draped in the folds of the Union Jack with tableau curtains of red, white and blue silk as the luxury surround". Predictably in the year marking the centenary of Wolfe Tone's rebellion, such Unionist paraphernalia succeeded in antagonising local nationalists. O'Connor also took particular exception to the tribute to Newburn's dubious world record and was said to "grouse daily about the bit of wood in the window". Before long someone threw a brick through the shop window, shattering the provocative display. Though Jack Gordon may initially have intended the exhibit to be temporary, following the brick incident he decided to keep it there permanently, giving it an overt political significance. The offending articles would remain in Gordon's windows until another Irish athlete surpassed Newburn's jump.[6]

CB

BY NOVEMBER 1898 THE HYPERBOLE surrounding Newburn was beginning to irritate a number of people. The final straw seems to have come when it was reported in *Sport* that Newburn was jumping over 25' 2" in "semi-public and 26' in private". Such claims got up the noses of the various elements who were annoyed at Newburn's attempt to have his Mullingar jump of 24' 6¾" ratified as a world record. A certain Pat Lydon of Salthill, County Galway felt honour-bound to put pen to paper and pulled no punches in his correspondence to *Sport* magazine.

> I was standing by when the jump was made, and I unhesitatingly say that it was not genuine, in as much as the ground was not level, there being a very perceptible gradient, and that a strong breeze was blowing directly in the jumper's favour. Newburn recognizing these two very potent factors actually changed the original place selected for the jump, which was perfectly level, to another part of the grounds in order to take full advantage of them, with the result that he did I believe cover the distance. . . . If Newburn can do 26 feet in private how is it that he cannot go within 2 feet of that distance in public excepting his jump in July last? The less of such bombast on Mr Newburn's part the better, as it lessens his reputation in the eyes of the public, and serves to make him appear an extreme egotist. . . . With all the booming about Newburn's 26 feet, I honestly believe that were O'Connor and Leahy to give over high jumping which is totally opposed to improving their long jumping powers, and had the same opportunities which Newburn has of being trained by such a capable trainer as Mr Brierly, they would prove themselves equal if not superior to Newburn.[7]

Lydon's comments directly supported O'Connor's contention that Newburn had changed the jumping ground "at his own convenience". With such a swirl of controversy surrounding the affair, the Mullingar jump was not destined to be recognised as a new world record. Even at the time when Lydon was writing, Newburn's valid world record jump of 18 July against Scotland had not yet been ratified. The awarding of records was a slow and methodical process, undertaken jointly by the GAA and the IAAA. If there was even the shadow of doubt surrounding a possible new record, more often than not the records committee favoured the standing record. Though O'Connor maintained that he was not acquainted with Lydon, supporters of Newburn thought otherwise. Replying to Lydon, the anonymous "APO" writing from Mullingar, who was clearly a Newburn supporter, claimed in *Sport* that it was O'Connor who had changed the jumping ground and he also maintained that, contrary to reports, the crosswind had neither favoured nor hindered jumpers. APO's allegation that O'Connor knew Lydon and may even have instigated him to write his loaded letter to *Sport* received a firm denial from the Wicklowman, who disparaged those seeking to create "rancour" between Newburn and him.[8]

After the various controversies surrounding the Mullingar sports were reported in *Sport* and the *Midland Reporter*, O'Connor found his word and reputation under scrutiny and his version of events being questioned. Further, as many people in Mullingar supported the push to get Newburn's jump ratified, O'Connor probably felt somewhat isolated. An innocent bystander, he found himself dragged into a divisive dispute with political undertones. Not only had Newburn supporters tried to blame O'Connor for shifting the jumping ground, O'Connor also resented the manner that victory over the English sprint champion Cooper had been snatched from him under extremely questionable circumstances. Whether these events led to O'Connor's decision to leave Mullingar in November of 1898 is hard to say for sure but they may well have been contributory factors.

While the merits of Newburn's Mullingar jump were being contested in the national press, O'Connor decided to move to

Waterford city, home to one of Ireland's busiest ports. There he took up the position of managing clerk in Daniel Dunford's Solicitor's practice situated in the heart of Waterford city on O'Connell Street. Because Dunford was a bachelor and had no sons who might take over his office following his death or retirement, O'Connor probably saw his new position as a promising opportunity to further his legal career. There was also an active Athletic Harriers Club in Waterford city that he joined soon after his arrival. For O'Connor, the transfer to Waterford promised the chance to start afresh, after a turbulent few months in Mullingar.

The rest of the 1898 season was played out under the long shadow of Newburn. O'Connor had gained the reputation for being one of Ireland's best athletic prospects at jumping but Newburn's sudden arrival on the scene somewhat removed him from the limelight. Despite being taken unawares, O'Connor responded well to the presence of a new rival and Newburn's success and consequent fame seems to have galvanised him to train even harder. The 1898 season was not particularly memorable from O'Connor's perspective, until the final big sports of the year when he made an important breakthrough.

In the week before the Dublin Metropolitan Police Sports at the Royal Dublin Society grounds in Ballsbridge, it was rumoured that Newburn had been trained "to the pink of perfection" and that he was specially reserving himself to set a new sensational record. On the day in question, this was given the lie as both O'Connor and Pat Leahy cleared 23 feet, easily beating Newburn, who was obviously nowhere near record form. Most likely he was now beginning to feel the effects of his rollercoaster season. Newburn's lapse was an important psychological moment for O'Connor after a season of many ups and downs. Newburn had been invincible all season, but O'Connor now saw that even the Ballinrobe man could have his off days. Since the Mullingar jump was most unlikely to be approved, O'Connor could quite realistically set his sights on Newburn's official record of 24' 0½". For the first time, O'Connor had a clearly defined goal.

4

Starting Over in Waterford

AFTER MOVING SOUTH TO WATERFORD city, Peter O'Connor found himself in a large, bustling and vibrant city, a world apart from remote Clifden or the flat Midlands. Founded in the ninth century, Waterford was Ireland's first city, the generously proportioned and sheltered River Suir ensuring that the city established itself as one of the island's most important ports. Unlike many other Irish cities, Waterford had a long royalist tradition, underlined in 1495 when Henry VII rewarded Waterford with the motto *Urbs Intacta Manet Waterfordia*, for resisting a siege by Perkin Warbeck, pretender to the English throne. Throughout the Reformation, Waterford's civic leaders managed for the most part to resist interference in religious matters and the city's independent spirit and tolerance were emphasised in the late eighteenth century when Protestant and Catholic cathedrals were both built within a few years of each other. The city that Peter O'Connor came to in late 1898 was one with a long and proud tradition of relative autonomy and economic prosperity, thanks to its loyalty to the British Crown.

On his arrival O'Connor took up lodgings in the old Viking city quarter and that winter set about exploring new social outlets, attending dancing classes and "hops" on a regular basis. His entry into Waterford social life was eased by the many new friends he met in the Waterford Harriers Athletic Club. They invariably met at the bandstand in the People's Park and practised on a scientifically designed and cambered cycle track, that had been built by

local philanthropist Sir William Goff in 1895.[1] The track was considered one of the best in the British Isles, and now that he was in
the company of like-minded sports lovers with access to great
training facilities, O'Connor was very much in his element.

Spurred on by his victory over Newburn in the DMP sports at
the close of the previous season, in the winter of 1899 Peter
O'Connor began to develop a unique and revolutionary method
of training to improve his results in the long jump. Previously he
had relied on basic all-round training, including cross-country
running and weights, to improve his level of fitness and results.
Throughout the year, rain or shine, he would rise each morning at
seven, eat breakfast and then go for a walk of three or four miles
and a "gallop through the fields" before going into work at 10.00
am. He also consistently "trotted about high on the balls of his
feet so as to cultivate his 'spring' and elasticity of muscle", an innovative and extremely useful exercise now considered essential
to avoid ankle injuries.[2] This all-year training, coupled with an
immense natural ability and spring, had already made him one of
Ireland's leading jumpers.

Despite the strong tradition of athletics in Ireland, there was
little in the way of a scientific approach to training or preparation.
Sport science was essentially non-existent in Europe and athletes
had to develop their own training regimes and work out ways to
improve their technique by themselves. As such, there was no one
in Ireland who could offer advice which might radically improve
his jumping. The only coaching O'Connor ever received was
when Tom Kiely wrote to him at the beginning of his athletics career, outlining what he felt were the finer points of jumping. The
Tipperary man's advice no doubt set O'Connor off on the right
track, but throwing and hurdling were Kiely's chief areas of expertise and his advice, therefore, would have been necessarily
limited. What little knowledge O'Connor had about long jumping
was gleaned through the reliable time-worn tradition of trial and
error, a laborious but nonetheless effective path to self-
improvement. After some four years' experience of competition in
the long jump, O'Connor came up with a decidedly novel method

of training which he hoped, in time, would enable him to demolish Newburn's record.

He probably knew that his all-round long-jumping technique was far from perfect, but at the same time the best technique would not necessarily make him a world-class athlete. Obviously speed was an important factor in jumping. Without sufficient velocity, a jumper would sink under his own body weight while in mid-air and cover only a relatively short distance. Nonetheless experience had shown that speed alone was not enough to make a champion long jumper. Good sprinters were not necessarily capable of transferring successes on the track to the jumping pit. On that account, O'Connor reasoned that the height a long jumper could reach and maintain was critical in achieving long distances. He who jumped highest and remained there the longest inevitably would cover the greatest distance. Although this basic physics may not seem like ground-breaking reasoning, O'Connor had identified what was perhaps the most critical factor in long jumping, that of being able to remain airborne for as long as possible. And it was to this particular aerodynamic conundrum that he concentrated his mind and energies.

After much thought and critical analysis, O'Connor hit on the idea of making a second "leap" when in mid-air, just at the moment when he had achieved maximum height. Then, instead of simply losing height and beginning a natural descent, this jerky action would momentarily prolong the time spent at maximum height, as well as propelling him forward before descent. In order to put this theory into practice and to get used to the idea of rising further while in mid-air, he began experimenting in training by placing a wooden lath across the designated jumping zone at various heights. This was a highly unusual and somewhat precarious undertaking, as failure to clear the bar would result in being unceremoniously clattered to the ground. This kind of training was particularly hard going, especially in winter, as he practised, trained and competed almost exclusively on grass and only rarely had the luxury of landing on a comfortable bed of sand. Whatever misgivings or doubts he may have had about the efficacy of this kind of training, within a short time he began to see a marked improvement in the distances he could achieve. In competition there would be no wooden lath to act as a guide, so he would have to condition his mind and body to such a degree that when competing, despite the absence of an obstacle halfway, he would produce the vital mid-air knee jerk reaction to propel him that little bit farther. It would take both time and patience to adopt and refine this new style of jumping, but he hoped it would give him a crucial edge over the opposition. It was something of a gamble, but before the year was out, O'Connor began to see some interesting results.

Perhaps owing to the pressures involved in his new job as managing clerk at Dunford's Solicitor's practice, O'Connor did not compete extensively in the 1899 season. He took no part in the IAAA Championships at the RDS Ballsbridge where Newburn won the long jump and 100-yard sprint. Since this was the principal qualifier for the annual Ireland–Scotland match, O'Connor was lucky to make it into the international Irish selection that travelled to Edinburgh in mid-July. At the Powderhall grounds in Edinburgh, O'Connor made his debut for Ireland on foreign soil. It was also the first time that he had set foot in Great Britain since his birth in Millom. From the time the annual contests began in 1895, the Irish team had won every year and had taken a 4–0 lead. Understandably, the Scots were desperate to stem the flow of successive defeats and that year's contest was to prove the closest yet. After ten events, with the two sides tied at 5–5, only the long jump competition remained. After winning the 100-yard sprint earlier that day, it was generally believed that Newburn had decided the contest in favour of the Irish athletes. The previous year at Ballsbridge, he had made his world record jump of 24' 0½" in the same event. When the competition began, however, Newburn inexplicably "broke down" leaving O'Connor to take up the challenge. O'Connor led his Scottish opponent, Hugh Barr, right to the last until the Scot, in his final jump, snatched victory from the Irishman, jumping 23' 2". In the most unlikely of circumstances, Scotland had at last registered a victory. There was much discussion in the Irish press as to the reason behind Newburn's sudden loss of form in the long jump. He was supposed to have "strained a sinew", but he may already have been feeling the pressure of having to defend his Irish record against O'Connor. Belvedere, a noted Irish sports correspondent, conspicuously noted that:

> Newburn would have been beaten in any case, because Barr beat him on his very first jump. Newburn was more afraid of O'Connor than he was of Barr, a very keen sense of rivalry existing between the two Irishmen.[3]

O'Connor had been unable to secure victory for Ireland in Edinburgh, but he had once again finished ahead of Newburn. So when he returned to Ireland, he renewed his training with vigour and set his sights on Newburn's world record. By that August, O'Connor realised that he was making significant progress when, at the Charleville Sports, he jumped 24' 8½". This jump, which was eight inches greater than Newburn's, was made on ground with a downhill gradient and could not therefore stand as a new record. O'Connor probably did not mind because he had never before approached such a distance in competition. He now knew that his new training regime was paying off.

In the last big sports meeting of the season, the GAA Championships at Thurles, O'Connor showed that his jump at Charleville was no fluke when he took the GAA long jump title with a distance of 24' 3". Although both these jumps were far in excess of Newburn's record, neither the jumping grounds at Charleville nor at Thurles had been properly laid out by the organisers and they did not conform to specifications necessary for establishing a new record. The fact that the Thurles record would not stand was extremely unlucky, considering that it had been made at a national championship. As the 1899 season closed, O'Connor was determined that, come the next season, Newburn's world record distance would fall to him. That winter, however, brought news from across the Atlantic that someone had pipped O'Connor to the post and Newburn's world record had been surpassed. Alvin Kraenzlein, a noted hurdler and all-round athlete from the

University of Pennsylvania, had set a new distance of 24' 4½" and both Irishmen now had a new rival.

⚘

UNBEKNOWNST TO MOST EUROPEAN athletes, a veritable renaissance was taking place in the United States whose effects would soon reverberate around the world of sport. Athletics was about to move up a gear and into the spotlight. The catalyst for this explosion of interest in athletics came from a few highly ambitious and successful Ivy League schools which were the driving force behind these currents of change, and it is largely thanks to their efforts that the US soon emerged as the single strongest sporting nation in the world. Many of the American college athletes who were about to impact on the international scene attended universities with strong sporting traditions, cultivated and developed over many years. These American schools had shown a commitment to sport and the pursuit of athletic excellence since the early 1870s which was in stark contrast to European attitudes. By 1900 Ivy League athletes would change the face of international athletics, bursting on the scene and eclipsing almost all European athletes in track and field. O'Connor was about to become acquainted with an entirely new breed of athlete.

The most important and progressive of the Ivy League schools at the time was the University of Pennsylvania, which had opened its doors in 1751. Unlike the other American colonial colleges, it did not focus on education for the clergy but, under Benjamin Franklin's guidance, it set out to prepare students for careers in business and the public service — providing the first de facto liberal arts curriculum in America. As early as 1873, Penn, as it was known, recognised the importance of sport in the development of young men and the necessity of forming an association to promote and foster athletics and to engage in intercollegiate competition. Though initial seasons were hampered by a lack of funding, in 1885 Penn threw its weight behind sporting pastimes, providing some $15,000 so that a ground might be prepared which would be suitable for baseball, football and athletic events. The college fathers must have been of the opinion that a healthy body led to a healthy mind because in 1894 a gymnasium was opened and all students were obliged to attend a "mild form of compulsory gymnastics". Not only would such activity improve the all-round fitness of students but it might also enable coaches to identify potential athletes. Alongside the new gymnasium was a swimming pool that would prove a particularly astute investment, since it was to remain in use for intercollegiate competition until the 1960s. Penn's generous expenditure did not stop there, however, and in 1895 a new sports ground, called Franklin Field, was unveiled at an estimated cost of some $100,000.[4] Few if any places in the world could boast such ideal facilities for promising athletes to develop and realise their potential.

Penn was perhaps the first Ivy League school to recognise that sport, and in particular success on the sports field, could raise the profile of their academic institution. Through financial and institutional support, the university invested heavily in the cultivation of a sporting tradition that could bring prestige and fame to the Penn name. Crucially, the sports infrastructure that evolved there allowed athletes to develop and mature without compromising their amateur status. Under the umbrella of an academic institution, student athletes could receive training from professional coaches, avail of superb facilities and eventually become coaches themselves if they decided against completing their studies or using their qualifications. The University of Pennsylvania was the kind of place a man such as O'Connor could only dream of. It was also the breeding ground for some of his greatest rivals.

Not all Ivy League schools at this time viewed sport and athletics in the same positive light. In 1896, Harvard, regarded as perhaps the most prestigious Ivy League school, went so far as to expel one of its students for travelling to the inaugural Olympic Games in Athens. The student in question was James B. Connolly, an upwardly mobile and ambitious Irish-American from a poor district of Boston. Connolly was told that if he left for Greece, he would have to re-enrol in the university on his return. Determined not to let red tape stand in his way, he walked out of Harvard and weeks later became world famous as the athlete who bridged the gap between the ancient and modern Olympics, when he won the hop, step and jump, the first event at Athens in 1896. Connolly's victory ensured that an American flag was the first to be raised in victory at the newly reinstituted games. On his return Connolly did not bother to return to Harvard. Ten years later, when as an established writer he was invited by the Harvard Union to speak on the subject of literature, and somewhat belatedly on the occasion of his year's fiftieth anniversary he was presented with a sweater bearing the university's insignia.[5] Harvard's harsh action in 1896 might be ascribed to the fact that the Olympic Games had not as yet captured a special place in the public imagination. In the short space of four years, however, attitudes were quick to change and as the Paris Games loomed on the horizon, there was fierce competition amongst the leading Ivy League schools to secure places for their students on the American Olympic team.

Predictably, Pennsylvania was at the forefront of the hungry pack anxious to win international acclaim on the athletics' field. By 1900 Penn's investment had begun to pay dividends in domestic competition, but the university had not as yet been granted the chance to showcase its sporting talent in an international arena. Their determination to put on a good show at Paris was further fuelled by the fact that Harvard and Yale had only recently been invited to compete against Oxford and Cambridge in a transatlantic inter-varsity contest. This snub was a direct insult to Penn athletes, who were clearly a major force in American domestic athletics, having dominated the annual intercollegiate games for the previous three seasons.[6] The 1900 Paris Games would provide the ideal scenario for Penn to redress the balance and stake its claim as the strongest university of both the Old and New World. In American college athletes' quest for Olympic glory and international recognition, the line that was drawn between amateurism and professionalism would become blurred. Athletics would witness the beginning of a new era, and one American athlete in particular, the Pennsylvanian all-rounder Alvin Kraenzlein, would symbolise the success of Ivy League schools in producing and nurturing athletic talent.

Before 1900, O'Connor had had no opportunity of competing against Americans or seeing this new breed of athlete in action. Since the inaugural modern Olympics of 1896 and the considerable success of American athletes at those games, much had been made of the training facilities available to leading American sportsmen. As the 1900 season opened, there was considerable excitement in Irish sporting circles. Apart from the usual Irish sporting calendar, which would see athletes competing the length and breadth of the country in both GAA and IAAA events, there were also several appetising international encounters to look forward to. That year was Ireland's turn to entertain Scotland in the annual duel between the Celtic cousins and this extremely popular and closely followed event was to take place in Belfast. Within days of meeting the Scots, most of the leading Irish athletes would contest the English AAA Championships at Stamford Bridge, perhaps the best athletics venue in the British Isles. It was rumoured that the Americans would put in an appearance at the English AAA Championships before heading to Paris for the second modern Olympics, scheduled to take place some days later. O'Connor had never competed at an English Championship, and was no doubt anxious to make his mark at Stamford Bridge, since the games were then effectively considered world championships. In 1905 an athletics commentator declared:

> To win an English athletic championship is the greatest honour an athlete can aspire to. Unlike other countries which confine their championships to athletes born or resident six months in the country in which they are held, the English Championships are open to the best athletes the world can produce, and they are therefore universally regarded as the world's championships. This is why American, French and other foreign athletes are attracted to England year after year to gain the "blue ribbon" of Amateur Athletics.[7]

In 1900, with the participation of a large group of American athletes en route to the Paris Olympics, the global dimension to the championships would be self-evident.

In the run-up to the Stamford Bridge Championships, O'Connor had two high profile sport meetings in Ireland in which to judge his form. At the IAAA Championships in Ballsbridge, for the first time in years the annual championships were blessed by fine weather, attracting a "splendid company" of holidaymakers eager to witness numerous sporting "deeds of derring do" on the bank holiday. As in previous years, the championships took place in the hallowed surroundings of the exclusive Royal Dublin Society. Ballsbridge was one of Dublin's most affluent suburbs and amongst the members of the society were many of the leading political and cultural figures of the day. Sports held at the RDS were always extremely well attended and proved particularly popular social gatherings for Dublin's elite and ruling class. For those with a mere passing interest in athletics, there were always plentiful diversions and entertainment at hand to amuse and tickle the fancy. Much like a day at the races, social animals would flock to Ballsbridge in order to see and be seen, gossip and connive. People from all walks of life, united by a love of sport, would mingle and jostle for the best view. If the weather was good, this was definitely one of the best places in Dublin to relax and be entertained.

O'Connor was one of the busiest competitors, not restricting himself to his pet discipline but competing in the 100 yards, 100 yards handicap and the high jump before the long jump contest took place. In the high jump he squared off against his old friend Pat Leahy from Charleville. Leahy, whose father had only recently died, was clearly off form, so when he could manage only 5' 9¾", O'Connor retired in sportsmanlike fashion, not wishing to take the championship from the holder when he was at a disadvantage. It was a generous gesture noted not just by Leahy but also by an appreciative public and contributed to O'Connor's growing reputation as a steely but fair opponent. At the following year's championships, in a slightly different way, Leahy would return the compliment.

O'Connor's new and improved long-jumping style was now beginning to pay dividends but it was his intrepid high jump that created quite a stir. Unlike other athletes who approached the high jump from the side, O'Connor went straight for the bar, head on in a most uncompromising style, effectively demonstrating how he had been training for the long jump. He jumped so far when battling Leahy that he sailed past any soft surface prepared to ease the fall, crashing to "the hard jarring ground".[8] There were no special mats to soften the impact of landing, so a portion of the grass near the jumping bar was probably turned to ease the impact. With his kamikaze style, however, he inevitably sailed many yards blissfully past any soft landing area. Considering this almost reckless approach, it is amazing that he did not suffer serious injuries more often.

Though all events were extremely hard fought, the day did not produce any real surprises until the 100 yards sprint heats. Going in to the contest, Walter Newburn was the clear favourite as holder and was fancied to retain the title. Much to his and everyone else's surprise, a little known soldier by the name of G. Cutts stole the day, winning the sprint comfortably. Cutts was a Yorkshire Light Infantry man, who qualified for the event by residence. Newburn seems to have choked at the start of the qualifying heat, losing half a yard and after some 30 yards quit the race when it was clear there was too much ground to be made up in the home straight to catch the flying soldier. The pressure was beginning to tell and it was plain for all to see:

> If Newburn's pluck was in proportion to his length, he would be a fine man, but unfortunately it is in the inverse ratio. He abused the starter, the latter being the nearest to hand, but even granting that he lost more than half a yard at the start, it was foolish to stop at thirty yards.[9]

Newburn's nerves were on a knife edge, desperate not to disappoint his numerous Unionist supporters. Unlike O'Connor, he was not a good loser and took his defeats personally. When Cutts went on to win the final in a time of 10.4 seconds, the same as in his heat, the British soldier demonstrated that his victory was no flash in the pan. He was simply the best man on the day and Newburn had no one but himself to blame for failing to qualify for the final because he had quit halfway:

> As usual, when a "sojer" wins a big race, there were all kinds of rumours and objections, some saying he was an out and out pro, a Sheffield handicap winner, an American etc. It will probably be found that Cutts is all right.[10]

Since his purple patch in 1898, Newburn had become accustomed to winning and had developed many of the airs and graces of a sporting prima donna. Denied victory in the event in which he stood the best chance of winning, he seems to have lost his nerve, rattled by his unexpected defeat. The prospect of facing O'Connor in the long jump and possibly losing face still further was clearly too much for him. In such a "funk after losing the sprint championship, he refused to turn out in the long jump, probably saving himself a further beating".[11] Like many hasty decisions made on the spur of the moment and with emotions running high, it would prove a costly error. By declining to face O'Connor, Newburn effectively renounced his chance to compete for Ireland against Scotland, something that disappointed his many supporters. His tantrum following the loss to Cutts would prove a crucial moment in the turning of the tide for Newburn. Until now, most of the sporting press and public had been kind to him, excusing his various foibles, but these latest antics and his sudden withdrawal from the long jump contest were to have a devastating impact on his reputation. He had not only been ungracious in defeat but in some eyes seemed afraid to compete, turning tail against the first sign of decent opposition. The latter charge in particular would prove his undoing.

> In Ireland it is not thought that [Newburn] will ever beat O'Connor again, for even admitting that he is as good a jumper, he has no heart and shakes in his pants before competing. O'Connor on the other hand, is a light-hearted individual, who takes defeat as complacently as victory. Were he

to devote himself exclusively to jumping, as Newburn did in the last two years, he would beat the world's record in the long jump, and might even beat Leahy in the high.[12]

The big man from Ballinrobe was clearly suffering under the weight of expectation that his world record jump had engendered. Perhaps for Newburn success and fame had come too soon and too easily for him to comprehend what was required to remain at the top. His impressive physique and natural ability enabled him to reach the heights, but he seems to have lacked the psychological strength to remain there. When faced with defeat or a perceived injustice Newburn was clearly prone to stress and temper tantrums. Such behaviour is quite commonplace in the world of sport, at both amateur and professional levels. In 1900, however, Victorian notions of etiquette, reserve and decorum dictated that his actions were interpreted much less favourably. At that time there was no real understanding of the pressures experienced by top athletes.

O'Connor was at hand to take up Newburn's mantle and was beginning to demonstrate that he had the necessary psychological strength and character required to build on initial successes. After his exertions in the sprints and high jump, O'Connor showed that his energy reserves were not yet depleted for his favourite event. As Newburn quit the grounds, the Wicklowman began to deliver on the promise he had shown in previous seasons, covering well over 23 feet comfortably in consecutive tries, in what was a consistent performance in far from optimal conditions. There was no fussing on his part, he just got on with the job:

> The run up to the jump was uncared for, rough and bumpy, with long grass on it. All things considered O'Connor did well, and is a champion of the right type — a man that can put heart into his work and be depended upon not to turn tail at opposition, when that opposition takes the shape of good men and, it may be, also champions.[13]

O'Connor signalled that he was ready to move up a gear, coolly taking his first IAAA long jump championship with a distance of 23' 6½".

Within days of the IAAA Championships, the team to face Scotland was announced and included O'Connor and Pat Leahy. The Irish athletes would be given a chance to avenge the Scots surprise victory the previous year in Edinburgh where the Scots had sensationally snatched victory in the last event, the long jump, despite the presence of both Newburn and O'Connor. In Belfast, what should have been one of the most memorable meetings of the sporting season turned into one of the wettest and most miserable days of the summer. Despite the rain, some 3,000 spectators turned up at the Cliftonville Athletic Club to see Ireland comfortably win the fixture by seven events to four. The deluge was at its worst when O'Connor and Leahy were contesting the high jump. Conditions were so poor that their Scottish opponents were "washed out" at an early stage. The Scots' withdrawal effectively meant that Ireland had secured the high-jump contest but the two Irish crack jumpers battled on regardless. Neither O'Connor nor Leahy wanted to stop in spite of the downpour, such was their intense rivalry and mutual desire to outdo each other. The sight of the two Irishmen, battling it out in the lashing rain and vying for supremacy without any Scottish opposition, must have amazed the onlookers. No less stupefying were the contrasting styles of the two jumpers. O'Connor's unorthodox technique bemused all who watched him and was beginning to unnerve his opposition. The best high jumpers in the world regularly jumped over six feet and the world record stood at 6' 7¾". It was extremely doubtful if O'Connor could ever rise to those heights considering the limitations of his uncompromising style, although spectators found it extremely entertaining. Nonetheless, one suspects that it took its toll on O'Connor, especially in poor conditions. His new style would improve his long jumping, but simultaneously prove a restraint on his high jumping:

The contrast in style between the two jumpers was most remarkable. Leahy jumped with all that grace which has called
forth praise from every judge of jumping who ever saw him.
He never went an inch higher than was necessary, and took
off and landed within a few feet of the lath. O'Connor on the
contrary was jumping 5ft 9in, when the bar was 3in lower, and
the point from where he took off to where he landed was
nearly 17 feet. He was really broad jumping, and if he had
Leahy's style he would do wonders.[14]

Eventually, after much coaxing from teammates and drenched
officials, the two Irishmen decided to call it a day. On the toss of a
coin, Leahy was declared the token winner. Within a couple of
days they would have opportunity to continue their personal tus-
sle and perhaps settle the issue at the English Championships in
Stamford Bridge. Their hunger and enthusiasm for competition
was undoubtedly admirable, but one commentator could not help
but lament the disregard the Irish athletes showed for their health
and well-being.

That neither [Leahy] nor O'Connor could establish individual
superiority either at Ballsbridge or Cliftonville is not a matter
for surprise or sorrow . . . but it is a curious coincidence that
on both occasions a shocking shower descended just as they
were about to start. O'Connor would be dead now only for
me, as he threw his clothes aside out on the wringing grass before jumps, and I was barely in time to whip them up before
each of his efforts. I solemnly and sorely warn all athletes
against this careless practice, which is very prevalent in the
South. Take off your coat and give it to a friend or an umpire
to hold and having jumped or run put it on immediately, close
the neck and turn up the collar.[15]

This was undoubtedly sensible advice, since Irish athletes seem to
have been universally dismissive of taking precautions against the
effects of the elements. Perhaps they thought to do so might be
interpreted as a sign of weakness and diminish their hard-earned
reputation as tough Celts willing to compete in any kind of

weather and in the roughest or most primitive of sporting arenas. Nevertheless, the days of such cavalier, romantic and essentially foolhardy conduct were numbered. The forthcoming events at Stamford Bridge would dispel any illusions that such bravado was really necessary or productive.

5

A Rude Awakening

A FEW DAYS AFTER THE BELFAST meeting with the Scots, a sizeable contingent of Irish athletes made their way to Stamford Bridge to compete in the AAA Championships. They were joined by the cream of British athletes and a large contingent of Americans. After the comprehensive victory over their Scottish cousins, the Irish athletes were no doubt confident of putting on a good show and coming away with their share of the spoils at the English Championships. The Americans would, however, provide much stiffer opposition than expected. Indeed the meeting would prove something of a watershed in international competition, and a crucial moment of awakening for British and Irish athletes.

The presence of the American visitors en route to the Paris Olympics ensured plenty of coverage before and after the meeting. Though they had never been seen in competition before in Europe, many of the athletes were already well known. In particular, the Pennsylvania trio of Alvin Kraenzlein, Walter Tewksbury and Irving Baxter had fearsome reputations. Baxter was a noted high jumper and pole-vaulter, Tewksbury a renowned sprinter, and Kraenzlein was the man who had revolutionised the world of hurdling by developing a unique leg-before-body technique that left the opposition yards behind. All three were roommates whose lives at university were inextricably linked through a shared regime of study, training and athletic competition.

> The [Americans] are nearly all University men, or collegians,
> according to the favourite term employed across the water,

and though neither Yale nor Harvard is especially represented, practically the pick of the American athletic world will
figure on the Stamford Bridge track tomorrow afternoon.
Pennsylvania University has furnished the greatest number of
competitors and it is to their performances that English eyes
will be chiefly directed. "Old Penns", as is known, have long
and anxiously awaited an opportunity of measuring the capabilities of their chosen team against ourselves . . . and the very
men who carried the blue and red jersey to triumph in [America] are today preparing to wrest the title of champion from
our home-born athletes.[1]

The night before the competition, the Irish delegation, comprising athletes, officials and members of the Irish press, set out for
England by boat. The crossing was especially rough and proved an
inauspicious beginning to the trip. An anonymous correspondent
to *Sport*, signed "Athlete", later provided an illuminating and
hard-hitting account of the Irish experience on the way to and during the Stamford Bridge Championship. Exactly who the author of
this interesting and expert report was is not known but "Athlete"
could possibly have been Maurice Davin, who had travelled over
especially to see the contest at Stamford Bridge:

> They all travelled over to England on the night before, arrived
> about two hours before the contest, tired, jaded, and weary af
> ter the long sea and railway journey, and in addition some of
> them suffered from seasickness. After hurriedly partaking of
> dinner to try and allay the hunger and exhaustion consequent
> on a long continuous journey, they arrived on the grounds.
> They had not a friend to assist in rubbing them, but had to do
> as best they could themselves. I may here remark that the
> crude way rubbing down is indulged in by Irish athletes pre
> paratory to going out for a contest is more injurious than oth
> erwise. I actually saw one of our athletes applying the fresh
> glove so vigorously that he actually drew the blood.[2]

Until this time it was common practice, particularly amongst
Irish athletes, to arrive on the day of a sports, sometimes even
minutes before the beginning of a competition. Although it was

clear to all and sundry that such practices might jeopardise an athlete's chances of competing to the best of his ability, more often than not the IAAA did not have sufficient funds to cover the costs of accommodation for large groups over several nights. Indeed it was not uncommon for teams or individual competitors to travel large distances, compete and depart immediately after the finish. Such was the life of the amateur Irish athlete. There could not have been a greater contrast between the lot of the Irish athletes and that of the American visitors. While the Irish preparations were somewhat haphazard and left to the discretion of each individual, the Americans left nothing to chance:

> The Americans, who numbered close on fifty, had the advantage of actually training on the grounds for a whole fortnight twice daily before the contest came off. They were in [the] charge of experienced trainers, who were unceasing in their supervision and efforts to bring their men out as fit as the proverbial fiddle. They had about ten coloured attendants to rub them down and prepare them for their respective events, and I may here mention that the process was decidedly novel, strange and interesting to me, and wholly different to what I had been accustomed to see at Ballsbridge dressing room and elsewhere. After being thoroughly overhauled the Americans who were to compete came out on the grounds wearing a heavy bath robe or dressing gown with a hood on the back to go over the head, which completely enveloped them. Each carried with him a heavy grey blanket to protect him when lying on the grass from cold and damp, so that nothing in the smallest degree could militate against his chances.[3]

Such sights were unprecedented in the old-style genteel world of British and Irish athletics. The notion of even arriving a day or two before an athletic contest was a luxury amateur athletes such as O'Connor could only dream of. What employer in his right mind would consent to such a long period of leave, unpaid or otherwise? Further, the sight of so many dedicated trainers and masseurs must also have amazed the athletes from the home countries. It was clear that the Americans meant business and would do everything possible to ensure the best performances from their sportsmen.

The greatest number of American athletes came from the University of Pennsylvania. These Penn athletes were very much the focus of attention, roaming about the track and field in large robes, mysterious cloaked and hooded figures. Had their gowns not been blue and red, and inscribed with the letter P, some of the Irish competitors might have been excused for thinking that a bunch of Franciscan Friars had taken to the field. The peculiar chants which emanated from this group during the course of the day, however, would leave no doubt as to the allegiance of the athletes in question, "Hoo-Raa-Raa-Raa Penn-syl-vania". Never before had such American college calls been heard at a European fixture. In the politically correct world of British athletics, etiquette and manners were of the utmost importance and such tribal behaviour on the part of the American visitors was unprecedented and occasioned much comment. "It is a curious but interesting custom — and had no doubt an unsettling effect on the American athletes' opponents."

Over 10,000 people filled Stamford Bridge to see the athletes of the Old and New World clash. There was plenty of entertainment and spectacle but little to cheer about for the home crowd. British disappointment was tangible when it transpired that of the five runners in the 100-yard sprint, four hailed from America and the fifth from Australia. Throughout the day's proceedings the crowd was engrossed by the American athletes, each dressed in the colours of their respective university.

Against his better judgement, O'Connor was leaned on by IAAA officials who cajoled him into competing in the high jump because they reckoned his victory in the long jump, scheduled for later in the day, was assured. Since it was a cold wet day with constant drizzle, he would have been better advised to stay in the changing rooms, dry and relaxed. He could then emerge to take on the American long jumpers at the last minute. Anxious not to let the side down, O'Connor agreed to turn out in the high jump, although he intended to retire early from the event. When Leahy inexplicably faltered at 5' 7¾", it fell to O'Connor to uphold the honour of Ireland against Baxter. Unlike O'Connor and Leahy, the American did not have a particularly crowd-pleasing style, and his jumping even received a "chilly" reception from the crowd. Though Baxter's style may not have been as aesthetically pleasing as that of the two Irishmen, it was clearly superior and he comfortably beat O'Connor into (joint) second place. Following the disappointment of losing a long and gruelling high jump contest, O'Connor, who was now sodden and with his energy reserves somewhat depleted, had to face Kraenzlein in the long jump.

In contrast to the Americans, whom it was believed had arrived in London two weeks before, the Irishmen geared up to compete without any prior practice or knowledge of the grounds. The conditions were unfamiliar to both O'Connor and Leahy and they consequently struggled to adapt in the wet circumstances. The run-up was on a cinder path and the take-off was only about three inches in width, in contrast to Ireland where the run-up was almost always on grass and the board over six inches in width. The smaller take-off was particularly tricky, and neither O'Connor nor Leahy succeeded in timing their take-off accurately.

The unusual sporting paraphernalia and customs of the Penn athletes intrigued various onlookers, and the lengthy and ponderous manner in which the Americans prepared for the long jump seemed no less bizarre.

> Prior to the long jump coming off the Americans and their trainers were nearly an hour engaged measuring the run up with a tape, and practising until they were able to take off accurately, which showed how thorough and systematic they do things in order to ensure success. Leahy and O'Connor were all the time looking on bewildered, not comprehending the effect of what they saw until it was too late. The three Americans [during the progress of the contest] got off the lath or board with wonderful accuracy whilst the Irishmen could not get off the board at all. They sprang from about six inches behind the board on almost every occasion, and when they did on one or two occasions manage to get on it they fouled the

> trig and their jumps were disallowed. They evidently have
> adopted no system [to take off accurately] as they merely ran
> to the jump, chancing it to good luck that they would come
> properly to it.[4]

Throughout the long jump the two Irishman struggled to register
a decent distance. O'Connor was probably disgusted with his best
effort, a mere 22' 4¼", considering he had jumped over 23' 0½" at
every sports so far that season. Despite having held the world record for a short time at 24' 4½", Kraenzlein could do no better
than 22' 10". This unimpressive distance nonetheless proved
enough to beat O'Connor and Leahy into second and third place
respectively. O'Connor must have been beside himself with annoyance, particularly since one of his disallowed jumps was some
8 inches longer than Kraenzlein's best effort. As O'Connor faltered at Stamford Bridge, he lost a golden opportunity to make his
reputation against the American, who within weeks would become a living legend.

At the end of the day, eight of the ten events on the card had
been won by Americans; it was perhaps fortunate that the entire
American Olympic team was not present at Stamford Bridge.

O'Connor's defeat by Kraenzlein, the loss least expected, was a
huge blow to Irish morale. The team had been undone by a combination of fatigue and poor preparation. Arriving at the last minute
and still suffering from seasickness, their chances were scuppered
before they even made it onto the field. Just when it seemed things
could not get any worse, some of the team's disappointment
turned to dismay and disbelief when word broke that the Olympic
Games were due to commence within days of Stamford Bridge.
The Irish athletes were under the impression that they were due to
start on 2 September and some had hoped to compete in them. At
this late stage, no preparations, financial or otherwise, had been
made to travel to Paris. Finding themselves caught unawares at the
eleventh hour, there was considerable grumbling and discontent
amongst the group, with all "thoroughly disgusted with the affair".[5] The whole trip to Stamford Bridge had proved a shambles
and this final blow was the proverbial straw that broke the camel's

back. One can imagine the sense of disappointment and frustration that must have filtered through the Irish ranks when they heard the news. They were but a short journey away from Paris, but the IAAA had neither the time nor the funds to organise a last ditch effort to get them there. Had Irish athletes travelled independently of the English AAA to Paris, it is not clear if they would have been allowed to compete. Quite possibly any medals they would have won and points scored would have been attributed to Britain, as was the case in later Olympics.

Curiously, the only Irish athlete who had been entered at Paris was the one person who had no intention of competing. In the months preceding the 1900 Olympics, the English AAA had contacted Peter O'Connor several times to invite him to compete for Britain at Paris and had undertaken to pay his expenses.[6] Each time O'Connor refused because he did not want to compete under the Union Jack and he therefore was probably as much in the dark as other Irish athletes as to the precise dates of the Olympics. When O'Connor once again refused the chance to join the British team at Stamford Bridge, Pat Leahy accepted a last-minute invitation from the AAA to compete in Paris.

In some respects it was a pity that O'Connor did not follow Leahy's lead, since his absence effectively allowed American athletes to dominate the jumping events. By declining the English AAA's invitation, he had postponed his Olympics debut for another six years. Apart from the fact that O'Connor was determined to nail his nationalist colours firmly to the mast, he may also not have considered the Olympics to be of any great importance because this was only the second time that the revitalised Games was being held. In the coming years O'Connor would be far more concerned with winning the AAA and, effectively, the world championships. Though the Olympic movement had been revived, it had yet to establish itself in the public's consciousness as the landmark sports event it is today.

છ

DEFEAT TO KRAENZLEIN CAME just at the right moment in Peter O'Connor's sporting life. Recent successes had given him a taste of fame and celebrity, but now he was brought right down to earth, made to look ordinary, a pale shadow of the champion athlete he aspired to be. He certainly had much more to think about than most on his return to Ireland. He knew in his heart that he was a better jumper than Kraenzlein, but he also had become painfully aware that his all-round technique left much to be desired. His weaknesses had been exposed and laid bare for all to see. The experience could have adversely affected his development as an athlete, but fortunately he had the strength of character to learn from the disaster and avoid lengthy and futile recriminations. Though he may not have realised it at the time, this temporary setback was possibly the single most important formative experience in his athletics career. Defeat at the hands of Kraenzlein left a lingering, bitter aftertaste, but the Americans had revealed several important "trade secrets" in their brief but memorable invasion of Britain. A discerning athlete could learn much from the American display.

Crucially, O'Connor had witnessed an effective method of improving the chances of a clean take-off. Initially he had been amused and baffled by the way the American long jumpers and their coaches laboriously measured the run-up distance to the take-off board. Afterwards it was clear that this simple ritual greatly increased the chances of hitting the take-off board accurately, and it was this that proved the difference between him and Kraenzlein on the day. O'Connor had always trusted to lady luck and, deserted by her at Stamford Bridge, he had come unstuck. The Americans had kept themselves warm before jumping, so that their muscles would not stiffen up, a sensible precaution considering the sometimes unpredictable British climate. Significantly, some Americans competed in only one contest so as to reserve their energies for their best event. In short, the Americans were organised and prepared, the Irish and British athletes the opposite, turning up on the day and hoping for the best.

The American athlete believes that if a thing is worth doing it is worth doing well. He leaves nothing to chance and takes no risks. For instance, between jumps, say, he does not loll about on the cool turf, with nothing on but his athlete's costume. He carefully envelops himself in a long and hooded cloak and keeps sufficiently on the move to avoid stiffness and sluggishness, and when his turn comes makes his way to the mark, a reserve of energy, life and well-honed strength, backed by a grim determination to "get there", "go one better".[7]

The British and Irish sporting press did not unduly criticise the home athletes, recognising that training facilities and the sports infrastructures in Britain and Ireland were vastly inferior to those of American universities. Nonetheless, hard questions would have to be asked. Would extra amounts of grit and determination, the age-old weapons of the amateur athlete, be enough to combat this new breed of finely tuned and disciplined athlete, or was the era of the amateur athlete effectively coming to an end? If so, what future lay in store for Irish athletics, run more or less on a shoestring and with few if any training facilities? These questions and many more must have been to the forefront in the minds of the Irish entourage as they made their way home.

The 1900 AAA Championships at Stamford Bridge was something of a watershed in British and Irish athletic circles, and indeed the beginning of a new era in international athletics. The American Ivy League invasion squad had decimated almost all opposition and made many experienced and hardy athletes look like rank amateurs and dilettantes. For Irish athletes the debacle proved a bitter pill to swallow so soon after their fine victory over the Scots. The Americans' exhibition both on and off the field gave them much food for thought. Not only had the home side been beaten fair and square, they had been out-prepared and out-thought. Indeed the Americans' intensive preparations clearly redefined the state of play. From this moment, talent and determination alone would not suffice to ensure success.

CB

THE PARIS OLYMPICS, AS EVENTS TRANSPIRED, were not all that they were cracked up to be. In contrast to the inaugural Games in Athens four years before, which was run as a unique individual event, the French decided to incorporate the Games into the 1900 Paris Exposition Universelle Internationale, hoping the Exposition would increase awareness of the Olympics. Exposition organisers took control of the Games and relegated Pierre de Coubertin, who had almost single-handedly resurrected the Olympic movement, giving it a new lease of life, to a minor role. The Paris Games were a huge disappointment, never taking centre stage, and were dragged out over five months. Spread all over Paris in a disparate, haphazard manner, the Olympic celebration was treated with relative indifference by the French public. On a positive note, women made their debut in these Olympics, a not insignificant step considering attitudes prevalent at the time. In the ancient Olympics women had been forbidden from competing and initially from spectating. Female participation heralded a new era in the history of the Olympics, an early sign that big social changes were afoot as the twentieth century dawned. The inaugural 1896 Games in Athens had been run more or less according to the classical model, with few unusual competitions. Parisian organisers seem to have been much less concerned with historical accuracy and came up with some particularly bizarre events. Most notable amongst these were the equestrian long and high jump, as well as a swimming obstacle race that required contestants to climb a pole, scramble over a row of boats and under another flotilla. Flagrantly flouting the amateur ideals of the Olympic movement, there was a prize of 3,000 francs for the winner of the fencing event, the epée, for amateurs and masters. Coubertin must have been secretly delighted when the Games finally came to an ignominious end without a closing ceremony. Though the Paris Games at times had threatened to descend into farce, one suspects Coubertin learnt much from the experience. For the Games to be a success both financially and culturally they would have to be run over a shorter period of time as well as having a clearly identifiable "locus" such as a stadium.

Despite the organisational and logistical difficulties facing the organisers, the Games themselves were extremely hard fought, though the Americans proved the dominant force in track and field. The American delegation was officially led by A.G. Spalding, whom President McKinley appointed as the first American director to an Olympic Games. Spalding had been a professional baseball player in his youth before setting up a giant sporting goods company with his brother J. Walter Spalding. Spalding's appointment was most likely honorary and it was his assistant, James E. Sullivan, who was effectively in charge of the American campaign. Sullivan was not only the long-standing secretary of the American Athletics Union, but from 1892 he had been employed permanently by Spalding and was in charge of the advertising and promotion of Spalding goods through one of their subsidiaries, the American Sports Publishing Company.[8]

After his excellent performances at Stamford Bridge, Alvin Kraenzlein continued his good form and became the star performer of the Paris Games, taking four gold medals. Universally applauded for his first three gold medals, his fourth gold in the long jump sparked perhaps the biggest controversy of the Games and set the stage for one of the most legendary feuds in the early history of track and field. At the time of the Paris Games, Kraenzlein was the best all-round athlete in the world. In hurdling he was in a class of his own and untouchable. Likewise he was an exceptionally fast sprinter. Although he had broken Newburn's world record, establishing a new distance of 24' 4½", long jumping was probably his weakest discipline. Apart from O'Connor who was not present in Paris, the one man who could beat Kraenzlein in long jumping was his compatriot and Syracuse University rival, Myer Prinstein.

Though he was selected for the American team, Myer Prinstein almost didn't make it to the Paris Games. His university, Syracuse, which had a strong sporting tradition similar to Penn, although it was not one of the big eight Ivy League schools, was not willing or able to send Prinstein and three other athletes to compete in the Games. Because the Syracuse men could not afford the expensive journey to Europe without sponsorship, the Paris Olympics was destined to remain an elusive pipe dream. With the situation seemingly hopeless, a wealthy American oil baron intervened and offered to give them free passage on one of his oil tankers. It was just the break they needed. Not only would they make it to Paris in the nick of time, they would be able to train on the tanker while crossing the Atlantic. Though Prinstein was only 5' 7¾" and 145 pounds, relatively small for a long jumper, he was extremely well built and a gifted athlete.[9] Already that season he had become intercollegiate champion at the Penn relays, not only beating Kraenzlein on home ground but smashing the former's long jump world record by almost three inches, with a distance of 24' 7¼". The Paris Games were expected to provide the opportunity for an epic long jump encounter between the two, with Prinstein the marginal favourite. As it transpired, the event was to be a memorable encounter for entirely different reasons.

In the qualifying round for the long jump which was held on a Saturday, Prinstein showed good form, taking the lead with a jump of 23' 6½". The final was due to be held the following day. There had been much consternation from numerous quarters that events were to be held on the Christian Sabbath. Since Syracuse was a Methodist University, some officials who were present forbade their student athletes in Paris from competing. Myer Prinstein was Jewish, but as a student of Syracuse he found himself under considerable pressure to boycott the event. Interestingly, he did not seem to mind competing on the Jewish Sabbath. It must have seemed absurd for Prinstein to have travelled such a long distance and not be able to contest the final of his speciality event. Eventually, after much persuasion, Prinstein agreed to respect the Sabbath. It was reasonable to expect that no one would surpass his distance. The only man present who could realistically do so was Kraenzlein, but he had allegedly given his word to Prinstein that he likewise would not compete on the Sunday because he was a Christian.

The following day tensions rose as Kraenzlein turned out for the long jump, reneging on his promise. Prinstein was furious, forced to watch from the sidelines as Kraenzlein gradually crept up from behind and closed in on his qualifying lead. With his sixth and final jump, Kraenzlein overtook Prinstein's qualifying jump, robbing the Syracuse man of gold. Incensed, Prinstein stormed onto the field to demand a "jump-off" for first place the following day. When Kraenzlein refused, Prinstein punched him and a mêlée ensued. Kraenzlein was undoubtedly one of the greatest athletes of the early Olympic era but his finest moment, taking a fourth gold medal at Paris, would remain somewhat tarnished by accusations of brinkmanship. It may well be that at the last minute Kraenzlein had been ordered by officials from his university or perhaps by J. E. Sullivan to contest the final, to make sure that America took gold as Syracuse had sidelined Prinstein. Whatever the case, to this day the affair remains shrouded in mystery but there can be no doubt that the experience left its mark on Prinstein. Whether or not this incident may have had a bearing on a future controversy between O'Connor and Prinstein at Athens in 1906 is open to question. The parallels between the two incidents are, however, clear.

As Kraenzlein and Prinstein exchanged blows, Pat Leahy quietly took the bronze medal. The only Irish athlete at the Games, Leahy acquitted himself creditably in Paris, also taking silver in the high jump. He might well have expected to do better in both events, but Leahy, whom O'Connor described as the "enigma" of Irish athletics, was never able to achieve top form in international competition.

ଔ

ONCE BACK ON IRISH SOIL AND having missed out on the Paris Games, Peter O'Connor set his sights once again on Newburn's Irish record and the dream of an eventual world record. There may have been a lack of stiff competition for O'Connor in Ireland in the long jump, but the generous odds offered his opponents were incentive enough for him to improve. Life was not always plain sailing as at the Royal Irish Constabulary sports, O'Connor, "the scratchman",[10] had to concede some eight inches to Leahy, though the Charleville man was fresh from his Olympic victories and was now jumping over 23 feet consistently. When Leahy jumped 23′ 1″, O'Connor was forced to find some special reserve of energy and came up with a jump of 23′ 11½″, an enormous improvement on his previous best and within an inch of Newburn's record. O'Connor was becoming extremely consistent and his jumping that day averaged 23′ 7¼″.

Only a week later in Ballinasloe, it looked as if Newburn's Irish record was once again done and dusted when O'Connor jumped 24′ 4½″ at a sports organised by the local St Michael's Abstinence Society. The jump was immediately heralded by all present at the meeting as a new Irish record.

> It was generally believed that O'Connor of Waterford would, by developing a better turn of speed, equal if not excel Newburn's long jump record. He has ever since been gradually but steadily breaking the crust of clay which lies between 23ft 6 inches, his then best jump and 24 feet, Newburn's record. This little strip of ground was the one spot of earth which barred O'Connor's way to athletic prosperity. It was the writing which he saw on the walls of his room at night, but the whalebone-like muscles of this superbly built athlete has at last surmounted the dread obstacle. At the Ballinasloe sports last week O'Connor came to the trig with the action of an affrighted deer, and with an enormous bound and flexible figure covered a distance of 24ft 4½ inches. A civil engineer testifies to the legal formation of the ground, and Lord Clancarty vouches also for the accuracy of this phenomenal performance.[11]

The accolades were premature, however, as the records committee in Dublin still had to sanction the jump. O'Connor probably thought that the clarification of his new record would be a formality, as all necessary measures seem to have been in place. He was to be sorely disappointed, however, because the Records Committee found the new record inadmissible on technical grounds, when on inspection the jumping grounds did not conform to specifications.

O'Connor soon discovered that his new-found reputation and improving form brought with it certain drawbacks. He had become so consistent of late over 23 feet that handicappers began to penalise him heavily, making it increasingly difficult to take home any first prizes, even against vastly inferior opposition. At times the absurdity of the handicapping system became clear to even its fiercest advocates, as when O'Connor faced Newburn in the long jump later that summer in Tramore. Owing to recent poor form, Newburn was offered a six-inch head start against O'Connor. It was the first time the two had met in competition since Newburn had walked out in Ballsbridge and, although O'Connor was at a considerable disadvantage, he was determined to underline his supremacy. Newburn was odds-on favourite to beat the Wicklowman and perhaps regain some of his old confidence and form. Although he jumped creditably he could manage no more than 23' 0½". When O'Connor jumped 24' 0" the competition was effectively decided. It was an ignominious defeat for Newburn and signalled that he was now very much a spent force in athletics. In his other main event, the 100-yard sprint, he could only manage second place. At this time Newburn was probably trying to bounce back from injury, but it may be that psychological as well as physical factors played a part in his loss of form. Newburn's transformation from man of the moment to fallen idol had been swift as a commentator at Tramore noted: "Newburn is a man hard to please, and a more consistent grumbler I have not met in my time. He appeared to be displeased with everyone and everything, and certainly was not on the best terms with himself."[12]

After Tramore, O'Connor and his numerous supporters began to wonder if any of his unofficial "world record" jumps would ever be officially recognised. The Records Committee was jointly chaired by GAA and IAAA officials, but the two organisations had slightly different rules regarding the long jump, so this may have created a certain amount of confusion. For instance, the GAA made allowances for clay, whereas the IAAA did not. Many nationalists felt that the IAAA was an organisation with strong Unionist sympathies and associations. As such, it might be reluctant to see O'Connor take Newburn's Irish record. Most of the grounds that O'Connor competed at may not have fulfilled the precise specifications laid down by the Records Committees, but the consistent and repeated rejections of so many record claims were now becoming suspicious in the eyes of many. There was probably little truth to the rumour that the IAAA were intent on seeing Newburn's record remain, thereby depriving a Catholic pretender of a Unionist throne.

Following the jumps at Ballinasloe and Tramore, O'Connor competed at a sports meeting in New Ross where he once again broke Newburn's record. When this latest record was rejected, the tensions between the IAAA and O'Connor's supporters finally reached boiling point. Once again the jumping grounds were not perfect, although the conditions did not always work in favour of the hopeful record breaker.

> The run to the board was slightly down the hill, the fall being so slight as to be almost imperceptible, but any advantage which he gained in this respect was more than compensated for by the unevenness of the turf. In fact O'Connor had to run in zig-zag fashion to avoid the numerous miniature kopjes with which the ground was studded.[13]

O'Connor was now beginning to think there was some truth behind the conspiracy theories. To be denied a record once was unfortunate, but to be denied so many times smacked of intrigue. After New Ross, his case made its way into the national newspapers following a short anonymous letter from a Waterford reader hiding under the pseudonym of "Intacta". Whether or not it was O'Connor who initiated proceedings is not known but "Intacta's" comments that the Record Committee intended Newburn's record to remain "permanent" started a lengthy and divisive debate, clearly drawing the lines between his supporters and IAAA officials.[14] The IAAA was quick to rebut the claims, pointing out that none of the grounds where the records were made was acceptable. At the time it was common practice for long-jumping areas to be selected by the competitors themselves when they arrived at a venue, so the chance of finding a completely level area that could satisfy the numerous technical requirements of the Records Committee was slight. At Ballinasloe there had been a slight fall in the ground in the run-up to the jump and an engineer at the New Ross sports certified that there was a gradient of 3½ inches that was imperceptible to the human eye in approach to the jumping pit.[15] There was only one officially sanctioned jumping pit in Ireland — at the RDS grounds in Ballsbridge. If O'Connor's records were to stand, they would have to made there, right under the noses of the Records Committee. So as to limit the damage caused by the controversy, the IAAA officials undertook to prepare the Ballsbridge grounds for O'Connor to make a record attempt at the last major sports meeting of the season, the Clerys & Co. Sports. This was the best O'Connor could hope for. Unfortunately when the opportunity presented itself, O'Connor was unable to repeat his earlier form of the season, battling a stiff breeze to no avail and managing only 23' 3½". His lacklustre close to the season was a sign that he was tired and his exploits that summer had at last taken their toll.

The season ended in frustration and disappointment for O'Connor. It had been a topsy-turvy year in which he had promised much but failed to deliver at the crucial moments. He had underperformed at Stamford Bridge, missed out on the chance to pursue Olympic glory because of his nationalist beliefs, and Newburn's Irish record was still hanging by a thread. Nonetheless, in the person of Kraenzlein, and American athletes in general, O'Connor had new opponents by whom to set his standards. He had successfully eclipsed Newburn, his first great rival in the eyes of the public and the sporting press, and his name was beginning to become known throughout Ireland. This new-found celebrity was no doubt a solace to O'Connor in the cold winter months when he resumed his relatively anonymous working life in Dunford's solicitor's office. He had been granted a taste of the kind of recognition and fame rarely afforded someone from his social background and working life. This attention would fuel his ambition to advance up the social ladder. He would remain focused and train hard right throughout the winter months. If he was going to make it in sport, 1901 would be a make or break year. He knew he was on the cusp of greatness, but also that he could just as easily fade into obscurity as Newburn had done. He was determined not to suffer the same fate.

6

On the Touchstone of Mastery

THE IRISH ATHLETICS SEASON WAS traditionally considered to start every year on Whit Monday with the annual IAAA Championships. Though many athletes would just be waking up from sporting hibernation, O'Connor was unusual amongst the top athletes in that he trained throughout the winter months. The season was relatively short and it was important to make a good start. O'Connor had been disappointed not to have officially broken Newburn's record the previous season and it was rumoured that he had even considered retiring, presumably to focus his energies on his career.[1] C.P. Redmond, the editor of *The Waterford News*, seems to have played a pivotal role in dissuading him from any such action, and exactly four weeks before the IAAA Championships O'Connor began his specialised training regime in earnest. For the first week, every second day he ran 440 yards and a half mile at a slow pace, always stepping "very high" on his toes. He also restricted himself to two sessions of 35–50 yard sprints the first week and only really began jumping the second week. Up to five days before the event he had "his eye on", he made make six jumps each evening, always using a lath placed four feet high, so as to jump only 21–22 feet, some two feet short of his best. In the remaining days before the championships, O'Connor pushed himself to the limit, always falling well short of 24 feet. He was not unduly worried, however, because he knew from experience that the adrenalin rush of competition as well as his excitable temperament were key factors in producing his best.[2] As Whit

Monday approached, O'Connor was primed to peak and ready for any and all opposition.

Anyone who had ambitions to gain a coveted place on the Irish team to face Scotland in the annual showdown would have to impress at the IAAA Championships, which served as the principal qualifier. National titles would be on the line as well as the chance to represent Ireland. As the first highlight of the sporting calendar, a great deal of organisation usually went into the day.

This year the Dublin Metropolitan Police Band and the Carriglea Industrial School Band had been given the honour of playing during the day's proceedings, the former's presence underlining that this was very much an establishment occasion. Although the IAAA was always considered to have a strong Unionist background, they were not overtly political, unlike the GAA. For O'Connor, the Ballsbridge venue would give him a chance to compete and try for the world record in arguably Ireland's best jumping ground. Further, most if not all of the officials responsible for certifying records would be there on the day to witness his efforts at first hand.

There was a lot of hype in the sporting press in the run-up to the championships about Newburn, who was rumoured to have returned to form after intensive training. Anxious to re-stake his claim as Ireland's best jumper, Newburn had allegedly spent two weeks practising his jumping in the Ballsbridge grounds. If O'Connor needed any extra motivation to show the world what he was capable of, the promise of Newburn's return was it.

As Whit Monday, 27 May, drew near, he was in top form, and possibly at his physical peak. Just over six feet tall and weighing 158 lbs, O'Connor possessed a physical fitness and well-toned body that probably did not escape the attentions of the female readership.

> He is a splendid type of athlete. He is almost as hard as iron, or as near being that metal as any human being could be. With no superfluous flesh, he looks like a racer of the finest brand . . . a greyhound, well formed, thin, wiry and a mass of sinewy muscles. [3]

Such was his commanding physical presence that O'Connor was beginning to become a draw for crowds in his own right. If the rumours regarding Newburn were true and he was indeed making a comeback, the first sports meeting of the season was guaranteed to be explosive.

Preparation for the IAAA Championships was meticulous and ordered. An attractive sports programme was drawn up, encompassing both athletic and cycling events. The elements of speed and danger in cycling always brought in a good crowd and, considering the interest Newburn and O'Connor were generating, it was not unreasonable to expect that there would be a very good gate. The ultimate success of the day would, however, be dictated by the weather. By Whit Monday, unfortunately, dark clouds ominously loomed over the Irish metropolis and a steady stream of rain and drizzle put a dampener on proceedings. The conditions deteriorated to the extent that the organisers reluctantly had to cancel the cycling events, the principal crowd-puller. Seldom had such weather blighted the annual meeting.

> There was a big falling off in the attendance of the spectators, but that was only a natural consequence of the erratic manner of the weather clerk, who showed no more consideration of the athletes who had trained in anticipation of the events than he did for the pretty toilette of the fair ones who had courage enough to brave the elements and make Ballsbridge their rendezvous for the day.[4]

In spite of the downpour, it was decided to go ahead with the athletics programme since athletes had travelled from the length and breadth of the country to compete. While the wet conditions had made it too dangerous for cyclists, officials maintained that the rain improved the running track which only two days before had been as "hard as cement". Considering the inclement weather, it was hardly surprising that the expected throngs of spectators did not materialise, but a sizeable number decided to brave the elements and looked on from the relative comfort of the sheltered stands.

As the hour of combat drew near, there was as yet no sign of "Niagara" Newburn. At length word came that he had strained a sinew and would play no part in the day's proceedings. The crowd, who had braved the weather to see the two legendary jumpers square off, must have been bitterly disappointed as the news seeped through the ranks. O'Connor no doubt shared their disappointment that an in-form Newburn had not materialised, since there was no better way to break a record than in the heat of battle and against stiff opposition. Fortunately, Pat Leahy decided to compete because otherwise O'Connor would have had to jump on his own, deprived of the rush of adrenalin that tough opposition creates. Leahy's chief talents lay in the high jump, but he was also becoming a distinguished long jumper and latterly had begun training specifically for that event, something that contemporary pundits noted was to the detriment of his high jumping. Leahy was well capable of clearing 23 feet, so there was no room for complacency on O'Connor's part.

As Leahy and O'Connor moved to the jumping area, the crowd began to cheer loudly, waiting expectantly for something exciting to happen to rescue the dreary afternoon. In the light but persistent drizzle, several officials took up their positions by the jumping pit, bowler hats and umbrellas to the ready. A white marker was put down in the pit to mark the distance of Prinstein's world record. The sand was raked, the jumping board wiped dry. Everything was in place. The IAAA had fulfilled its side of the bargain. Now it was up to O'Connor to honour his.

The competition between Leahy and O'Connor was consistent, with no jump of less than 22 feet being recorded. After each jump and a big applause, a silence enveloped the grounds until officials announced the distance covered. In his third jump, O'Connor cleared 24 feet, effectively making the result of the competition a foregone conclusion. The sense that a world record hung in the balance must have been tangible, the tension never far from the surface, in spite of the constant rain. So as not to upset O'Connor's rhythm and give him a much-needed breather between jumps, Leahy decided not to retire. He probably had not forgotten

O'Connor's gesture the year before when the Wicklowman had sportingly chosen to share the high jump title with him, when he might easily have won it. This time it was Leahy's turn to repay the compliment. O'Connor was gradually creeping up on the elusive white mark to the side of the pit and he still had a further three jumps.

Behind the façade of his usual stony and determined demeanour, O'Connor was evidently feeling the full extent of the tension. After all the agonising misses and disappointments of the previous year, he was deeply suspicious of certain officials whom he believed were in league with Newburn. Now that he was so close, these suspicions resurfaced and O'Connor momentarily and uncharacteristically lost his cool. When his fourth jump was disallowed, he exploded and declared openly that the judges did not want him to erase Newburn's Irish record. The crowd looked on in bewilderment as the argument raged, so many grown men, officials and athletes standing around, arguing in the pouring rain. O'Connor was furious, feeling that his last jump had beaten the record. He was so annoyed that he refused to continue the competition. His concentration was gone and the controversy was not just wasting time but valuable energy. Eventually, after much "absurd coaxing" from Leahy and others, O'Connor changed his mind and thought better of storming off the field in disgust. This outward display of emotion, though it almost ended in his withdrawal, must have eased his nerves because he now renewed his task with even more determination.

The long jump is one of the most exacting disciplines in athletics. An athlete must judge his run-up correctly, accurately hit the take-off board and land without falling back into the pit or disturbing his mark. In O'Connor's day, the ultimate success of any jumper was down to presiding officials, who were expected to judge if the jumps were valid or not. There are many factors which come into play each time a long jumper thunders down the track and takes off for destinations unknown. In modern times, television and playback, as well as precision instruments, remove the chance of error or underhandedness on an official's part. In the early days of athletics, however, there were no photo finishes, no foolproof method of ensuring that justice was served. An official's honesty and integrity were all one could rely on. In O'Connor's world, a man was judged by his actions and bound by his word. Clearly by now the divisive and lively debate that had taken place in the national press the previous season had shaken his trust in certain IAAA officials. His outburst was therefore understandable, although poorly timed.

As O'Connor steadied himself for his fifth try, he once again set about regaining his composure and mentally preparing himself. The presiding officials took up their positions, somewhat hotter under the collar, but relieved that the argument had not led to the day's only remaining entertainment finishing in dispute. Such an eventuality would no doubt have led to another litany of irate correspondence in the national newspapers. Such publicity the IAAA could certainly do without. Behind the pit a photographer for *The Gael* made ready to catch O'Connor in mid-flight. Close to the pit Leahy watched, sheltered beneath a long warm overcoat that afforded some respite from the rain. The crowd looked on in silence as O'Connor carefully measured out his traditional run-up of 40 feet, retracing his steps on the sodden track. After several deep breaths and momentarily bowing his head, he burst into a sprint. Within seconds the take-off board resounded with the thud of his running shoes and all present held their breath. Rising to at least five feet in height, O'Connor gave his characteristic scissors kick and sailed towards the white marker.

> In the last 10 yards he gathered himself up for the spring, rose high in the air, like a ball, midway in the spring he gave a sudden jerk as if performing a second spring, and then shot his legs forward like a flash, the momentum as he landed pitching him forward on his face and hands.[5]

Caught mid-air, O'Connor saw the white marker and "felt a thrill of joy knowing that he would land beyond it". As he fell to the ground and bundled himself forward, it would have taken him only a split second to realise that the judges had ruled the jump good. Realising what their silence signified, O'Connor was ecstatic, jumping around wildly, "dancing the fandango". The crowd did not yet know the distance but they were aware that it had been a good jump.

The judges made doubly sure the jump was measured accurately and, following consultation, declared that not only was it valid but he had set a new Irish and world record of 24' 9"! O'Connor's dream had come true and the crowd, who had so patiently braved the elements, were treated to a new world record in the most unlikely of circumstances. All requirements of the ruling bodies were complied with, and with almost all the record committee present to witness the jump, the ratification of his new record should be merely a formality. When the committee eventually convened to discuss the jump, two somewhat disgruntled officials questioned if it was right and proper to award O'Connor the record because he had initially declined to continue the competition after his war of words with them. Their argument was that he had technically withdrawn from the competition, so his successive record-breaking jump was invalid. Fortunately, their protests were not taken seriously and the new record stood.

൚

FOLLOWING O'CONNOR'S TRIUMPH, his name hit the headlines and the managing clerk from Waterford suddenly found himself the man of the moment. The Irish media in particular seemed to relish the opportunity to remind their American cousins that athletes from the "auld country" were still a force to be reckoned with. The world long jump record, long considered a national treasure, had briefly been held by the Americans Kraenzlein and Prinstein but now O'Connor had set matters straight, as official handicapper T.W. Murphy regaled:

> Just get a tape and measure it off on the ground, reader, and realize for yourself what it means. Ireland once more takes its place at the head of a sport she has made particularly her own, and America takes a back seat.[6]

Within days of the Ballsbridge championships, O'Connor became a household name across the English-speaking world. All
the hard work and dedication had finally paid off and the accolades streamed in.

> His style of jumping is complete. Like a whirlwind he runs to
> his jump, gathers himself like a ball, and with a mighty spring,
> high into the air, soars along, and then, with grace and ease
> descends, not the slightest difficulty being apparent.[7]

There was wonder at his dramatic improvement in such a short
period of time. How was it possible for an athlete who had only
begun competing so late in life, within the space of a few years to
become the world's leading jumper and for the most part against
men who were much younger than him? Only a few discerning
commentators noticed that the all-conquering Waterford athlete
had a style that was unlike any seen before.

O'Connor had proven himself not just a hardy and determined
athlete but also an innovator. The gamble to retrain himself to
jump in an entirely different way had paid dividends and the
hard lessons of Stamford Bridge had been absorbed. Now at last
he had finally delivered on his promise. He had a world record to
his name but, most importantly, he felt that he could jump even
farther and with the whole season just ahead, he would have
every opportunity of doing so. One excited reporter of the time
exclaimed that one day the Irishman would "jump to another
planet". Such hyperbole was clearly over the top; interstellar
travel was not on O'Connor's mind. His heart was nonetheless set
on a leap of more modest proportions: to America, the Western
Republic. There, with the best facilities and the huge support of
the Irish-American community, who knows what records he
might set? And should he decide to stay permanently, like many
other Irish athletes before him, he might even have the opportunity to start his career afresh and pursue the American dream.
With all these emotions and aspirations buzzing about him,
O'Connor returned to Waterford to great acclaim. A stranger in
his adopted city when he first arrived in 1898, now his name was

on everyone's lips, his exploits swiftly becoming the stuff of legend. An unforgettable period in his life was just beginning.

છ

THE PREVIOUS JANUARY when Canon Flynn, the Parish Priest of Ballybricken, proposed organising a bazaar to mark the occasion of the Waterford Presentation Convent's centenary, there was great support for the project on a local level since the nuns had made a valuable contribution to Waterford life in the previous hundred years, teaching the poor children of the city. Recently they had extended the school premises, incurring significant debt. The bazaar would present a pleasant social occasion and also alleviate the financial burdens of the Presentation nuns. The prospect of doing a good deed and the additional bonus of several nights on the town attracted a great deal of interest amongst Waterford's leading citizens. The city's celebration was scheduled to take place at the county courthouse the following June and a committee chaired by Canon Flynn was formed that would meet each Thursday over the ensuing five months in Barronstrand Street.

Peter O'Connor, who was never one to miss an opportunity to promote sport and raise the profile of athletics, took time out of his busy season, offering to organise a Gaelic tournament as a prelude to the bazaar's main events, and assuming the role of secretary to the sports committee. Assisting him in this undertaking was his friend and fellow sports enthusiast, C.P. Redmond, who ensured that the event was well publicised. Large numbers were expected to attend the Gaelic tournament because the day's events included a match between the local De La Salle College and a visiting team of "Commercials" from Clonmel.

O'Connor sought out a suitable venue that could cater for large crowds and whose perimeters could be easily controlled, eventually settling on a location known as Hennessy's Field on the outskirts of the city. The venue not only provided a level open space but was conveniently bound on three sides by thickset hedges presenting a natural obstacle to would-be gatecrashers. It was decided to host a Gaelic football tournament, as opposed to an athletics meeting, because the former would appeal to a wider audience and require less organising. On 19 May 1901 the Gaelic Tournament Sports took place in Hennessy's Field at Ballytruckle. Owing to the good publicity surrounding the event and the exceptional weather, some 2,000 spectators turned out to support the fundraiser. The Barrack Street Brass Band were on hand to entertain the assembled crowd. O'Connor's tournament was a resounding success and the crowd impeccably behaved despite "the inevitable ditch climber [who] was in evidence every time he got a chance, which was not very often considering the arrangements made for his special benefit".

On the pitch there was great excitement as the Waterford Commercials second team played out a nail-biting match, narrowly losing by one point to Gracedieu II, and the Clonmel Commercials lived up to their fearsome reputation, hammering the De La Salle school contingent by 1 goal and 10 points. As the crowds were engrossed by the afternoon's sporting spectacle, O'Connor worked behind the scenes to ensure the smooth running of the day, his high-profile role an opportunity for the Wicklowman to ingratiate himself with those locals who may still have considered him as something of an outsider, though he had now been in Waterford for three years. The presence of a great number of young female spectators no doubt gave him an extra incentive to show his organisational flair and "indefatigable" energy in discharging the "lion's share of the arrangements". His efforts did not go unheeded and O'Connor received a generous proportion of the credit for the day's success, being "here there and everywhere during the day looking after the teams and the arrangements generally; tireless in his efforts to keep things straight, which he did, and courteous to all who approached him for information or advice".[8]

On 25 June, the Presentation Convent bazaar was officially opened by the mayor of Waterford, Richard Hearne, and the citizens of the city were invited to peruse the various stalls and marvel at the courthouse's unprecedented transformation "into a perfect little paradise of beautifully arranged stalls laden with valuable prizes and flowers".[9] It was a grand occasion, the local industrial school band providing the first of many entertainments for patrons of the bazaar. Over the two days, Peter O'Connor was responsible for organising the various amusements. After the successful sports at Ballytruckle and his world record success at Ballsbridge some weeks before, O'Connor's name was on everyone's lips. With "quite a bevy of fair and daintily costumed ladies"[10] frequenting and involved in the bazaar, he no doubt enjoyed being at the centre of attention. Each of the stalls at the bazaar displayed attractive prizes and O'Connor probably took the opportunity to acquaint himself not just with the wares on display but also with the numerous ladies running them. One in particular, Mrs Keogh's "Fancy Fair and Children's Stall", seems to have caught his attention. The prizes on display included a drawing room chair, a gold-mounted walking stick, a smoking cabinet and a lady's watch, as well as numerous children's toys. Helping Mrs Keogh were two sisters, Maggie and Statia Halley, who came from one of Waterford's wealthiest farming families. O'Connor probably made a mental note that both young ladies were single, and though he may not have known it at the time, in the person of Maggie Halley he had met his future wife.

CB

FOLLOWING THE BALLSBRIDGE CHAMPIONSHIPS, the IAAA had announced the team to face Scotland in Glasgow. As always, it was hoped that the strongest possible team would travel to do battle with the Scots, because experience had shown that, although they were the weaker team on paper, they were notoriously hard to beat at home. The showdown with the Scots was the most important international contest of the year involving Irish athletes, so the IAAA made sure that the Irish team arrived in Glasgow in good time and well rested. Since 1895, when Ireland and Scotland had first met in a friendly athletics showdown, the annual bout had flourished and become the highlight of the Irish and Scots sporting calendars. It provided both Irish and Scots athletes with the only chance of competing under their national colours in an international event. The large amount of press coverage given to the event in pre-match predictions and lengthy post-mortems is testament to the interest which the Celtic duel generated. Though this annual fixture would continue to be held for many more years, the competition in Glasgow in 1901 marks the apex of its importance as an event.

As the Irish athletes, officials and pressmen left Dublin for Glasgow, the eyes of the world were already trained on the rapidly growing city and industrial hub. The most extravagant and important exhibition of the twentieth century thus far was in full swing, adding an extra dimension to the annual Ireland–Scotland contest as Scots sports fans were sure to turn up in force for the occasion. Ever since the first exhibition of its kind at Crystal Palace in 1851, the public appetite across the world for this kind of showcase event remained unabated. Paris had hosted the first great exhibition of the twentieth century the previous year, but Glasgow's effort would prove a far grander, more impressive affair, better organised and concentrated in one area rather than dispersed over a vast metropolis. Much like modern theme parks today, a whole city was constructed close to Glasgow University, where the Victorians could display their wares, inventions and Oriental exotica. The exhibition opened on 2 May 1901 and ran until early November, some 11,000,000 people passing through its gates, marvelling at the wonders the Victorian world could muster for its eager public. The exhibits encompassed the worlds of science, industry, architecture, music and fantasy, as well as catering for the Victorians' interest in Eastern cultures. Amongst the more extravagant buildings designed specially for the exhibition were a Russian village containing a model farm with a working dairy, a windmill and a grieve's house, and a concert hall with seating for more than 3,000 people. In preparation for the exhibition, a new sports ground situated close to Glasgow University had been specially constructed, with a four-lap cement cycle track, a cinder pedestrian course, football pitch and stand accommodation for over 25,000 spectators.[11] The sheer scale and organisation that such an enterprise required were testament both to the expertise and imagination at work in Glasgow in 1901.

The last time the sides had met in Scotland, the Scot Hugh Barr had snatched victory from the jaws of defeat in a last gasp effort in the long jump, turning the tide for Scotland. As always in the weeks before the contest, the Irish and Scots sporting press gave extensive coverage to the merits of the two sides. The Scots conceded that the Irish were the favourites but the home side would certainly be no pushovers.

> Paddy is such a bounder to argify that it is hard to resist rubbing in a few facts to disturb his confidence if that is possible, but that he will not have such a walkover can be seen at a glance from the respective championship performances.[12]

As the Irish and Scots athletes readied themselves for battle, some 20,000 spectators turned up to see the day's action. The meeting officially got underway with the half-mile event. All around the grounds the music of the pipers of the 2nd Highland Light Infantry resounded with the traditional *Banks of Allan Water*, setting the nationalistic tone of the day. It would be a stirring contest, the eyes of the crowd riveted on the performers, the conditions excellent, the crowd finding vent for their pent-up feelings in salvoes of approving cheers.

Still fresh from his sparkling form in Ireland, Peter O'Connor once again demonstrated his superiority in the jumping events. His chief rival for the high-jump contest was a diminutive Scot, 5' 6" in height, "Milne of Dundee who is gallant as he is game".[13] J.B. Milne was considered an acrobatic "wonder" and showed he was more than capable of causing an upset, matching O'Connor blow for blow until they both had cleared 5' 11⅝". The pair "almost brought down the house", their different styles and statures resonating with the crowd. J.B. Milne made up for his lack of height by having a particularly unusual and gymnastic style of jumping, "which did not find favour with some of the judges, but all the same, even allowing for tricks, was deserving of praise, for he appeared but a midget when seen beside O'Connor". Eventually after a long and gruelling fight, O'Connor finally beat Milne, jumping 6' 0⅝", a new Scottish high-jump record.

> Milne, who looked like a pocket pistol in comparison to the other competitors, worried O'Connor to the finish, but the Scotchman's jumping was achieved more by tricky work than honest jumping. In the high jump the wind was blowing from the left and by jumping at that side the Scotchmen had a slight advantage. Even so, O'Connor accommodated himself to the conditions and went straight at the lath. [14]

It is interesting to note the manner in which Milne's acrobatics found disfavour with many of the sporting public, who seemed to have strong preconceived notions about how their sports stars should perform. Acrobatic jumpers were invariably viewed with suspicion, particularly by Irish sports fans, their achievements often put down to trickery and guile rather than ability. The demand by the Victorian sporting public for athletes' performances to be aesthetically pleasing and visually spectacular may seem absurd from a modern perspective. The leading athletes of the time were often portrayed as modern gladiators with almost superhuman abilities and, as sporting icons, were expected to compete "honestly". Thus O'Connor's spectacular "caveman" approach to the high jump was applauded wildly, while Milne's more refined acrobatic style, which enabled him to compensate for his lack of height, was greeted with less enthusiasm. The contest between the two was of epic proportions, and in the language strikingly resonant of later Marvel comics "elastic man" (Milne) was vanquished by the "royal lepper" (O'Connor).[15]

In the long jump O'Connor easily defeated his rivals with a jump of 23' 9¾". His closest rival was Pat Leahy with a jump of only 21' 4". Leahy had already failed to make any real impression in the high jump event, his loss of form being attributed to his recent concentration on the long jump. One wonders what made Leahy, such a talented and skilled high jumper, neglect his best discipline and first love, to concentrate on the long jump which was so dominated by O'Connor.

O'Connor was the only dual winner of the day, but Tom Kiely was the other mainstay of the Irish effort, putting on a sterling performance that excited the 20,000-strong crowd. In his best event, the hammer, he extended the Scottish record he already held by a farther four feet, beating his previous record of 141' 4" made in 1899.

> Whirloon Hurro and such like exclamations burst from the crowd as T.F. Kiely whirled the 16lb hammer through space, to the wonderment of the beholder and to the dismay of those within the arena, who gave the Irish giant a very wide berth. He whirled the toy like a twig . . . covering no less than 145 ft 4 in. [16]

In the hurdles the top Irish runner Denis Carey was unable to compete, so, rather than give the Scots a walkover, Kiely lumbered towards the starting blocks, to the surprise of the Scots. The Scottish crowd no doubt imagined that their hurdling aces would make short shrift of the Irish giant, but Kiely showed he was not a man to be underestimated.

> Due to Carey's absence or injury Kiely contested the hurdles which created quite a stir as few thought Kiely, already quite old and heavy, capable of posing a challenge. Nonetheless he ran the Scotch favourite close. For a man of Kiely's age and weight who gives little attention to running it was a grand performance. While the Scotchmen complained of the ground being bad, Kiely, used to the rough tracks of the South of Ireland, found it too fast, and when he put on steam in the middle he nearly came over.[17]

Kiely had a terrific burst of speed for someone of his build and though already in his thirties, he often competed in hurdling events. Since seeing Kraenzlein in action the previous year, he had changed his hurdling style, adopting the American's innovative technique, enabling a man of his bulk to seriously challenge the Scottish hurdlers.

With only one event to go, the four-mile race, Ireland and Scotland were all square. As at Edinburgh two years before, the contest would have a tense, nail-biting finale. The chief protagonists of the four miles were John Daly, the long-distance runner from Galway, and the Scot, Mill. After two miles and six laps from home, Daly lost one of his shoes and had to finish the race on the hard cinder track in a sock. Slipping a "pump" at such a crucial stage made Mill, the Scottish runner, clear favourite. Daly did not let him out of his sights, however, his running "an exhibition of true grit, as his sock was coming off at every stride, and at the finish there was a couple of inches of it in front at his toes". Eventually, Mill prevailed and he ran away with the race in the home straight, winning by 12 yards in a time of 20 minutes 47⅗ seconds. His victory dashed Irish hopes but delighted the home crowd, who most likely had never seen such a hard-fought, stirring athletics contest.

> The scene at the end was simply indescribable. The crowds broke over the track; they cheered themselves hoarse; the excitement intense, the enthusiasm unbounded. [18]

Daly had lost that day but his gritty performance and international debut indicated someone to be reckoned with in long-distance events in the future. The day's proceedings officially came to a close as prizes and medals were presented by the Provost of Glasgow University. Before the athletes and officials left for their annual banquet, and as the crowds streamed out of the grounds into the vast expanse of the Great Exhibition, one of the Scottish heroes of the day paid a special tribute to all present. M.N. McInnes, who had won the shot put from Galavan by three-quarters of an inch, had sensationally put the Scots back in contention, beating one of the Irish favourites. Since he was shortly due to leave for South Africa, this was to be his farewell performance. In a moving final gesture, he took up the pipes, playing some traditional airs, thereby bidding all adieu. Emotions were running high and with Scottish pride brimming, one suspects there was hardly a dry eye in the house. It had been a fine victory for Scotland against probably the strongest Irish squad ever assembled. The Irish could take solace from the fact that after the event all the Scottish field records were held by Irishmen, a not inconsiderable achievement! Belvedere, Ireland's most respected athletics pundit, was at hand to report and put some perspective on the Irish performance. In his estimation, there were still some visible chinks in O'Connor's armour, and consequently further room for improvement:

> O'Connor will some day jump off the earth. He is the greatest jumper that ever lived and, though I do not say it in any captious spirit, he has even yet something left to learn. There is such a thing as a psychological moment in long jumping, and O'Connor has not quite grasped the fact that reducing trigging, or in other words, taking off to a fine art, is absolutely necessary to attain to perfection at the game. A man must be prepared to take off a sixpence if necessary, and the day O'Connor will do that he will do a jump that will stand maybe forever.[19]

☙

AFTER THE EXCITING CONTEST AT GLASGOW, O'Connor and Kiely stayed on in England to compete in the English AAA Championships at Huddersfield the following week. The chance to beat English athletes on home ground was always highly prized by Irish athletes, particularly those of a nationalist outlook. One suspects that the likes of O'Connor and Kiely probably viewed the English titles as even more important than the GAA or IAAA ones. Not only was there stiffer competition at the English Championships, Irish victories were often hailed back home by nationalist elements as strengthening the case for an Irish identity distinct from the English. For O'Connor as a Redmondite and staunch Home Ruler, winning the English AAA Championships had a special significance because, in many people's eyes, Irish victories over the English on the sports field strengthened the case for an independent Ireland. Through athletic achievement, old scores could be settled in bloodless yet symbolic battles and provide the nationalist press back in Ireland with further ammunition for arguing their case.

On a personal note, O'Connor hoped that the English AAA Championships would provide an opportunity to exorcise the ghosts of Stamford Bridge and avenge his defeat by Kraenzlein. After the American's four gold medals at the Paris Olympics, American newspapers had carried reports that the Pennsylvania phenomenon had decided to retire from athletics at the peak of his fame and with his reputation intact. It was not thought that O'Connor would ever have the chance to compete against him again. Within weeks of O'Connor's world record, however, newspapers carried reports that Kraenzlein had decided to postpone his retirement and intended to travel to Europe to defend his English hurdling and long jump titles. The news of Kraenzlein's imminent arrival in Europe spread like wildfire in Irish athletic circles and created considerable excitement in the sporting press. When Kraenzlein had won the English AAA long jump championships at Stamford Bridge, he had not just beaten O'Connor but to some degree had hurt Irish pride. O'Connor would be charged with taking the long jump title and restoring Irish pride. He knew well what was expected of him:

> Our crack jumper will be afforded the much wished for opportunity to wipe out the fluky defeat he sustained last year. I have seen it stated that it was funk that beat him twelve months go. If there is one thing less than another the Waterford wonder can be accused of it is want of grit and pluck, and from what I have seen of him his heart is as big as his record jump of Whit Monday. I am confident that O'Connor's heart and his jump will be big enough to bring the English championship back to Ireland, where it has been held for so many years. Denis Horgan went all the way to America to retrieve the laurels he lost to Sheldon the same day that O'Connor succumbed to Kraenzlein, and he duly defeated the Yankee weight-putter on his own ground. O'Connor, I have no doubt, will be equally successful when he meets the Pennsylvania phenomenon next month.[20]

The air of expectancy and consequent pressure on O'Connor to bring home the English AAA Championships title must have been enormous. The story of Denis Horgan's remarkable trip to America to re-establish his reputation after a single defeat to the American Sheldon was indicative of the combative spirit expected of Irish athletes at the time.[21] O'Connor was equally determined to set matters straight. Following his good form at Glasgow, he trained intensively in the week before Huddersfield, hoping to capitalise on his recent superb form. Unfortunately, during a training session in Manchester, O'Connor suffered an injury, jeopardising any hopes of being on optimum form for his showdown with Kraenzlein. O'Connor blamed the gruelling and "severe" high jump competition with Milne at Glasgow as having brought on the niggling injury to the back muscles of his jumping leg. While stopping off in Birmingham, he sent a telegram to Redmond at the *Waterford News*, giving him an update on his condition:

> Should I be able to get one jump, I might succeed as I feel convinced that my leg will give way after the first effort. Am distracted over it, as I expected doing sensational performances in both long and high. If I lose I shall never rest until I again meet and vanquish the Americans in a long jump contest.[22]

O'Connor's sense of determination and duty were clear, but would his leg hold up under the pressure of competition from Kraenzlein?

Kiely and O'Connor were geared up for the encounter, but despite careful planning they almost didn't make it to the competition. The previous year's lead-up to the competition had been a disaster, as we have seen. O'Connor and Kiely clearly decided that this year things would be different and they would take matters into their own hands, stay on in England at their own expense and arrive at the AAA Championships fresh for competition. Ironically, in spite of the best of intentions, yet another comedy of errors scuppered any chance the two had of arriving in Huddersfield early and in a relaxed mood. Instead, the Irish duo were destined to make a late and spectacular entrance.

Unintentionally misled by an Irish friend in Birmingham, O'Connor and Kiely ended up missing the train for Huddersfield

by a few minutes. When they realised what had happened, they
rushed about the different platforms, trying desperately to find
out the time the next train was due to leave. Since there did not
seem to be any scheduled trains that could get them there on time,
the situation looked extremely serious. The friend who had
caused them to miss the train was no less anxious for the two to
get to Huddersfield on time, because he was being threatened
"with all sorts of pain and penalties". Just when it seemed that all
was lost and their mutual acquaintance was no doubt contemplating his fate, an excursion train pulled into the station that would
get the pair to Huddersfield in the nick of time. For all concerned,
a last minute reprieve was at hand.

The journey to Huddersfield was a tortuous one as the excursion train was filled to the brim with passengers, and conditions
were extremely cramped. As the small, packed train ambled towards its destination, stopping at all the small stations en route,
O'Connor and Leahy knew they were in danger of missing their
events. When the train eventually pulled into Huddersfield and
creaked to a halt, the two Irishmen jumped out and hastily in-
quired where the championships were being held. To their dismay they discovered they were taking place in a cricket club over
a mile away and their events were due to start within minutes.
With the seconds ticking away, they needed a means of transport
and fast. Luckily there was a horse-drawn bus at the station waiting to meet people off the train, and with the promise of a double
fare, the driver set off at a wild gallop hurtling through the main
streets of Huddersfield in a race against the clock. When they finally arrived at the grounds, Kiely rushed straight onto the field
with the intention of throwing the hammer without putting on his
racing togs. It must have been quite a sight for English officials to
see a man of Kiely's size and bulk, brandishing a large hammer,
bursting on to the cricket grounds and careering towards them.

Fortunately, rain had delayed proceedings and their events
had yet to start. As O'Connor and Kiely entered the changing
rooms, prospective opponents who had been "anxiously enquir-
ing" about the failure of the two Irishmen to materialise were

evidently "much disturbed" at their sudden entrance. Casting a glance around the dressing room, O'Connor noticed that Kraenzlein was being rubbed down by his trainer. He approached the American and asked him if he would mind waiting a few minutes until he was ready to compete because he had only just arrived. To his amazement Kraenzlein told him he did not intend to defend his long jump title, since some days before he had suffered a thigh strain and was out of form.[23] O'Connor's immediate disappointment was nonetheless soon tempered by scepticism. Why then was Kraenzlein being rubbed down by his coach? If he was indeed suffering a thigh strain, surely he wouldn't contest the hurdles either? In spite of all the talk, hype and media coverage about a showdown between the two great jumpers, O'Connor would be obliged to jump alone. Despite Kraenzlein's contention that he was injured, he won the hurdles in magnificent style in a time of 15.4 seconds, a new English Championships record which also equalled the world record.

In the aftermath of the Huddersfield meeting, the English media could report that "the Britishers had come out much better than last year" and had regained some of the pride lost at Stamford Bridge. In light of the excitement generated by the Americans the previous year, numerous journalists, photographers and even cinematographers with new-fangled equipment made their way to the championships. Poor weather did, however, manage to cast a dampener on the day.

Putting the Huddersfield championships in perspective, there were far fewer Americans competing than at Stamford Bridge and those who made the transatlantic journey walked away with their events. Kraenzlein once again showed that he was in a class of his own in hurdling, while Arthur Duffey of Georgetown University was reported as winning the 100 yards "with ridiculous ease". The other Penn athlete, Irving Baxter, regained his high jumping title of the previous year, as well as coming joint first in the pole vault, despite having mislaid his pole before the competition and having to use an improvised one.

Apart from British successes in the long-distance running events, the most important "home" successes were those of O'Connor and Kiely. Both Irishmen left their mark on the championships, O'Connor setting a new English record and Kiely defeating his nearest rival in the hammer by a huge margin of 25' 32"! English athletics may have made progress since the American stampede at Stamford Bridge the year before, but much work still remained to be done if they were to become a force in international athletics. The AAA may have wondered if it was such a good idea to let American and Irish athletes contest home championships because no doubt their presence had a demoralising effect on English athletes. Attempts in the English media to claim the Irish successes as British victories were met with scorn and incredulity by Redmond in the *Waterford News*:

> The English papers are loud in their praise of the great English success . . . but surely it is a stretch of the imagination to describe O'Connor as a common or garden Saxon. A truer, a better or a prouder man because of being an Irishman, is not alive today. Kiely's great victory in the hammer throwing is also put down as a success. How our friends on the other side clasp us to their bosoms when they pretend to claim "Kudos" because of our efforts. Kiely, like O'Connor, is an Irishman who loves the dear old country, and who fought at Huddersfield not for England but for the land he loves so well.[24]

O'Connor could return to Ireland with his head held high. He had brought the English long jump championship to Ireland where many believed it rightfully belonged, and although he did not have the pleasure of facing Kraenzlein on the day, the American was on his way to compete in Ireland, so it was only a matter of time before their paths would cross again.

⊗

ONLY DAYS AFTER HIS TRIUMPHANT return to Waterford, O'Connor made the short journey to a Sports at Maryborough (now Portlaoise) on 8 July. Starting with respectable jumps of 23' 9",

23′ 8″ and 24′ 0″, the "Waterford wonder" then showed why he was increasingly being referred to as one of Ireland's greatest athletes. In his fourth jump, to his and the crowd's delight, he sailed across the magical 25-foot barrier, which no man had ever crossed, registering a jump of 25′ 0½″. O'Connor had always maintained he would break the 25-foot barrier some time, but must have been amazed by how quickly he had done it. His improvement that summer had been incredible and people began to wonder just how far this 29-year-old Irishman would jump. Unfortunately, owing to an incline on the Maryborough grounds, the record could not stand, but O'Connor now knew what he was capable of and determined to be the first man to set a new world record of over 25 feet.

O'Connor's next scheduled event was at Kilkenny one week later. It had been publicised that Kraenzlein would put in an appearance and he had sent a telegram to that effect. In consequence there was huge excitement and Kilkenny city and county were covered in posters billing the Sports as a chance to see "The wonders of the century", "the great long jump contest between the representatives of America and Ireland". "Don't miss the only chance Kilkenny ever got!" Kraenzlein did not show up, however, leaving O'Connor to entertain sports fans. O'Connor had been expected to defend "The Land of the Shamrock" against the "Greatest Sprinter of the Age" and supposed claimant to his world record, but he nonetheless put on a sterling show despite the absence of the American.

෨

THE DUBLIN METROPOLITAN POLICE SPORTS was to all external appearances the most successful sports meeting of the 1901 Irish season. With superb weather, the RDS grounds at Ballsbridge quickly filled with thousands of enthusiastic athletics fans eager to catch a glimpse of some of the world's leading athletes in action. Such a mass of spectators had not been seen since 1887 when a crowd of 25,000 came to watch a legendary four-mile race between the

American middle-distance runner Eddie Carter and Ireland's first world-renowned runner, Tommy Conneff of County Kildare.[25] On a similar fine day some fourteen years later, there were queues at the gates of the RDS, the atmosphere electric in anticipation of Kraenzlein and O'Connor. "Cheers re-echoed again and again, hands were clapped, handkerchiefs were waved, and it was a great function, one that will be talked of with pleasure when most of us are dead."[26] With all the recent press coverage, the chance to see both O'Connor and Kraenzlein compete at the same meeting was clearly hard to resist. Kraenzlein was undoubtedly the star attraction, having agreed to run a number of handicap hurdles. The organisers had put together a mouth-watering programme of athletic and cycling events and mooted a possible three-way long jump contest between O'Connor, Newburn and Kraenzlein as well as some handicap hurdles. Those who had followed the recent twists and turns in the world of long jumping probably suspected that neither Newburn nor Kraenzlein would risk taking on O'Connor in his present form and in front of a partisan crowd.

As always, the American athletes created a huge amount of curiosity thanks to the ritualistic way in which they prepared and the monastic-style robes they donned. Even though it was a hot day, and the sun was beating down, they remained shrouded in their robes and in the shade until called to compete in their events, just like modern-day professional boxers before they enter the ring.

> They are thin and long with a curious sort of greyhound appearance, and apparently lack muscular development, and a weird uncanny sort of impression is created when watching them at their favourite items. Both of them [Kraenzlein and Baxter] came on the ground swathed in great thick dressing gowns, but dressing gowns of a peculiar sort, for they had very thick and high collars, and there was a hood attached.[27]

The first glimpse that most spectators had of Kraenzlein was when he burst out of the starting blocks and began hurdling in his own inimitable style. In an exhibition race against Denis Carey, the Irish hurdling champion, Kraenzlein conceded his opponent a six-yard start with one hurdle down. Those who had never seen the American in action before thought Kraenzlein had set himself an impossible task. At the starter's shot, however, he was away like a bolt, passing Carey halfway and smashing the old Irish hurdling record with a time of 15.4 seconds, the same as his Huddersfield and world records. His performance "simply electrified the spectators", who marvelled at the American's approach to hurdling. His fellow collegian, Irving Baxter, created a similar flurry of interest with his unusual jumping technique in the high jump. People had come in their droves to see the American superstars in action and were delighted by the Pennsylvania pair. All who saw Kraenzlein's blistering speed and athleticism in the hurdles must have secretly relished the prospect of the American legend taking on the local hero of the hour, O'Connor, in the long jump. Once again, however, he declined the opportunity, his inaction speaking volumes.

> It seems that Kraenzlein tacitly acknowledges O'Connor's supremacy as a long jumper seeing that on Saturday he had again an opportunity of trying conclusions with the Irishman but did not avail himself of it. It will be remembered that at the British championships a strained sinew prevented the American from facing O'Connor, and on Saturday although he competed in the high jump, yet he stood down at the long jump. Being thus indisposed to try conclusions with O'Connor admits of but one interpretation — Kraenzlein knows he cannot equal O'Connor, but is unwilling to have it practically demonstrated. [28]

Many years later, Joe Deakin, who came second in the mile event at Ballsbridge that day, recalled an amusing interchange between O'Connor and Kraenzlein. When O'Connor jumped 23' 6" against a stiff wind, he turned to Kraenzlein and said, "Your jump." Kraenzein replied, "No fear; no man can beat that" and declined the offer. A little later when the high jump was taking place, the bar had been raised to 6' 1" and O'Connor ran straight at it like a long jumper, clearing it by about a foot. Seeing O'Connor in blistering form, Kraenzlein turned to him and joked, "I don't think I'll jump, you're too hot." It was a great moment for O'Connor — a clear acknowledgement from the world's greatest living athlete, Alvin Kraenzlein, that when it came to long and high jumping O'Connor was his superior. As Joe Deakin observed on his ninetieth birthday in 1969:

> Kraenzlein would have had to jump 6ft 2 ins to equal him, and that wanted some doing then. Nothing like this American [Dick Fosbury] now jumping backwards and landing on his head. That wouldn't have been allowed then. We would have called it acrobatting.[29]

The day came to an end as always with an awards ceremony. In recognition of their visit to Ireland, the organisers of the sports presented Kraenzlein and Baxter with two special silver-mounted blackthorn sticks. The generosity afforded the American athletes was in stark contrast to the prizes awarded to the Irish winners, which in light of the significant gate on the day, were uncharacteristically poor. This annoyance became more widespread amongst the Irish athletes when it was rumoured that the Americans had received payment to appear at the sports. An indiscreet official had allegedly been seen passing money to the American coach. The home athletes clearly felt neglected and taken for granted since they had provided the lion's share of entertainment on the day. For the time being, the matter would be allowed to rest. This blatant infringement of the laws of amateurism would not be forgotten, however, and was a time bomb waiting to go off. It would take over a year for the scandal to come to light, but when it did it the affair would cause an international controversy.

ᴄᴈ

AFTER HIS NEW RECORD AT the English AAA Championships, O'Connor was royally received at Ballsbridge. Nonetheless, his greatest welcome would be from his own people in Wicklow on the occasion of a "Monster Gaelic Carnival". There, in front of his family and old school and childhood friends, he received an entirely different type of reception. A public monument to Billy Byrne, one of the leaders of the 1798 Irish rebellion, had recently been erected in Wicklow town, but the monument had incurred considerable debt. Therefore it was decided to hold a sports festival at Annacura in County Wicklow to try and clear the debt. When O'Connor was asked to support the festival, he immediately agreed, delighted to get a chance to jump in his native county. Posters advertising the sports were plastered all over Dublin, with O'Connor's name splashed across them. Trains were laid on specially for people to go and see him jump. In a gesture that left little doubt as to the tone of the meeting, the poster advertising the event concluded in Irish: *Dia Saor Éire!* — God Save Ireland! The day would be a celebration of Irish language, sports and pastimes, and a large number of Gaelic football teams journeyed from Dublin to tackle local Wicklow teams. In typical nationalistic terms, the event was described as a Gaelic invasion of Wicklow and a monster Gaelic carnival demonstrating that the spirit and memory of 1798 was as strong as ever in the county. Six football matches and one hurling contest were scheduled, each game lasting 45 minutes. With such enthusiasm for the sports as well as the cause, the special trains laid on were filled to the brim, carrying vast masses of surging Gaelic life. At the station in Aughrim, the trains were met by the local fife and drum band which played athletes and spectators to the field. On arrival, O'Connor was accorded a tremendous reception, which was repeated throughout the day whenever he jumped. Although the applause was as heartfelt and the cheering much like he had experienced at Ballsbridge, this was his real homecoming amongst his own people, outside the Pale, a world apart from the RDS. Jumping on home turf, he was credited with over 24' 11" in his final jump, sending the crowd wild, and ensuring boundless applause.

છ

THE FINAL BIG MEETING OF THE YEAR was the Royal Irish Constabulary Sports, once again at Ballsbridge. Some 350 entries had been received for 36 events and the day promised to be an exciting one. Though the early sports were restricted to members of the RIC and the military, subsequent events were open to all-comers. The RIC sports were popular with athletes, particularly because of the generous prizes on offer. One such trophy, the Aberdeen Cup, was worth £25, an increase of £5 on the previous year. By guaranteeing good prizes, they knew the top athletes would compete and ensure a good gate. All profits on the day would go to the orphans and widows of deceased members of the forces. To facilitate O'Connor, the organisers included a special long jump event with a grass take-off to give him the chance to beat the Newburn record of 23' 3" set on 15 August 1898 in Monasterevin. Under the stewardship of a certain Sergeant Whisker, time was rigidly enforced. With so many events and numerous spills in the cycling events, necessitating several ambulances, a certain amount of military precision was required to ensure that the day ran smoothly. Amongst the crowds were members of the nobility from the metropolis and surrounding districts. There was an eclectic mix of music, comprising airs from Donizetti, Balfe, English tunes and military airs such as the "Empress of India's March", as well as the 21st Lancers' own march and signature tune.

In the backdrop to all this pomp and splendour, O'Connor readied himself for his last sports event that summer in Ireland. Clearly feeling in excellent form, he decided to run the 100 yards as a warm-up and finished just five yards behind Denis Murray, Ireland's current fastest sprinter. His form in the sprint augured well for his jumping in the long jump with a grass take off as he finally eclipsed Newburn's last remaining world record with a distance of 23' 10¼". His best, however, was saved for the long jump proper where he achieved a distance of 24' 11¾" — a huge improvement on his own world record and just a tantalising shade short of 25 feet. As in the case earlier in the summer, the officials from the Records Committee were present to witness the jumps, so it was most likely the record would be allowed to stand. The following day, when a newspaper report in *The Irish Times* erroneously suggested that he might have been helped by a strong crosswind, O'Connor responded by writing directly to T.W. Murphy, an official handicapper and timekeeper for the IAAA. Murphy set any concerns O'Connor might have to rest, assuring him that the Records Committee, most of whom were present at the RIC sports, would not be influenced by a newspaper report "by a new and inexperienced man". Furthermore, any efforts by Newburn or his supporters to oppose the new world record would fall on deaf ears. "With regard to Newburn he has no more right to oppose you than the man in the street. The Records Committee would not give him a hearing."[30] The new world record of 24' 11¾" would go into the record books. Little could he have imagined that this new world record would stand for over twenty years and become the longest national record of all time, only being surpassed by another Irishman, Carlos O'Connell, in 1990. All the years of training and perseverance had finally paid off.

ೞ

AN ANONYMOUS CLERK JUST A FEW YEARS before, now O'Connor was about to become one of the most famous athletes in the English-speaking world. As he celebrated his second world record at Ballsbridge in the space of a few months, behind the scenes the final preparations were being made for him to travel to America. There he hoped to achieve new heights and officially break the magical 25-foot barrier. Before the RIC sports, it had been rumoured that O'Connor would be leaving Ireland. Irish-American athletics associations had been in contact with him trying to secure his presence at the world championships in Buffalo and there was also a good deal of speculation that he might not return. Whether or not the crowd knew of O'Connor's impending departure for the US, they gave the Wicklowman an ovation he was not likely to forget — the perfect send-off.

In the twenty-first century, it is difficult to comprehend the significance of or interest in O'Connor's achievement in 1901. In an era before mass media, radio or television, athletics was very much on a par with sports such as football and rugby today in terms of popularity. Within the athletics field, the long jump also held a special place. Somehow the notion of a man jumping the huge distance of 25 feet struck a chord in the public imagination more than other world records in running, throwing or hurdling. In Ireland, the recent domination of Irish athletes in long and high jumping went some way towards explaining the popularity of the discipline, although a likely contributory factor in the public's fascination with long jumping was the event's strong associations with Irish mythology. O'Connor's latest accomplishments rekindled the age old debate as to whether modern athletes were on a par with their predecessors, either mythological or actual.

> The theory of "laudator temporis acti" that men were stronger and more active in the old days than they are now will hardly stand the test of recent experience. Day by day, old athletic records yield to new. . . . Unfortunately we have no definite information as to the times or distances at the Olympian games. But judging by latter-day experience, athletics are becoming an exact science, in which the old Greek athletes would have no chance with some of our champions of the present time. So we may conclude that if those whom Oisín [in his lament for the heroes he had known] designated as the "sons of little men", can achieve such feats, it is easy to conceive that the performances attributed to the heroes of antiquity were not so mythical as some of our modern commentators would represent them.[31]

Yet the likes of Oisín were not the only mythological figures O'Connor could be compared to, as Redmond noted after the Annacurra Monster Gaelic Carnival:

> In our school days, that is before intermediate cramming came to the front, the youngsters had a belief in a mythological personage known as Spring Heeled Jack. His strides were enormous and once he went on the run he could place leagues

between himself and all pursuers by one or two mighty springs.[32]

If associations with Celtic myth were contributory factors to the sudden celebrity thrust on O'Connor in Ireland, in the English-speaking world comparisons with the mysterious jumping phenomenon Spring Heeled Jack ensured his feats struck a chord in the public consciousness. Spring Heeled Jack was one of Victorian London's most puzzling and enduring urban folk legends, a phantom-like menace, first sighted in 1837, who was allegedly capable of jumping inhuman distances, across fences and hedgerows as well as from rooftop to rooftop. After a spate of incidents in 1838, the Lord Mayor of London saw fit to warn the public that a strange man or "creature" whom he nicknamed "Spring Heeled Jack" might be roaming the streets of the vast metropolis by night.[33] Until his last sighting in Liverpool in 1904, one suspects the mere mention of this shady urban folk legend's name was enough to send a tingle down the spine of several generations of Londoners. It is little wonder that as O'Connor reset the boundaries of human achievement in long jumping in 1901, he became an immediate celebrity and an object of curiosity.

O'Connor in America

AFTER HIS FIRST WORLD RECORD JUMP at Ballsbridge on 27 May 1901, O'Connor attracted the attention of an Irish-American organisation based in New York. When news broke in America that Prinstein's world long jump record had been broken by an Irishman, the Greater New York Irish-American Club initiated correspondence with C.P. Redmond and O'Connor, in the hope that he might visit America.

O'Connor could only undertake such a trip if given protracted leave from his place of work. Though Daniel Dunford was probably pleased by all the publicity which O'Connor's athletic feats attracted to his Waterford office, he may have been less enthusiastic to see such a valuable and trusted employee embark on a trip to America for a couple of months. Not only was there the problem of finding a suitable caretaker for O'Connor's post, there was also the distinct possibility that the Wicklowman might not return. Prior to his departure, before he had even laid a foot on a transatlantic steamer, a newspaper referred to him as having "a tendency to live in the States". Whatever O'Connor's intentions were at this time, he was anxious that his situation in Dunford's office would be secure until his return. To alleviate any worries that O'Connor may have had that Dan Dunford might dispense with his services in his absence, C.P. Redmond took matters in hand.

The first time his employer became aware of O'Connor's impending trip may have been from Redmond's editorial in the *Waterford News*. The following excerpts testify to the subtle yet manipulative way Dunford may have been cajoled into releasing

O'Connor for a few months and so delighting sporting enthusiasts
on both sides of the Atlantic:

> I have received from Mr M.J. Tierney, New York, who used to
> be a member of the Waterford Town Council, a very interest-
> ing letter, from which we feel privileged to give a few extracts.
> He says — "I suppose you are aware that the greater New
> York Athletic Association have written to P. O'Connor, invit-
> ing him to come over here to take part in the many athletic
> contests which are to be held here this year, and also represent
> this club at the Pan-American Exposition at Buffalo. Now I
> don't know what chance the club has of getting O'Connor, but
> should you help us in our ambition to have him here, every
> member, many of whom are old friends of your own, will be
> rightful thankful to you."[1]

In the ensuing paragraph entitled "Mr Dan Dunford", Redmond's
masterful yet discreet cognitive powers came to the fore:

> O'Connor being in England we cannot, of course, say anything
> definite, but are perfectly certain that our sporting friend —
> the best of the best — Mr Dan Dunford, whose managing clerk
> O'Connor is, will do his level best to let the Irish champion
> away for a few weeks in order to put the climax to a remarka-
> bly brilliant career in Athletics. The New York Club is in such
> good hands as Judge Brown, and Senators Dowling, and P.J.
> Conway. The secretary is by the way, an old friend of our
> own, Mr D. Madigan of Limerick, and was secretary of the
> Rowing club there.

O'Connor's invitation was engineered by Dan Madigan and P.J.
Conway, two Limerick men who had only emigrated recently to
America, and whose names and faces would still have been fresh
in the minds of many Munster folk. Despite humble beginnings,
Conway had become an important figure in New York's Irish-
American community, and is credited with founding the Irish-
American Club that received its charter from the city of New York
in 1897. Having left Ireland at twenty years of age, Conway
worked as a journeyman before saving enough money to develop

his own successful business as a farrier. As President of the New York Irish-American Club for all but one term until the 1908 London Olympics, Conway was symbolic of "the increasing prosperity and respectability of turn-of-the-century Irish immigrants".[2] The links between the Irish diaspora in America and the old country were extremely strong. For O'Connor to be blocked from travelling to compete for the New York Irish-American Club in Buffalo would be a blow to the aspirations of Irish-Americans, who were hoping to further raise the profile of their community in American society through sporting excellence.

Whatever reservations Dunford may have had about O'Connor's proposed American trip, in a gesture of goodwill, and perhaps wary of incurring the wrath of C.P. Redmond, he was seen publicly at least to give his blessing to the venture and drafted in an assistant from his Dublin office to act as temporary managing clerk. Redmond had played an important role in securing the chance for O'Connor to travel to America to compete. Yet in the course of his American adventure, O'Connor would experience at first hand the potency of the media and become aware of the dangers associated with prolonged and excessive exposure to it. The instrument that had been so conveniently employed to occasion his trip, once outside of his control, would prove a far less amenable entity.

The costs of O'Connor's voyage would be paid by the Irish-American club he was to represent in Buffalo. It was a unique opportunity for a man of O'Connor's age, profession and background, a chance to visit the New World with a guaranteed return ticket. Most young Irishmen who sailed to America at this time did so on a one-way ticket, with the prospect of a hard working life in front of them.

Though the official reason for going to the United States was to try to win the long jump world championship in Buffalo, O'Connor was fulfilling a dream that he had harboured for a long time. For years he had heard many stories and collected newspaper articles that raved about the superior facilities for training and competing in the United States. American stadiums were said to

have the world's best cinder tracks, the ideal surface for maximising the speed that could be generated in the run-up to jumping.
The opportunity of training and competing in such an environment must have excited O'Connor, who was hoping to break the
magical watershed of 25 feet. Now, at the peak of his career, the
temptation of competing with the world's best facilities at his disposal was hard to resist.

A further inducement was the prospect of competing against
both Kraenzlein and Prinstein, the two greatest jumpers in the
world after the Irishman. Kraenzlein had avoided meeting
O'Connor in competition thus far that season but was rumoured
to be preparing to face him on his own turf. Although he had not
yet met Prinstein in competition, it was the Syracuse man's record
that O'Connor had broken the previous May. O'Connor was well
aware of the necessity of competing against quality opposition if
he was to maintain his new world record. In his quest to become
the world's greatest long jumper, his intense rivalry with both
Newburn and Pat Leahy had proved crucial. Direct competition
with Kraenzlein and Prinstein during his American sojourn might
provide just the competition required to push O'Connor beyond
25 feet. Should he beat the Americans on home ground, O'Connor
would succeed in finally avenging his defeat at Stamford Bridge
the previous year. The ideal time and place for such a showdown
would be the world championships at Buffalo, where the question
of who the world's greatest long jumper was might be settled
once and for all.

O'Connor's trip as an athlete to America was by no means
without precedent. What differentiated his visit to the United
States from previous sorties by Irish athletes was that he went as
an individual rather than as part of a group. Notably, in September 1888, the GAA had dispatched some fifty athletes to the States
to raise funds for an inaugural Celtic Cultural Festival, to be held
subsequently every five years, and that would also include the
participation of athletes from Wales, Scotland and the Isle of Man.
Despite the warm welcome the expedition received on arrival in
New York, the fundraising attempts of the GAA were thwarted

by the powerful combination of adverse weather conditions and an ongoing presidential election campaign.[3] The former led to exhibitions being held in torrential rain and the latter distracted the attention of many American sports enthusiasts. The trip was not just a financial disaster but had more far-reaching effects for Irish sport in general, as some 17 of the 45 hurlers and athletes who had travelled decided to remain on in America permanently. This collective desertion set a precedent for future Irish athletes who would make the transatlantic crossing to display their athletic talents and be tempted by attractive offers to stay on and compete for America. Much Irish native talent was lost in this way as a whole host of Irish athletic stars chose not to return to the old country and continue living as British subjects. At Buffalo, O'Connor would compete for the same club as hammer-thrower John Flanagan, another recent high-profile Irish sporting émigré. Flanagan, originally from Kilsheedy, County Limerick, had emigrated to the United States and become an officer in the NYPD. A noted athlete before he left Ireland, Flanagan had won Olympic gold in Paris the previous year for the US and was but one of a significant number of Irish sporting champions competing under the Stars and Stripes. The extent of sporting talent that Ireland lost due to emigration in the final decades of the nineteenth and early twentieth centuries is inestimable and it could be argued that Irish athletics and field sports in particular never recovered.

On a personal note, O'Connor's visit to America would give him the opportunity to visit his older brother Arthur, who had emigrated some five years before. This was the first personal contact that O'Connor would have with him since he had moved to America. O'Connor no doubt was curious to see at first hand how his brother was getting along. Though Peter considered himself to be quite well set up in Ireland, having relatively good prospects, both financially and socially, he may secretly have harboured ideas of following in his brother's footsteps. Still a young man with no ties and at the peak of his powers, the future must have seemed bright and full of possibility as he made his final preparations for his American voyage.

On 9 August, one day prior to sailing, O'Connor left Waterford by the 2.40 train for Queenstown in County Cork. Numerous
friends and admirers gathered to send him on his way and wish
him "God-speed, good luck and a happy return to Waterford".
Notably, the occasion of his departure was marked by a short letter from John E. Redmond, the Irish MP and leader of the Home
Rule Party, hoping his trip would prove a success, both on and off
the athletics field. Such a show of sentiment and goodwill from
both friends and a national figure gave fresh inspiration and a
second wind to O'Connor after a long and gruelling season.

The voyage, which took a week, would prove an eventful one
and leave an indelible impression on O'Connor's memory. It was a
"terrific voyage, nothing but storm and rain up to Wednesday
night". One of 296 second-class passengers on the voyage, lodged
on the lower decks of the *Lucania*, O'Connor described the manner
in which he and his fellow passengers "became like members of a
big family" as the storm raged outside. There were several anxious
moments, such as when the vessel was struck by a freak wave in
high seas. There was considerable damage to the steamer and one
of the sailors was left in a critical state, "dashed on deck, receiving
terrible injuries and breaking a leg".[4] In a separate incident, high-
lighting the dangers inherent in transatlantic crossings, several of
the crew were injured by the violent rolling of the steamer. Once
safe on dry land, O'Connor would quip humorously that he really
thought he would make a record trip — but to the bottom! Despite
his hardy seafaring genes, he lost a considerable deal of weight
due to seasickness, a circumstance that would be remedied with
zeal when he was once again on terra firma.

O'Connor's recent exploits had made him something of a celebrity and, somewhat unusually, several first-class passengers descended to the lower decks, curious to meet the Irish jumping
phenomenon. One such passenger could have been Sir Thomas
Lipton, who was making his way to America to take part in the
Americas Cup yacht race on behalf of the Ulster Boating Club,
which he was entering for the second time. Lipton, whose name is
nowadays synonymous with tea, was a self-made millionaire of

Irish-Scots descent, whose parents had fled the Great Famine in Ireland in 1849 and sought refuge in Glasgow. Proud of his Celtic roots, Lipton had named his boat *Shamrock II*. Curiously, O'Connor and Lipton would also return to Europe on the same ship some months later, both having experienced comparable misfortune in their respective sports. The duo nonetheless received a huge amount of press coverage during their stay in America.

On the morning of 17 August 1901, Peter O'Connor had his first glimpse of America, as the *Lucania*, a little worse for wear but still intact, made its final approach to New York. Little could the Irishman have known the reception that awaited him as the ship docked and he said farewell to the many new friends with whom he had passed the previous week. He probably expected to be welcomed by several club officials and may even have hoped to see his brother Arthur waiting dockside, but he surely could not have anticipated the media circus that eagerly awaited his disembarkation.

As he made his way down the gangplank, O'Connor had a pair of field glasses slung over his shoulder, a mackintosh hung over one arm, a watch chain and one of his championship medals dangling from it, the latter a symbol of his athletic credentials. Last but not least among O'Connor's paraphernalia was "a blackthorn stick remarkable for the length and number of the thorns" brought as a gift for his hosts. Waiting to welcome him to America were several representatives of the Irish-American Club, the President P.J. Conway, D. Madigan and M. Tierney, the Waterford man who had made representations to Redmond on behalf of the club. Before they had a chance to greet him, O'Connor ran foul of the custom house officers who wanted to charge duty on the field glasses. As O'Connor had an animated discussion with the customs officials about the relative merits of not charging him duty on the binoculars, one of the waiting Irish-American contingent quipped to the press "that he carried the field glasses to look for Kraenzlein". Once past the customs officers, O'Connor was greeted by a huge number of admirers, officials, reporters and photographers.

His arrival in America is very well documented as the event was covered in great detail by several American newspapers. In particular, one newspaper, *The New York Sun*, gave him much complimentary coverage, delighting the Irish-American Club officials who had gone to great measures to entice him across the Atlantic. *The Sun*'s cartoons of O'Connor literally leaping to shore from the *Lucania* and jumping over the clubhouse at Celtic Park were extravagant and sensationalistic. Indeed, O'Connor was particularly amused by the article and sent it back to his friend Redmond in Waterford. The editor of the *Waterford News*, who was never one to miss an opportunity to cause a stir, placed the newspaper cutting in a shop-front window in Waterford, so that the city's residents could marvel at America's perception of O'Connor. Hardly a day went by in the first weeks of his stay when his name did not appear in print, not only in *The Sun* but also in the *New York Herald*, *The World*, and the *New York Journal*. O'Connor was questioned and interviewed by many leading coaches and newspapermen who were trying to divine the secret of the Irishman's phenomenal accomplishments. The *New York Journal* provided perhaps the most in-depth analysis, after noting that "Broad jumping is an athletic exercise for which Irishmen are naturally adapted, . . . due to a peculiar 'springiness' in the Celt, a physical endowment but rarely possessed by any other nationality". Talking to the *New York Journal*, O'Connor suggested two theories behind his success. His first was that taking off from the left leg — what people in Ireland call a *ciotóg* — he received some extra propulsion power from the cardiac arteries, as the left leg was underneath the heart. O'Connor's second theory provides a fascinating glimpse into his philosophy towards competition and preparation and describes how he would psyche himself up so as to "get into the zone" (as modern sports psychologists might term it):

> To do anything great, whether mentally or physically, the act must absorb a man's entire being. An athlete can never do a big performance in a slipshod manner or with his mind preoccupied. He must have his very soul riveted on what he is about to do and make the effort with his brain as well as with

his muscles. When I am about to jump I like to walk around undisturbed and key myself up for the trial. I don't measure my strides to the take off. Somehow, perhaps by intuition, I have learned to strike it right always. If I chance to pass the trig the failure does not bother me like other jumpers. My secret of jumping so far? Well, you can see for yourself. An easy run, a nice easy rise from the trig and a sort of jerk forward at the finish. That is all.

His interviewer, however, preferred to rely on a more scientific explanation for O'Connor's success. By studying photographs of O'Connor taken while he was jumping, he came to the following conclusion:

It is while his body is in the air and the method in which he takes off that the great jumper gains the advantage. Striking the take-off board with his hands held behind him he gets a splendid smooth rise without any ungainly twist of the back or contortion seen in other jumpers. Consequently, he starts through space as evenly as a feather arrow. With his hands still behind him he travels on, but when about to land, brings them forward with a swish the impetus of which nearly throws him on his face and hands. This final movement unquestionably adds about a foot to the length of O'Connor's jump. Most great jumpers, especially Kraenzlein and Prinstein, [come to the] take-off with great speed and create a lot of fuss in the air, but with O'Connor it is different. He slips through the atmosphere without any apparent difficulty.[5]

The *New York Journal* correspondent was undoubtedly fascinated by the Celtic race's unusual predilection for jumping but he was nonetheless quick to recognise that O'Connor's success probably had more to do with his innovative style rather than with genetic or mythological factors.

Over the course of the next weeks, O'Connor was accommodated in the clubhouse at Celtic Park. This was the first athletic park built specifically for Irish games in New York and was ideally situated in the Laurel Hill section of Queens, a short ten-

minute ride from the Long Island city terminus of the 34th Street
ferry, making it convenient for all Irish-Americans in the Manhat-
tan and Brooklyn catchment areas. The impressive sports grounds
and clubhouse had recently been completed and were becoming a
focal point for Irish-Americans in New York, many of whom visited the grounds on Sunday after visiting Calgary Cemetery, "the
City of the Celtic Dead", to visit the graves of loved ones.[6]

The clubhouse at Celtic Park was a particularly impressive
structure that catered not just to the sporting needs of the Irish-
American community but also to their social and cultural requirements. In the first week of his stay in Celtic Park, O'Connor,
whose room overlooked the dancing floor, had the opportunity to
witness first hand a jig and hornpipe contest between parties from
Tipperary and Kerry.

As he had hoped, the training facilities at Celtic Park were superb. He was also especially pleased to be assigned a coach, Alfred Copeland, who could supervise his training for the world
championships in Buffalo. This was a new experience for him as
he was largely self-taught. Copeland was a former athlete with an
impressive sporting pedigree, having held the American long
jump record for a number of years at 23' 3". O'Connor would later
credit him "as having given him some rare and good old tips".

He did not train alone in Celtic Park but was joined by John
Flanagan, the legendary hammer-thrower. This would mark the
beginning of a friendship between the two athletes and O'Connor
would always talk of his fellow athlete in glowing terms.
Flanagan's form was also at its peak at this time and he was beginning to break records on a regular basis. In an extraordinarily
long and distinguished career, Flanagan would dominate the
sport of hammer-throwing and win three consecutive Olympic
titles, an achievement that would not be equalled until 1964.

The Irish-American club at Celtic Park must have been secretly
delighted to have such distinguished athletes in their fold. Apart
from the fact that the mere mention of O'Connor's and Flanagan's
names was enough to guarantee a full house at any athletic meeting, the club stood a good chance of cleaning up at the world

championships. In addition to their good fortune in successfully attracting O'Connor to the United States to represent them, just one month before the Buffalo games were due to commence, they had successfully enticed Flanagan to resign from the New York Athletic Club and compete under their colours. Thus the Irish-American organisation that was seeking to establish its sporting credentials had achieved something of a double coup in the world of American and international athletics.[7]

O'Connor's description of his first impressions of America reveals his fascination with the place. The vast bustling metropolis of New York filled him with awe, "a truly wonderful city, how to describe the hundreds of thoroughly strange sights, strange customs, strange everything". Another object of amazement for him was the amount of food and drink consumed by the native population, leading him to declare that Americans can "consume as much in a day as the biggest men in Ireland could do in a week". The abstemious Irishman particularly noted how American men seemed to "drink, drink eternally", though the price of liquor was four times that paid in Ireland. In an uncharacteristically self-deprecatory gesture, O'Connor confesses to feeling something of a "greenhorn" in this new and unaccustomed environment. Indeed his heavy linen suit, that one observer noted was more suited to a wet and cold climate, would have made him conspicuous in the intense heat and humidity that engulfs New York in mid-August. An unexpected dimension to his stay in America was the somewhat surreal predicament of finding himself in a foreign country yet surrounded by compatriots. In correspondence home he would note that at times he scarcely believed he was in America at all, so surrounded he was by Irishmen. If he could fault it at all it was only the "stifling heat" and "air that seems hot" such that "one can hardly breathe at times".[8]

A menace to O'Connor's athletic form in these weeks were newspaper photographers who loitered around Celtic Park and were encouraged by club officials to take as many photographs of the Irishman in action as they wished. Thus O'Connor felt obliged to jump an excessive amount in training to cater to the needs of

the press. This constant inconvenience, invariably during the hottest part of the day, eventually took its toll and began to jeopardise his form. Often against his better judgement, he was cajoled
into pandering to the whims of photographers and pressmen. One
week after he had begun training with Flanagan, O'Connor unexpectedly collapsed, suffering from heatstroke and a serious fever.
He had been struck down by a malaria-like illness, his fresh Irish
blood evidently much to the liking of the local mosquitoes. With
his fair Celtic complexion, O'Connor would have been better advised to court the shade than to brave the midday sun. "Those
dreadful mosquitoes who have displayed a liking for my unfortunate anatomy which I don't at all appreciate"[9] were a nemesis
O'Connor had never faced before. His hosts were extremely em-
barrassed that O'Connor should become so ill within days of arriving at Celtic Park and decided to transfer him to a quieter
location to recover. Far from the prying eyes of photographers
and pressmen and away from the intense humidity of Celtic Park,
O'Connor made a relatively speedy recovery in the quiet seaside
town of Rockaway Beach, some 26 miles from New York, in the
borough of Queens. Until he was fully recovered, he would commute each day to train in Celtic Park and then return to pass the
night in the quiet hideaway. This compromise seems to have
suited O'Connor, as removed for the most part from the dual
menaces of photographers and mosquitoes, the Irish jumper could
concentrate on his goal of setting a world record over 25 feet.

On 2 September O'Connor made his official debut at the Irish
Association Sports held in Celtic Park, Long Island, and there was a
huge turnout to witness the occasion. Since the ground had been
opened, its Sunday sports events had attracted a huge following
amongst New York's Irish-American community. As it was also
Labor Day, an American national holiday, thousands of New York-
ers flocked to Celtic Park for the Sports. The whirlwind of publicity
that had enveloped O'Connor since his arrival in America had
done much to excite the curiosity and heighten the expectations of
many Irish-Americans. Much would be required of O'Connor to
live up to his reputation as a "jumping wonder", a "veritable

Spring Heeled Jack" and the reigning "King of Spring", because his abilities were already being talked about and portrayed as the stuff of legend. Some 10,000 spectators flocked to Celtic Park, filling it to bursting point in anticipation of spectacular feats of athleticism. There had been high hopes that, between O'Connor and Flanagan, a host of new records might be set that day on American soil. The Irish-American officials were delighted by the huge numbers congregating at Celtic Park, but it soon became apparent that there were not adequate security measures in place to deal with the assembled crowd. Many seem to have been attending a sports meeting for the first time and were particularly unruly and boisterous. The publicity surrounding O'Connor had created a frenzy of excitement around his first American appearance. Although he initially intended to compete in several events at Celtic Park, following his illness he decided to save all of his energies for the long jump. Considering the importance of the occasion, O'Connor sought to concentrate his mind before the contest, remaining in the quiet confines of the dressing room, away from the boisterous clamour until it was time for the long jump event.

When the appointed time came, O'Connor emerged from the clubhouse and made his way towards the jumping area. Once the crowd became aware of his presence, in a sudden, sweeping motion, spectators stormed the field so as to get a better view of him. Within seconds, despite the desperate efforts of police and officials to keep the multitude back, O'Connor found himself completely surrounded and trapped in a swarm of people. He was stunned by the unruliness and hysterics of the crowd, whom he later described as the "most enthusiastic and excited multitude I ever saw". Their enthusiasm almost spelt disaster, however, as O'Connor was nearly crushed by the heave and narrowly escaped injury. When officials and police finally managed to extricate him from the unruly mob, O'Connor was directed to the clubhouse as there was no immediate hope of re-establishing order and clearing the spectators from the field.

The long jump was put back until the end of the day's card. Some two hours later O'Connor was called. Just as before, however, the crowd forced their way through the barrier of police and officials, engulfing the jumping area. Though O'Connor was given some room to manoeuvre a second time round and was not in danger of being crushed or suffocated, in their eagerness the crowd trampled all over the jumping pit and destroyed the precious cinder path right in front of his eyes. O'Connor was speechless, bowled over by the sheer chaos of the occasion. In such circumstances, O'Connor could easily have refused to jump and retired indefinitely to the clubhouse, but he had come too far to turn back now and he set about doing his best despite the risks. The fraught situation O'Connor experienced at Celtic Park that day is documented not only in his own correspondence home but also by several independent observers. The following report, from a well-known athlete of the time, John Joyce, testifies to the disappointment and disgust felt by genuine lovers of sport as events unfolded at the meeting:

> I was very sorry for the way the crowd [behaved] when O'Connor went to jump. It was disgraceful but somewhat characteristic of the people here. It springs from their "hoggishness" and insane curiosity about everything. They could have seen the jumping to better advantage had they stood wide, but no, all hog, they must have it all and so crowd the run. I was rather surprised that he attempted to jump at all considering the circumstances.[10]

Despite the antipathy that O'Connor must have felt towards the crowd as the meeting descended into chaos, the competition went ahead. Another observer, Henry Harding, brother of the athlete P.J. Harding, apportioned a good deal of the blame for the debacle to the officials themselves, describing the day's proceedings as "one of the worst conducted affairs" he had ever attended:

> The crowd was in possession of the field most of the time, and the badge-wearers were continually inviting in any friends of theirs. When the jump came off, the crowd nearly tore the clothes off one another in their efforts to get on the inside of the push. The result was that O'Connor could not get room enough

in the lane between the two sides for a fair run down. There was
also a large round stone about eight inches in diameter in the
middle of the run, and one of the committee put a programme
over it and called to Peter to "look out for the stone".[11]

The stone had become imbedded in the cinder path as the crowds
trampled the jumping area. The need to negotiate such an obstacle
while executing a run-up would, one suspects, concentrate the
mind, yet O'Connor also had to watch out for an additional menace. The crowd had encroached on the jumping area to such a de-
gree that he had to run through a channel "scarcely five feet in
width and had to dodge in order to escape from colliding with
persons thrusting out their heads for a better look". Further, to
add insult to injury, the reluctance of the crowd to move back
meant that O'Connor was unable to have a sufficient run-up, having to make do with an approach of a mere twenty feet. Under the
circumstances, O'Connor could do no better than 22' 8½" and was
understandably annoyed at being denied the chance to demonstrate his true ability. In addition to performing well short of his
best, O'Connor found himself in the absurd situation of being in
danger of not qualifying for the final as some of his opponents
had been given a handicap of 3' 6".[12] He would have to risk everything on his final jump, despite the numerous pitfalls that had to
be avoided en route. The pressure was mounting and O'Connor
probably felt his reputation in the United States was on the line.

As if to fulfil Murphy's Law, the day finished in unmitigated
disaster as O'Connor, desperately trying to reach the final in near-
impossible circumstances, strained his jumping leg badly on his
third and final qualifying jump while approaching the trig on the
now furrowed and uneven cinder path. The injury brought an end
to his jumping that day. As the crowd spilled from the grounds of
Celtic Park many must have wondered what all the fuss and hype
was about this Irish jumper. After all, he hadn't even reached the
final of the long jump, let alone broken 25 feet. A day that had begun with such promise had descended into farce and disappointment. Disillusioned and disconsolate, O'Connor hobbled off the
field in excruciating pain in the direction of the clubhouse. The

Irishman's American debut was a baptism of fire that he would never forget.

In the immediate aftermath of the Celtic Park games, O'Connor realised that his injury would take time to heal. With only four days to the world championships in Buffalo, he was adamant that he could not and should not compete. He would have little chance against Prinstein and Kraenzlein in his current state. Another defeat and further humiliation would be inevitable and cast both him and Irish-Americans in a poor light. His misgivings, however, fell on deaf ears and the club insisted on his participation in the games. Despite his injury, O'Connor would still attract a great deal of attention and interest, particularly from Irishmen attending the Pan-American Exposition in Buffalo. The Wicklowman would have to grin and bear the pain and get on with the job.

Cʒ

THREE DAYS LATER, O'CONNOR SET off for Buffalo with Flanagan and four club officials. To his delight they took the Empire Express, billed as the fastest train in the world, with an average speed of a mile a minute. After the eight-hour journey, the Irish troupe arrived in Buffalo, which was home to yet another World Trade Fair, following hot on the heels of the Glasgow Exhibition. As the club had failed to book any accommodation in advance, they soon discovered that every hotel and hostelry was full to bursting point with visitors to the Trade Fair. The nearest accommodation that could be found was in Niagara Falls, a 40-minute journey by rail from Buffalo. The hotel was situated on the Canadian side adding an extra dimension to the world championship expedition. While passing through customs, "into English territory", the members of the troupe had to submit their luggage to a minute examination by customs officials and pay a toll bridge charge of ten cents each. This bureaucratic process amused O'Connor somewhat as he recalled with some nostalgia crossing the Waterford Bridge over the Suir with none of the fuss he had to submit to here. The inconvenience of not being able to stay in Buffalo turned out to be a blessing in disguise, because O'Connor got an opportunity to see Niagara. That day the Irish group explored the beauty spot, marvelling at the countless falls, rapids and whirlpools. Overawed by the magnificence of the wonders of nature, O'Connor declared that this experience alone made his trip worthwhile.

That night there was great commotion and excitement in Niagara, as two daredevils were intending to brave the Falls. A man named Carlisle Graham intended to swim the lower rapids from the whirlpool at Niagara to Lewison. Accompanying him on this most perilous journey was a friend, Maude Willard, who intended to make the trip in a barrel with her pet dog. The next day as the Irish contingent were leaving Niagara to make their way to Buffalo they could see the crowds gathering in anticipation of Miss Willard's attempt. As to the success of the venture, O'Connor would have to wait until it was reported in the newspapers.

On reaching the grounds at the Exhibition where the games were to take place, O'Connor recognised Prinstein among the spectators. There was no sign of Kraenzlein, however, as once again newspaper reports that he had returned to training specially to face the Irish champion proved false. When O'Connor observed the list of competitors due to take part in the long jump, he was amazed to find that Prinstein had not entered and had merely come to spectate and see at first hand the man who had broken his world record. At the time, O'Connor could not understand why Prinstein was so reluctant to face him, particularly in light of the fact that bad news travels fast and the American star must surely have heard of his misfortune at the Celtic Park games. There were, however, certain unforeseen political factors behind Prinstein's non-participation that day. Alfred Copeland, the man charged with coaching O'Connor upon his arrival in America, had received a letter the previous May from Prinstein which explains the American athlete's reluctance to compete. This most illuminating of letters, found among the assorted papers in O'Connor's scrapbooks, was most likely given to O'Connor by Copeland. In it, Prinstein expresses his disaffection with his university who had, to his mind, been unjustly harsh and critical of him. He refers to his "antic university" who believed he had in some way treated them unfairly and tells Copeland of his intention not to compete at any games that took place in Buffalo that year. Prinstein's disagreement with Syracuse no doubt stemmed from the Paris Olympics the previous year when they had not allowed him compete on the Sabbath, effectively denying him gold in the long jump. The letter is dated 28 May 1901, just one day after O'Connor broke the world record with a jump of 24' 9" in Ballsbridge. At the end of the letter, Prinstein acknowledged that his record had been "broken well" by the Irishman and that he would have to work all the harder to keep up with O'Connor. Prinstein also expressed the hope that O'Connor would come to America so the two could meet in competition. Whether O'Connor was aware at the time of the ongoing backroom politics between Prinstein and Syracuse University is not known, but he must have been extremely relieved, given his injury, to see that Prinstein was going to stick to his principles and not compete. One wonders what was in the American's mind as the long jump competition progressed. Had he competed and not become embroiled in a squabble with Syracuse, he could easily have beaten O'Connor and added the world title to the list of his achievements.

The absence of both Prinstein and Kraenzlein from the field meant that, despite his injury, O'Connor was in with a fighting chance of winning the championship. The only real threat in the field was an American named Harry P. McDonald, whose career best was 22' 10". O'Connor set his mind to the task, hopeful that his legs would see him through. In his initial qualifying jump, however, he could only manage a jump of 21' 4¾", collapsing in agony from the pressure exerted on the strained tendons in his jumping leg. The jump placed him in pole position for the time being, though it seemed unlikely he would be able to jump again if his distance was surpassed. Such a meagre distance could hardly be sufficient to win the world championships. While the other competitors closed in on O'Connor's mark, it became apparent that his initial jump had seriously aggravated the injury sustained at the Celtic Park games, and his leg became intensely swollen. Though it seemed for a while that O'Connor's first jump, mediocre as it was by his usual standards, could suffice to win the event and world title, McDonald shattered this illusion by jumping 21′ 5″, a mere quarter inch more than the Irishman. Things, it seemed, could not get worse. Riven by injury, with a leg reputedly swollen to almost twice its normal size, O'Connor faced the prospect of losing the world title by a quarter inch. To have come so far and be defeated by such a paltry margin was simply inconceivable.

He rallied his strength and made two further efforts to jump, pulling up each time in incredible pain. Squirming in agony on the sidelines as the other competitors tried to match McDonald's distance, O'Connor decided to give it one last try. In a concerted effort by the Irish team to salvage the situation and avoid the "disgrace" O'Connor always identified with ignominious defeat, he was laid out on the ground and copious amounts of alcohol and a stiff rubbing were applied to warm up the muscles of the injured leg. As O'Connor stood for the last jump, the assembled crowd, many of whom were of Irish descent, could plainly see the pain he was experiencing, with tears welling in his eyes. Despite later describing the run-up to this momentous jump as "something of a lame trot", O'Connor succeeded in jumping a distance of 22′ 5½″, thereby securing the world championship title. For years to come Peter O'Connor would recall with pride that the crowd could not have given him a better ovation had he jumped over 26 feet!

Despite the joy of victory, O'Connor had to be helped from the field and attended to by a doctor for quite some time. As *Sport* would subsequently report to a proud but concerned Irish readership, the doctor who attended to O'Connor in the aftermath of the Buffalo games thought it was sheer madness to have jumped, given the intense swelling of the leg. O'Connor was very lucky, narrowly avoiding the necessity of an operation to relieve the swelling, a precarious treatment which might have signalled a tragic and untimely end to his athletics career.[13]

⚬

THE HEROICS PERFORMED BY THE IRISHMAN that day would, however, be eclipsed by a tragedy which overshadowed the entire Pan-American Exposition itself. As with the 1900 Olympic Games in Paris, the world championships in Buffalo were incorporated into a Trade Fair and would have been seen as providing an extra attraction or even distraction to the commercial activity taking place. Thus a sizeable crowd, encompassing genuine sports enthusiasts and other curious parties, witnessed the day's proceedings. The previous day, numbers at the Exposition had soared to 116,000, some 50,000 gathering in the Esplanade to hear President McKinley's speech. The following day, as the athletics events were drawing to a close, the US President was due to perform his final official function in Buffalo, a short handshaking ceremony at the Temple of Music. The "music conservatory", as O'Connor called it, was one of the star attractions of the fair, an ornate extravagant construction, built in Byzantine style. In its close proximity to the Esplanade, at the centre of the Exposition itself, it was considered an ideal spot for the President's last engagement. Despite the considerable precautions needed to protect America's first citizen from potential hazard, disaster struck as a lone assassin, that spectre in American history, shot McKinley twice at close range. In a panic, the thousands of people who had crowded the Temple of Music in the hope of meeting the President, streamed out onto the central esplanade. There to witness the frenetic exodus was O'Connor, resting after the day's exertions. The anarchist whose actions had cast such a dark shadow over the Pan-American exposition was a disaffected young American of Polish descent, Leon Czolgosz. When McKinley died a week later, Czolgosz's infamous place in history was secured, although he would pay the ultimate price for his atrocity.

On a further tragic note, the woman whose courage and daring O'Connor had marvelled at had perished in the whirlpool at Niagara. Though the barrel had made it through the falls intact, it took such a long time to extract the barrel from the whirlpool that Maude Willard suffocated in the confined space, though her pet dog survived the ordeal. When the barrel was finally brought to shore and opened, Miss Willard was found unconscious and the little dog jumped out unscathed. Newspaper reports of the day reported that her companion, who had also braved the falls that day and was returned safely to shore, was said to be devastated and still at the pool mourning his plucky companion. In the space of a few short hours, the American President had been shot and fatally wounded, a perfectly healthy woman had perished after willingly throwing herself over the Niagara Falls in a barrel, and O'Connor's career looked to be in grave jeopardy after he was forced to jump against doctor's orders. America was proving to be a formidable country and the sights, sounds and events he experienced during his first trip there would linger long in his memory.

 os

IN THE IMMEDIATE AFTERMATH of the Buffalo games, O'Connor was entrusted for a time to a certain Mrs O'Donnell, a Waterford woman whose daughters still ran a business on the quay. In correspondence home, O'Connor sings the praises of this Waterford woman, crediting her with his recovery and with saving him from being crippled for life. Once he had recuperated sufficiently from the Buffalo ordeal, O'Connor spent a week with his brother Arthur in Fall River, Massachusetts. Seeing Arthur again seems to have reinvigorated him. The brothers had much in common, being very outgoing personalities — each in his own way loved the limelight. Arthur was graced with a good singing voice and composed many airs and ballads which were published in various periodicals and local newspapers in America. Peter O'Connor's lifelong passion for pipes, his only vice, may have come from his older brother, who opened a cigar emporium on his arrival in America. A newspaper excerpt of 1900 encapsulated the O'Connor family's preoccupation with tobacco, or as O'Connor used to refer to it, "the fragrant weed":

> Whether in training or out of training O'Connor smokes like a veritable steam engine. It is indeed a wonder to all judges of

athletics how, under the circumstances, he can accomplish
such splendid feats.[14]

The fact that O'Connor had won the world championships was a
source of satisfaction for his Irish-American hosts, yet back home
in Ireland the applause was somewhat muted. There was great
dissatisfaction that he was forced to compete despite being injured. Indeed, elements in the Irish press feared that O'Connor
might be lame for life. *Sport* declared that:

> There is such a thing as killing a man with kindness and we
> believe that O'Connor has been the victim of too much kind-
> ness on the part of his club men. He was also made to serve as
> an advertising medium to his own disadvantage.[15]

Certainly it must have been galling for O'Connor's friends and
admirers in Ireland, who had seen him accomplish world record-
breaking feats just weeks before, to hear reports of a possible end
to his career. In a move calculated to defuse considerable criticism
in Ireland, Dan Madigan wrote to Redmond making him an honorary member of the Greater New York Athletic Association, in
appreciation of his services in inducing O'Connor to visit America
and uphold the fame of the "old sod". In his tribute to Redmond,
Madigan tried to present O'Connor's visit in a positive light and
dismissed any notions that the New York Association had failed
to take care of the Irish world champion. From a purely athletics'
perspective, he pointed out that O'Connor's jumps on Labour Day
at Celtic Park and at Buffalo on 6 September were still the best
achieved in America that year. The victory at Buffalo was "entirely due to Irish heart and grit", an unforgettable moment of
sporting spectacle and theatre. In relation to the chaotic Celtic
Park meeting, Madigan denied accusations of impropriety on the
part of the organisers and hoped that O'Connor would undertake
"to discredit false statements" levelled at his association, though
he acknowledged that O'Connor could not have been expected to
jump well under the conditions of the Labour Day games. Madigan's description of the great hysteria that was evident that day

echoed that of other independent observers, "No words of mine could describe to you the enthusiasm of the 10,000 spectators who were present at Celtic Park to witness two such famous athletes as O'Connor and Flanagan."[16]

Indeed, nobody could have predicted that the crowd's enthusiasm that day would quite literally spill onto the field. The roots for such unprecedented chaos were probably due to the extraordinary amount of newspaper coverage and hype O'Connor received in his first weeks in America. Madigan seems oblivious to the fact that such overexposure to the media might have a negative effect: "I may aver without any exaggeration that no athlete has ever received so much attention from the press as he has, and he is worthy of it all."

O'Connor was perhaps one of the first sports stars to suffer from what we know now as "paparazzi" and "spin doctors". On leaving America, the Irish athlete would be left in no doubt as to the dangers inherent in being flavour of the month and becoming the darling of the press. In building up O'Connor's celebrity, papers like the *New York Sun* had pictured him as larger than life, an almost mythical figure. It was thanks to the media that O'Connor had become a household name in such a short time, but being the object of such curiosity had its drawbacks. To be in the focus of the American press was to live indefinitely in the eye of a relentless storm. With the shooting and subsequent death of McKinley, however, the bubble that had surrounded O'Connor finally burst and the storm shifted focus. McKinley's assassination jolted American society; Czogolsz's senseless act left a nation in shock. As reality set in, the press's attention was redirected to matters of national importance. Almost all sporting fixtures were cancelled in the ensuing weeks after the attack on McKinley and many American newspapers accompanied their print columns with sombre black bands. The only sporting event of any importance to take place was the Americas Cup yacht race in which Lipton's *Shamrock II* was participating, though once again he would fail to bring the much cherished cup home to Europe.

In the month prior to his departure, O'Connor had plenty of time to do some sightseeing in New York, and also resume training in the hope of regaining some form. These efforts would prove fruitless. At the 67th Fall Games of the New York Athletic Club at Travers Island on 6 October, O'Connor thought he was approaching good form and was described by one sports correspondent as "appearing to have all the spring necessary for a big jump". Indeed, in his qualifying jump he covered a respectable distance of 22 feet. Nonetheless, due to the long layoff and his various misadventures, O'Connor's technique had suffered and he could not get within a foot of the take-off block in two subsequent jumps. In his final attempt, instead of falling short of the wooden take-off block, he overstepped it and twisted his ankle awkwardly. It was a final blow to any aspirations he might have had to reproduce his earlier form of the season, and a clear sign that he needed a break. In a perfunctory newspaper roundup of the sports, it was reported that "a surgeon worked over the swollen ankle long after the spectators had left the Island. It is unlikely that O'Connor will be seen again in a jumping event in this country."[17]

The best medicine for a speedy recovery was to quit competition for the time being and give his body time to heal. Nonetheless, the Irish-American Club prevailed on him to change his ticket home just two weeks after the Travers Island debacle to compete in a further Celtic Park games. This somewhat ill-advised request was made, according to press releases, "so that the patrons of the Greater New York Irish-American Athletic Association will not be disappointed by any change in the programme of track and field athletic contests". O'Connor had reputedly recovered fully from the "mishap" sustained at Travers Island, so at the last moment on the eve of the departure of O'Connor's ship the *St Louis*, he put aside his misgivings in order to facilitate his hosts one last time. However, O'Connor knew better than to tempt fate and so settled for the more attainable distance of 21' 5¼". Still, the last big sports meeting of the season was a resounding success for the Celtic Park Club. Over 5,000 people turned out for the games to see O'Connor, Flanagan and a Seneca Indian called Jerry Pierce, who was attempting to break the American five-mile record. Treading carefully and making sure not to overdo it, O'Connor could enjoy the spectacle of his friend Flanagan adding a new world record to an already long list of honours, as the Limerick man threw the 56 lb weight 36' 9½", smashing the previous record held by J.S. Mitchell by nearly a foot.

Reminiscent of O'Connor's experiences on Labor Day, Pierce's five-mile world record attempt was ruined by the unwarranted interference of the crowd. Starting out in the three-mile handicap, he intended to continue for a further two miles at the finishing line of the three-mile race. Reserving his powers for the extra distance, Pierce was content to finish in second place in the three-mile handicap some 12 yards behind the winner. Unfortunately, a large crowd assembled at the finishing post to congratulate the winner and Pierce found his way blocked for about 10 seconds, losing his momentum and focus. Though he continued valiantly for a further mile, officials stopped him when it became clear the record was out of reach. As in the case of O'Connor's debut at Celtic Park the previous month, Pierce's record attempt was scuppered at the hands of a well-meaning but careless crowd.

Following his final appearance at Celtic Park on 20 October, O'Connor could sit back and relax as he waited for his ship home. He had experienced a fair amount of misfortune in his stay in America but had nonetheless fulfilled his mission to win in Buffalo. He had also been the recipient of great generosity on the part of Irish-Americans throughout his stay and would always refer to having been treated "royally" in America. Few if any athletes in modern times had ever received the kind of publicity and attention that he had experienced. Courtesy of the New York press and regardless of the fact he had failed to perform anywhere near his best on American soil, he had become a renowned celebrity overnight. How long the memory of the Irish champion jumper endured amongst Americans is not known, but O'Connor would certainly never forget America. The few months stateside had been something akin to a rollercoaster ride, a journey full of highs and lows in which he had both made and witnessed history. O'Connor had accomplished much in the athletic season of 1901 and now it was time to return home and further his professional career:

> I am quite tired of this country, and long to be back once more on my own congenial soil and pure air, far, far away from the maddening crowd, wild scenes of gaiety and bustle, stifling heat and abominable mosquitoes.[18]

On the morning of 29 October 1901, O'Connor's wish came true as the steamer *Celtic* carrying him and Sir Thomas Lipton amongst others docked in Queenstown.

Settling Back into Life in Ireland

O N O'CONNOR'S RETURN TO Waterford he took up residence in a boarding house situated on the edges of the old Viking city, run by a Mrs Foran, the widow of a sea captain, and her daughter. The lodgings in Bailey's New Street were beside the bustling quay and main thoroughfare, a stone's throw from the busy riverside. Close by was the ruin of an old Franciscan Friary that still stands today, lingering in picturesque decay, frozen in time.

Whereas in the past O'Connor had drifted from place to place, restless by nature, in 1902 a change seems to have come over him. The trip to America probably had a lot to do with bringing about this change of heart. He had a guaranteed return ticket. The vast majority of those he travelled with, less fortunate than himself, were no doubt on one-way trips seeking a new life. In his time in New York and particularly at Buffalo, O'Connor had seen that life in America was by no means as uncomplicated or plain sailing as many people thought. The experience seems to have cured his wanderlust and any ideas he might have had about emigrating to America were dropped. O'Connor had had an exceptional life as a bachelor, his gift in sport affording him the opportunities to travel far and wide despite a relatively low income. From the moment he returned to Waterford, he seems to have considered the city as his home and, now almost 30 years of age, he probably recognised that the time had come to put down some roots. Consequently he began to consider marriage in earnest for the first time. Towards the end of the nineteenth century and at the beginning of the twentieth century, marriage was a popular subject for debate in editorials both in England and in Ireland. In Ireland marriage was a state to be encouraged because the population had been in steady decline since the Great Famine of the 1840s, losing around three and a half million people over six decades. O'Connor was at the prime of life and beginning to tire of his life as a bachelor.

Of all of the letters and cuttings in his remarkably well-kept and comprehensive scrapbooks, perhaps the most curious entry is a long and humorous anonymous letter published in the *Waterford News* towards the end of 1902. In it, the author, "Disappointed One", shares his thoughts on matters and affairs of the heart, in particular that most venerable of institutions — marriage.[1] A prolific letter writer, O'Connor was never one to shrink from a good public debate, although at certain times, understandably, he chose to maintain his anonymity. In the early years of the twentieth century it was common practice for people to submit letters under *noms de plume* to the editors of newspapers, so correspondents could — and did — safely furnish personal details without the risk of exposure, and frank opinions could be freely expressed. The letter written under the pseudonym "Disappointed One" refers specifically to the dilemma faced by single men in the Waterford area. The sentiments expressed are those of a young bachelor feeling the pangs of solitude but well aware that the fundamental concept of marriage is "'til death do us part". "Disappointed One" laments the fact that in Waterford few young women are encouraged to develop the skills and habits necessary to becoming good housewives, attributing the "depressed state of the matrimonial market to the way parents bring up their daughters".

> They instill into their [daughters'] minds ideas much above their station, and grossly neglect one of the most important branches of their education — that is good housekeeping, good cooking — and to be thoroughly conversant with all other domestic duties!! The reason why young men *don't marry* is not far to seek. The present generation of ladies is composed of frivolous, conceited, unthinking creatures, whose whole ambition is to make themselves attractive and fascinating during their single blessedness; entirely forgetting that

their future happiness depends to a good extent on their being thoroughly equipped for the married state before entering upon it. Every artifice (some shady) is resorted to, every sub-terfuge requisitioned to the aid of the crafty maiden, of up to eight and twenty summers, to capture that much such sought after, but much abused creature called husband.

As O'Connor had no personal experience of the trials and tribula-tions of marriage himself, his "tongue-in-cheek" observations were possibly principally informed by life in Mrs Foran's boarding house. As a paying guest, O'Connor would have been used to regu-lar hours for breakfast, lunch and dinner as well as finding the house cosy and warm on his return from work. It is also possible that the stereotype for the crafty "unthinking" yet captivating crea-ture in the letter was Mrs Foran's daughter Annie. In the 1901 cen-sus Annie is listed as being 29 years old and thus would have seen some "eight and twenty summers". With a scarcity of eligible bachelors on the small Waterford social scene, Annie may have been on the lookout for a suitable man and quite possibly consid-ered her mother's lodger as a potential candidate. Many upwardly mobile young males of O'Connor's generation, with only minimal secondary education, ended up as clerks and more often than not as permanent guests in boarding houses. Interestingly, the tempt-ress described in O'Connor's missive also bears a striking resem-blance to the daughter of the landlady James Joyce later portrayed in his short story, "The Boarding House" from *Dubliners*. O'Connor seems to have had strong and clear ideas about the kind of person he would like to marry and settle down with, so there was little chance of him getting embroiled or ensnared in a relationship that was not of his own making and choice.

The letter, published a year after O'Connor's return from America, highlights the great dilemmas faced by his generation and is an interesting if slightly irreverent social document. At the time it was penned, some two-thirds of the Irish population were unmarried and a shortage of males in late Victorian Ireland due to emigration meant that many women with aspirations to marry and rear a family were destined to remain spinsters.[2] His preference for a wife and partner with practical skills as opposed to a delicately refined wife with artistic and musical leanings is somewhat conservative by modern standards but not unusual for Victorian times. Irish society in 1902 was still Victorian in outlook and mores, though the Queen herself had died the year before. It was still very much a man's world and the preference expressed by "Disappointed One" for a homemaker smacks of the kind of practical sensibility usually displayed by O'Connor. In the course of his life, O'Connor never had much time for grand shows of wealth or high fashion, nor did he approve of extravagant or superficial gestures. For the most part O'Connor's success in life was engendered by a practical, pragmatic philosophy and, great jumper though he was, marriage was one leap he would not undertake lightly.

The letter suggests that O'Connor considered himself an eligible bachelor and perhaps even a good catch. Despite this self-confidence, his future foray into the world of relationships would not be so smooth. Indeed, when contemplating who might be the ideal partner, "disappointed one" fails to address two key factors behind any marriage in Irish society: the social status of bride and groom and the attitudes of the prospective in-laws. O'Connor set high standards for any prospective partner, not realising that he was probably not quite as eligible as he contended. He may have been a strong handsome man who cut an impressive figure on the Waterford scene, but crucially he was still something of an unknown quantity in moneyed circles, a managing clerk with little or no fortune to speak of.

ଔ

AFTER THE INCREDIBLE HIGHS and lows of the 1901 season, O'Connor may well have expected a quieter less eventful summer in 1902. On the sports field he picked up where he had left off the previous season and easily dominated jumping events. Off the field, however, life would not prove so simple. Due to the death of fellow Waterford Harrier and friend Frank Furlong, O'Connor missed the IAAA Championships in Cork, leaving Con Leahy to take the honours in the jumping events. The sudden loss of such a close friend and supporter was a big blow to O'Connor and something of an omen as to what trials lay in store in 1902. Ill winds were blowing and O'Connor was about to get caught up in another of the many storms that would blight his athletics career.

At this time, the athletics world was an amateur one and cash prizes or appearance fees were strictly illegal. Despite the lofty ideals behind maintaining amateur status, the practical problems that this state of affairs gave rise to were obvious. There had been an explosion of interest in athletics in the previous six years since the revival of the Olympic Games and international athletics stars were in ever-increasing demand, particularly in Great Britain, Ireland and America. After his first world record at Ballsbridge in May 1901, O'Connor's popularity soared and, now a guaranteed crowd pleaser, he was one of a few Irish or international athletes whose presence could guarantee a good gate at athletics meetings. Consequently he expected that there would be reasonable prizes at athletic competitions to act as incentives to compete and train harder. Should the necessity arise, expensive prizes could be pawned so as to recoup the expenses of going to compete in Dublin or even farther afield. Leading athletes often came to an agreement with organisers that, if they should win, instead of receiving yet another set of carving knives they, would be given a stipulated amount of credit in a local shop where they could select something useful for themselves. Thus, in a somewhat roundabout way, the amateur status was maintained, the essential factor being that money would never grease the palm of an amateur athlete's hand. It also enabled world class stars to travel and compete against each other at home and abroad despite their lack of financial support.

While for the most part organisers gave prizes worthy of the victor, every now and again they reneged on their side of the bargain. The previous season at the DMP Sports, O'Connor and other athletes had received clearly substandard prizes. Despite winning the long jump and the high jump from the American ace Baxter, O'Connor was presented with a cheap second-hand gold chain and a faulty clock with mutilated works. What most annoyed O'Connor and several other Irish athletes at the same sports, however, as noted already, was the underhand way in which the American athletes had allegedly been paid for appearing. When DMP officials promised to repair or replace the broken clock, O'Connor let the matter rest for the time being. In the course of the next year, the repaired clock did not materialise and O'Connor was given the runaround on various trips to Dublin, adding insult to injury. Not one to be taken for a fool, O'Connor's patience finally ran out and he decided to make the matter public. What is most amazing about this episode is the way a storm in a teacup quickly grew into a major scandal. By targeting the officials of the Dublin Metropolitan Police Sports there would be significant collateral damage amongst the sporting fraternity. After a year of simmering tension and frustration, O'Connor now exposed the entire affair, embarrassing not just the DMP officials but also the supposed regulator of amateurism in Ireland, the IAAA.

> I have refused to enter or compete [in the 1902 DMP Sports] on the grounds that the prizes offered for competition to Irish athletes at the DMP Sports last year were simply scandalous, being of the cheapest and most unsuitable kind, while Yankee athletes, who were brought over specially from England to sweep all before them, won nothing, and for winning nothing received from Mr Blackhall, the then Hon. Sec., according to his own statement to several persons the almost incredible sums of from £30 to £50 each in cash. . . . I consider myself justified in letting the public know how I have been treated. I intend also to report the matter to the IAAA and hope to succeed in getting the DMP Sports on the 14th Inst. suspended, as it was in flagrant breach of the Amateur Athletic Laws for the Hon. Sec. to pay the Americans such large sums in cash. It is decidedly against my wishes to have to call public attention to and report this matter, but it is a monstrous state of affairs if "foreigners" can be paid £30 to £50 each, and first prizes of the value of £2 deemed good enough for "Irish" athletes, who have year after year been patronising the DMP sports.[3]

Following O'Connor's public exposure of the corruption of Dublin Metropolitan Police Athletics officials, he was called before the IAAA to provide proof of his allegations. Suspecting that it would be nothing more than a kangaroo court, hastily assembled to organise a cover-up and save the face of the IAAA, O'Connor refused to attend. Considering his previous acrimonious dealings with IAAA officials sympathetic to Newburn, O'Connor sensed he could be walking straight into an ambush. If he attended and furnished proof, he might be responsible for Kraenzlein and Baxter being banned indefinitely, something he would never do to another athlete. The Americans were bound to be made the scapegoats of the affair, so that attention could be deflected from the DMP officials. When he failed to attend, O'Connor received a public censure, the Americans were suspended and the DMP officials received a token slap on the wrist. O'Connor was living dangerously taking on the DMP and the IAAA, two unionist organisations with strong establishment links. He did not take the IAAA's snub lying down, however, and struck back through the most potent of media: the press. Though he was extremely adept and well practised in defending himself when caught in the maelstrom of controversy, O'Connor nonetheless regretted deeply compromising the American athletes in his assault on officialdom.

> I am very sorry for the Americans as they were led into a trap, and the very man who trapped them would have done the same to me had I given him the chance. I had no intention of injuring the Americans when I publicly made my charge against the DMP Sports Committee, as I have the greatest possible admiration for the Americans, who are in my opinion more genuine amateurs than we are in Ireland. The DMP officials who caused all the trouble are nominally suspended but then changing the title of their club, which at the time was a "Bicycle Club" to that of an "Athletic Club" which it is termed at present, the DMP sports officials practically escape harmless, and can go on holding their sports year after year, as if nothing occurred whilst American athletes are banished permanently from the amateur track.[4]

The IAAA suspended the Americans, claiming to have secret proof from an unnamed source regarding the DMP Sports. By refusing to name their source, they were effectively trying to lay the sole blame for the popular American athletes' suspensions at O'Connor's doorstep. It was an accusation O'Connor was anxious to refute, having refused to furnish any actual proof that could have warranted the suspensions. After he was treated so "royally" the year before during his stay in America, he no doubt wondered what Americans might think of his role in the affair. So he challenged the IAAA to come clean and report who, if anyone, had provided the proof against Kraenzlein and Baxter.

> They pass a vote of censure upon me for refusing to furnish any proofs whatever against the Americans, still they actually suspended them, and yet they maliciously represent to the public that I got them suspended, which is absolutely untrue. Now, I again ask, why has the IAAA deliberately concealed the name of the real individual who proved the charges or furnished the proofs which brought about their suspension?[5]

O'Connor need not have been overly concerned, however, as the news of the IAAA's suspensions of Baxter and Kraenzlein hardly made any news in America. Further, the American AAU would ferociously defend their champion athletes, demanding hard proof of any misdeeds. Indeed, once the controversy entered the public domain, it was the IAAA who were made to feel the pressure, as their activities and integrity as an athletic watchdog came under suspicion.

> The IAAA have fish to fry now, that they evidently never dreamt of, when they censured Peter O'Connor because — it seems to me and to the public generally — he drew aside a piece of the curtain and let a flood of light in on the amateurism of which they are such careful custodians. . . . I know a dozen so-called amateurs in Ireland who insist on having their expenses paid when competing at meetings. Their expenses have been paid regularly for years, and the gentlemen who pose as rulers in Athletic Ireland know, just as well as I do, the

offenders, yet they make a pretence of dealing with the question by making examples of Americans. This I consider distinctly shabby. Why let the Irishmen go free and tar visitors with the professional brush? — and this in hospitable Ireland![6]

Facing considerable public scrutiny and embarrassing publicity, the IAAA had no choice but to suspend Kraenzlein and Baxter. According to the understandings that existed between the English AAA, the American AAU and the Irish IAAA, the American athletes should have been immediately banned by their Amateur Athletics Union. Much to the surprise of the IAAA, however, James E. Sullivan, the man at the helm of the Amateur Athletic Union, demanded proof before he would suspend two of America's most famous and acclaimed sporting figures. When that proof was not forthcoming, he refused to take action. From today's perspective, Sullivan's reaction seems not only natural but quite appropriate. Up to this it was expected, at least by the IAAA, that a ban from one amateur athletics association would be recognised by their American and English counterparts. James E. Sullivan was arguably the most powerful man in world amateur athletics. He was a long-term employee of the Spalding Trust, and considering his vested financial interests, his stewardship of the AAU was often at odds with traditional amateur ideals. This is probably the chief reason why he and Coubertin, the founder of the modern Olympic movement, never saw eye to eye. The French aristocrat's approach to amateurism was idealistic. Sullivan's AAU outwardly upheld amateur ideals, but the American athletics body did not always practise what it preached, as the public would discover in a series of revelations and scandals in 1905–6.

Credited with being the driving force and organisational brains behind America's domination of the early Olympics, it is highly unlikely that he would punish the likes of Kraenzlein or Baxter without definitive proof. In his long tenure at the AAU, Sullivan had weathered much criticism and many storms. An Irish commentator in *Sport*, who was oblivious to the marked differences that existed between American and British interpreta-

tions of "amateurism", was extremely perplexed by Sullivan's reluctance to take immediate action against the American athletes.

> We really do not know why the Amateur Athletic Union of the
> United States should ask for the evidence in connection with
> the suspension of Baxter and Kraenzlein, and as a plain matter
> of fact the Union is not entitled to it, and should not get it.
> Both athletes are suspended by the IAAA and that is the end
> of it. The AAU are bound by the actions of the IAAA, and it is
> nothing short of mere childishness to be asking for evidence
> on the matter.[7]

The existing modus operandi of the world of amateur athletics
was receiving its first big test and as the American AAU did not
back down from its position; its unwillingness to act was a clear
sign that divisions and cracks were beginning to show in the hith-
erto pristine and clear-cut world of amateur athletics:

> People are now asking if the Americans will recognise the
> suspensions. I am inclined to say right off that they will, and
> even were the American Union disposed to act otherwise they
> will change their policy when the consequences of a refusal to
> do so are brought home to them. There is no direct agreement
> between the IAAA and the American governing body, but
> there is a general understanding between the ruling bodies of
> amateur sport all over the world to recognise sentences of
> suspension for offences committed within the jurisdiction of
> each other. It is not, therefore, within the power of the IAAA
> to compel the American body to recognize the suspension of
> Messrs Baxter and Kraenzlein, but should they not do so no
> American athlete would be allowed to compete in the cham-
> pionship of England, or any competitions held under the aus-
> pices of the AAA in England, or indeed in any other part of
> the United Kingdom. The American invasions have become so
> regular of late, and so uniformly successful that I am sure the
> governing body in the United States would hesitate before tak-
> ing any action in the defence of athletes, however eminent,
> that would result in shutting the English championships to all
> their men.[8]

Few people involved in the scandal or who took sides in it escaped unscathed from the controversy. By bringing the matter to light, O'Connor had effectively opened a can of worms, blowing the whistle on the hypocrisy that existed within Irish amateur athletics. The consequent inaction of the American AAU had given the affair a new twist. Either the American body did not recognise the integrity and ruling of the IAAA or it was unwilling to punish two high-profile athletes. The significance of this episode would not be fully understood until Arthur Duffey, the world's fastest sprinter, spoke out in 1905 following his suspension by the American AAU. O'Connor had inadvertently kindled the ashes of a fire that would be a slow-burner and eventually re-ignite. The principal outcome of the DMP affair was that O'Connor now became a *persona non grata* in the eyes of the IAAA. Equally, the affair may have encouraged Kraenzlein and Baxter to retire from active athletics competition, as both athletes seem to have quickly withdrawn from the sports limelight. Kraenzlein had by now successfully qualified as a dentist, and Baxter was already practising law.

❣

AFTER HIS PUBLIC FALLING OUT with the IAAA, O'Connor was not picked for the team to face Scotland in the annual bout between the two countries. O'Connor may have won the publicity war against the DMP and the IAAA, but his victory now came at a high price. His de-selection from the team, though not unexpected, hurt deeply. This contest was probably the most important fixture on the Irish sporting calendar, comparable to the Six Nations rugby matches of modern times. The annual sports created huge interest in the press and a place on the Irish team was considered highly prestigious. *Sport* would perfunctorily report that considerable changes had been made since the teams were first selected, and that the "most notable absentee from the Irish side" was Denis Carey. O'Connor's absence was simply ignored.[9]

O'Connor's de-selection was not favoured by all IAAA aco-
lytes, as was evidenced by one official IAAA handicapper writing
in *Ireland's Saturday Night*:

> Whatever may be the result of the International Athletics con-
> test at Ballsbridge this afternoon — be it victory or defeat —
> the feeling of dissatisfaction which the selection of the team
> has caused will not be wiped out. The committee deliberately
> departed from the well-established precedent for no other rea-
> son that I can see than to give places to certain members of the
> Dublin University Athletic Union. . . . O'Connor's name will
> appear on the programme as a substitute but whether he is
> present or not he is not likely to get a chance of jumping.[10]

It was alleged that the IAAA was heavily infiltrated by athletes
and officials with links to both Trinity College and Dublin Harriers and that the selection appeared to be skewed in favour of university students. To many it seemed that the IAAA were closing
ranks and punishing O'Connor and other leading athletes who
had lent him their support in boycotting the DMP Sports. Later
that summer, O'Connor went on the offensive with a "scathing
rejoinder to the IAAA".

> The IAAA refused to permit me to represent Ireland in the re-
> cent International Athletic contest with Scotland [in the long
> and high jumps], simply because I exposed the DMP officials'
> treatment of me through the public press. In order to give the
> IAAA no excuse, I wrote some weeks previous to this contest
> offering my services and stating that I was capable of winning
> the long and more than probably the high jump. It was well
> known that at the English championships in London, which
> were held exactly a fortnight before the Ireland v Scotland con-
> test, I easily beat Con Leahy and the two Scotch champions in
> both the long and high jumps. Notwithstanding this they re-
> fused to give me a place on the Irish team, so that it would ap-
> pear the venting of the spite of one or two members of the
> IAAA towards me was more precious to the Association than
> Ireland's athletic success. . . . The IAAA is supposed to put
> down with a strong hand professionalism in athletics and make

laws and rules, as its title implies, for the protection of amateurism. The IAAA however, instead of supporting me, vindictively
tried to injure my reputation for exposing professionalism, simply because the offenders happened to be such an influential
Sports Committee as the DMP's. I care not for their favour or
their censure, and I leave the sporting public to judge whether I
have done anything deserving of censure or not.[11]

In spite of numerous protestations in the Irish press and the surprise expressed by Scottish sports journalists before the contest, the
IAAA refused to back down or admit any wrongdoing. The political divisions and bitter infighting within the IAAA were early
symptoms of a new uncertain era for Irish sport, in which athletics
would become increasingly subservient to political concerns.

ଐ

IN 1901, WHEN PETER O'CONNOR helped to organise the Presentation Convent Bazaar in Waterford, a certain Maggie Halley had
caught his eye. Maggie's father, James Halley, was a prosperous
farmer who had made his home in Ballybeg, and farmed some 128
acres in the environs of Waterford City. James had moved his
family from Patrick Street in Tramore, where his father had several business interests including a victualler's and a cobbler's.
Like his father, James seems to have been a shrewd businessman,
since his wealth and property increased steadily in the course of
his life, culminating in the purchase of several farms in the 1890s.
Apart from raising cattle and running his numerous affairs, James
supplemented his income by acting as a rate collector, always a
lucrative, if unpopular, sideline. At the time O'Connor began to
show an interest in Maggie Halley in 1902, James Halley had
some £17,000 in the coffers in addition to numerous properties
and commercial interests and was considered one of the richest
farmers in County Waterford. As James and his brother Nicholas
were prominent figures in Waterford civic life, they had served on
the Grand Jury in 1897, and O'Connor would certainly have
known the Halleys by sight.

James Halley probably did not approve of this young man courting Maggie. O'Connor came from a different social class — artisans and craftsmen used to working with their hands and relying on their physical strength in the shipyards, and as small farmers. The Halleys were one of Waterford's richest farming families, with a good deal of property and a considerable income. Since O'Connor had set out in the world at the age of 14, he had managed to compensate for his minimal formal education through self-study and night classes and had become a fluent and articulate speaker. Though his courteous manner and educated comportment may have given the impression of a man from a comfortable middle-class background, in truth he was an independent man of relatively humble origins, schooled for the most part in the university of life. He was certainly not the kind of husband James Halley intended for his daughter.

In 1903 O'Connor would have seen little of Maggie as she and her sister Statia spent much time looking after their father who was ill. In early 1904, after two frustrating years of waiting on the sidelines and wondering if he would ever have the opportunity to declare his intentions towards Maggie openly, circumstances unexpectedly changed. That February, James Halley began to succumb to his illness. The ailing patriarch was attended regularly by a Dr Jackman of Waterford but, showing few signs of improvement, James decided it was time to set his affairs in order. Thus on the 26 February 1904 James Halley called two trusted friends to his bedside, his cousin Walter Halley and Nicholas Cummings of Kilmeaden, and then dictated his final wishes.

The last will and testament of James Halley is a fascinating and comprehensive document that provides an interesting insight into the man himself. He comes across as a strong patriarchal figure, who was not afraid to assert his authority even from beyond the grave. Though generous on the whole, some of the will's stipulations in regard to his children were somewhat draconian in nature. Apart from the usual responsibilities and duties involved in executing a will, the executors were also charged with evaluating the suitability of any prospective bride or groom of the deceased's children. The relevant charge was to "exclude from benefit or participation any children or child whose conduct shall not in the opinion of the trustees be satisfactory either for marrying without the consent and approval of the trustees or otherwise". Should the executors disapprove of any prospective suitor, they could threaten to exercise their veto and block any inheritance. The granting of such extraordinary powers to executors in such an entirely subjective matter as romance may seem excessive in the twenty-first century. It is important to remember, however, that Halley lived almost all his life in an era noted for its sober and formal approach to relationships, as well as clear class distinctions. Indeed, the notion that a good marriage required a sound financial basis as well as the tacit approval of society is distinctly Victorian in nature.

It is very likely that the peculiar and strict conditions laid down in the document were intended by Halley to scupper any prospective marriage between Maggie and Peter O'Connor. Certainly her father would have been aware of any contact between his daughter and the champion athlete. Waterford was not a large city and any girl seen with O'Connor was sure to set tongues wagging. Halley would have preferred to see his children marry into well-off farming families and thus build upon his prosperous legacy rather than allying themselves with people of inferior rank and status. In the will, Halley does not lay down any specific criteria for the executors to judge the suitability of his children's prospective partners — O'Connor was probably the only intended target of Halley's final decree, his name possibly passed on directly to the executors as a prime example of an unsuitable candidate.

Some three weeks after making his last will and testament James Halley died, leaving two sons and three daughters, heirs to a substantial estate. When their father's will was read to the Halley siblings there must have been considerable consternation, particularly for the two remaining girls at the Halley homestead. The fact that the trustees were given permission to rule in matters of the heart must have been an especially big blow to Maggie. Women of her position in rural Ireland in the early twentieth century had few realistic options in life. There was virtually no career open to Margaret, in spite of her education. Now at the age of 26, marriage was the best she could hope for. As her brother Walter stood to inherit the family home when he married, Margaret risked becoming a permanent house guest as she would have insufficient income and no property of her own. Only through marriage could she ever become mistress of her own house. Under such circumstances, many young unmarried women of the time chose to enter convent life or become governesses to obtain a secure position for themselves in life. Though Maggie was a devout Catholic, she did not have the vocation of her sister Catherine, who had become a nun some years before. In any case, a man considered one of the most eligible bachelors in Waterford and one of the finest athletes in the world was interested in her. Her father's stipulations in his will must have come as a huge shock, as she realised that to follow her heart could carry a high price, both economically and socially.

In the months following the death of her father, Maggie and Peter began courting openly, in spite of the disapproval of her family and no doubt the trustees of her father's estate. Eventually O'Connor proposed to his sweetheart and regardless of the furore their marriage would cause and the financial consequences, Maggie accepted. There was a good chance that should the will be contested in the courts, the extreme conditions laid down by her deceased father might be deemed unreasonable. As a clerk in a solicitor's office, O'Connor would have had access to much experienced legal opinion regarding the matter. Maggie most probably was more concerned about having the blessing of her family and their participation in her wedding. She also may have hoped that an acrimonious and public dispute might be avoided and her family and the trustees might warm to O'Connor. Both Maggie and Peter were to be disappointed, however, as old James Halley's influence still held sway with Maggie's family, for the time being at least.

A mere four months after her father's death, Peter and Maggie travelled to Dublin where they were married in Westland Row church on 28 September 1904. No member of the Halley or O'Connor family attended. Maggie had made her choice and now she was out in the cold. The ceremony was conducted by Canon Flynn, the parish priest of Ballybricken, County Waterford, who had organised the bazaar three years before, when the couple first met. Canon Flynn was assisted by Rev Andrew Moriarity of Clonliffe College, Peter O'Connor's old school friend and the son of his teacher Mr Moriarty. Only a small number of close friends made the trip to Dublin to join the celebrations, which suggests that the couple may have kept their marriage secret, possibly to avoid last-minute remonstrations or obstructions. For O'Connor, who had begun to think of Waterford as his home, it must have been with a great deal of sadness that he and Maggie had to steal away to Dublin to be wed. Had they married in Waterford, the Halleys absence from the ceremony would have been a humiliating blow for the couple. By marrying in Dublin, local gossips were denied a field day, but it must have been common knowledge that there was a rift between the newlyweds and Maggie's family. After the wedding, Peter and Maggie travelled to London for a two-week honeymoon. On their return from England the newlyweds moved into "Sweet Briar Cottage", situated in the Newtown area of Waterford city.

ය

WITH SO MUCH TURMOIL in O'Connor's private life, it was little wonder that he did not travel to the St Louis Olympic Games of 1904. He was still a formidable competitor and in very good physical condition, but he simply did not have the time, energy or money. The delicate and difficult circumstances surrounding his marriage to Maggie made a long and costly trip to the United States inconceivable. The various newspapers that speculated about O'Connor's possible appearance in St Louis were unaware that athletics was of secondary importance to him at the time. Any Olympic aspirations would have to be shelved this time, perhaps indefinitely. O'Connor knew it was extremely unlikely he would be competing internationally or at a sufficiently high level the next time the Games were due to come round in 1908. By then he would be 36 years old and almost certainly way past his best.

Few European athletes went to St Louis for the Games, the American athletes competing for the honours in many events against each other. It was perhaps fortunate that O'Connor did not undertake such a costly trip at this turbulent moment in his life, as the Olympic celebration proved the most disorganised to date, even more so than the Paris Games of 1900. In order to avoid a similar debacle in 1904, the International Olympic Committee, spearheaded by Baron Pierre de Coubertin, had awarded the Games to Chicago, the first time the Games would take place outside Europe. The choice of America to stage the Games backfired, however, as the city of St Louis, where the Louisiana Purchase Exhibition was due to be held, threatened to stage a sporting event to compete directly with the Chicago Games. When the St Louis bid received the backing of US President Theodore Roosevelt, the IOC's hand was forced and they voted to move the Games to St Louis. The change of venue would prove disastrous as the Games were spread out over four and a half months, with less than half as many nations represented as in 1900 and only 42 athletes travelled from outside America to compete.[12] As a result of the shift in venue, Coubertin, the IOC president, expressed his disapproval by absenting himself from St Louis and consequently James E. Sullivan the American AAU secretary and the Spalding Trust played an important role in running the event.[13]

Although there were many rumours that O'Connor would participate at St Louis, only Tom Kiely made the journey across the Atlantic to compete for Ireland and his native Tipperary. The English AAA had offered to pay the full expenses of his trip if he would compete for Great Britain, but Kiely refused. On his arrival in the US he was approached by numerous Irish-American athletics clubs who also offered to pay his costs if he would carry their colours at the Games. Despite all of these generous offers, Kiely did not yield. He paid the entire expenses of the trip himself and wore the colours of his native Tipperary during the Games. In a

Nellie Bywater's builders at Millom Shipyard in the UK, 1872;
Edward O'Connor, Peter's father, appears second from the right

Peter O'Connor's Wicklow home at Ashtown –
including the gravel path across which he first jumped

Peter O'Connor's world record jump of 24' 11¾" at Ballsbridge, Dublin, August 1901

Portrait of Peter O'Connor, John Flanagan and Dan Madigan, taken in New York, 18 October 1901

John Flanagan training in Celtic Park, 1901

Two cartoons from the *New York Sun*, 1901,
upon O'Connor's arrival in America

Peter O'Connor in 1902 sporting his most prized medals

KILKENNY R.I.C. SPORTS.

1904

O'CONNOR,

THE WORLD'S RENOWNED CHAMPION, IS COMING.

HE WILL ENDEAVOUR TO BREAK ALL PREVIOUS RECORDS.

In addition, the Brothers Leahy, Laurence Keily, Denis Horgan, Thomas Phelan, Laurence Roche, Denis Carey, P. Ferman, E. P. Colgan, and J. Garvey will be there.

Come and see the Greatest Athletic Struggle ever witnessed between Erin's choicest Sons at our Carnival in the Valley on the Nore.

REMEMBER THE 4th DAY OF AUGUST.

MODERATOR, KILKENNY

Poster for Kilkenny RIC Sports, 4 August 1904

Rochdale AAA Championships, 1904; O'Connor, the holder, ties for first place at 5' 9½"

Sweet Briar Cottage, Waterford,
O'Connor's home 1904-1913

British Olympic team on "steamer" to Athens, April
1906, incuding the three Irish participants, and also Peter
O'Connor's wife Maggie and her friend Bride Power

O'Connor and his wife Maggie
(in traditional Greek costume)
in Athens

Portrait of O'Connor proudly
displaying the first official Irish
cap and blazer at an Olympics

O'Connor takes gold in the hop, step and jump

William Sherring winning the marathon in
Athens, accompanied by Prince George

Myer Prinstein practising for the
long jump in the Athens stadium
as Martin Sheridan and another
US athlete look on

A.C. Kraenzlein demonstrating
his revolutionary leg-before-body
hurdling technique

The American Commissioner to Athens, James E. Sullivan,
and Matthew P. Halpin, Manager of the US team, in photo
taken by Prince George

Con Leahy takes Ireland's
second gold medal in Athens,
in the high jump

Martin Sheridan, Irish-American
hero of the 1906 Athens Games,
winning the shot-put

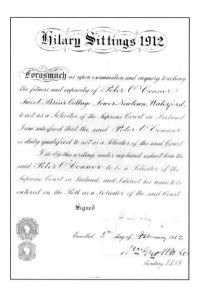

O'Connor's certificate to
practise law

O'Connor's home in Waterford,
"Upton", where he lived from
1913 until his death

Peter O'Connor and four
of his sons: (from left)
Jimmie, Walter, Arthur
and Peter

Peter and Maggie O'Connor with their nine children: (back row, from left) Arthur, Mary, Eddie, Kathleen, Walter, Madge and Jimmie; (seated, from left) Peter Jr, Maggie, Joan and Peter

Parade of Champions, photographed at Tipperary Garda Divisional Sports, Clonmel, 18 August 1929, including: (back row, left to right) J. Murphy, Pat O'Callaghan, Tom Kiely, Percy Kirwan, J.J. Ryan, General Eoin O'Duffy, Dan Fraher, Peter O'Connor (solr.), Pat Davin (solr.) and P. Stokes

Irish Olympians visit Fox Studios in Los Angeles and pose with cast
members of *The Golden West*; Maureen O'Sullivan also appears beside
General Eoin O'Duffy

Irish Olympians returning from Los Angeles Olympics; O'Connor is
second from the right in the bottom row

The Council of the Incorporated Law Society, photo taken in December 1933 when O'Connor was Vice President

Irish Athletics Championships in Clonmel, 1936; Eamon de Valera watches the parade of veteran athletes from the stand

O'Connor with his daughter-in-law, Dr Mary Ahern (wife of Peter Jr) and three of his dogs, *Perky* a brindle cairn terrier, *Barney* a smooth fox terrier and his most famous dog *Jumper* an Irish Red terrier

O'Connor with his son Peter, who took over the office, and two grandchildren, Rosemary (left) and Hilary (right)

Peter O'Connor's belt of gold medals, which he presented to Maggie on their wedding day *(Edmund Ross Images)*

Plaque dedicated to Peter O'Connor at
Waterford Athletic Track

Last portrait of Peter O'Connor, taken in 1956
when he was 84, in his garden at "Upton"

notable first for Irish athletics, Kiely took first prize and the gold medal in a competition billed as the "All Round Championship of the World" and which was later renamed and recognised as the Olympics' first decathlon event.

Although athletics was taking a backseat in O'Connor's life for the time being, the proposal that a triangular athletics contest might be held between England, Scotland and Ireland inspired him to make one of the most controversial moves of his athletics career. Following his falling out with the IAAA in 1902, he had declined to compete at further IAAA Championships, thereby making himself ineligible for subsequent international events. In that time he had continued to cross the Irish Sea each year, winning the AAA's long jump title and on occasion the high jump title. Since the dispute with the IAAA had effectively blocked his path to competing on an Irish team indefinitely, and to throw the cat amongst the pigeons, O'Connor wrote to the English AAA offering his services to compete for England against Ireland and Scotland. The triangular event would be the ideal platform for him to show the public that he was still the best jumper in the British Isles. It was an unusual move for someone who had refused to represent Britain at Paris in 1900, his controversial offer clearly born out of frustration at finding himself in the international wilderness. When the contents of the letter found their way into the public domain, there was much bewilderment amongst Irish sports fans and commentators, who were well aware of his nationalist beliefs. Though he had won the English long jump championships for four consecutive years, the titles themselves did not give him the right to represent Britain. It was assumed that O'Connor's Irish birth qualifications gave the IAAA first claim on his services and, although they might decline to select him, they could object to him representing their opponents. Unknown to all but a few, O'Connor was in fact entitled to represent both countries, England by his birth and Ireland by virtue of his residency. Though the notion of competing for Britain clearly did not appeal to him, the way the IAAA had treated him since the DMP scandal broke in June 1902 annoyed him greatly:

In 1900 the English AAA wrote and telegraphed me specially to Waterford offering to send me to the Paris Exhibition to compete at the World's Athletic Championships held there that year, and pay all my expenses, if I would go with the English team they were sending across as representing England. I unhesitatingly refused, and wires again came frequently, appealing to me to go, but they were of no avail. When they could not get me to go the Paris Exhibition they approached Mr P.J. Leahy, whom I defeated a few days previously in both jumps at the English championships, and he went as an English representative and got beaten in all the jumps. This is the same Mr P.J. Leahy who was selected in preference to me to represent Ireland. Owing to the scandalous way I [have been] treated by the IAAA, without any cause, I have ignored their championship sports ever since, and instead have gone to the English Championships, which are open to the world, where, I must admit, I have received respect, fair play and sportsmanlike treatment. I have now won the long jump Championship of England four years in succession, and when the Irish Association deliberately refuse my services why should I not offer my services to England as long and high jump champion of the United Kingdom? I maintain I'm perfectly justified in doing so, and I earnestly hope that the international contest between the four countries will come off when I shall prove my superiority as an Irishman, even though I have to represent England in order to do so.[14]

As the triangular tournament never got off the ground, O'Connor was not called upon to reveal his place of birth. Whether he would have done so or not is debatable. Never in the course of his life did he publicly acknowledge his English birth, choosing instead to be identified as a Wicklowman first and Irishman second.

ᗠ

THOUGH O'CONNOR HAD NUMEROUS battles to fight on the home front, he remained active on the domestics sports scene from 1902 to 1904. Since their war of words in public in 1902, O'Connor had ignored the IAAA's national championships. In 1904 he did, however, make a welcome return to the GAA annual Championships in Cork where he regained the long jump title that he had last won in 1900. Although he also entered the high jump and hop, step and jump, he failed to win either event, both titles being taken by Con Leahy, the younger brother of Pat Leahy. Since coming on to the Irish athletics scene Con Leahy was proving to be an even hardier competitor than his elder brother. Down the years, O'Connor had enjoyed close battles with Paddy in the high jump, but he knew he was no match for Con. He was still a dominant force in the British Isles in his speciality, the long jump, but in other events he was beginning to lose ground to younger athletes.

The following year, in 1905, O'Connor's absence from the annual Ireland–Scotland match was beginning to make itself felt as Ireland were beaten 8–3. The result might have been worse had Con Leahy not marginally edged out his Scottish opponent in the long jump, as one commentator noted:

> In the [long jump] Irish enthusiasts sorely missed the redoubtable O'Connor. In this event Leahy had all his work cut out for him, the opposition, strangely enough, coming from a raw recruit named Neilson, who at the 11th hour was prevailed upon to compete, and quite surprised everybody by being only 1½ inches behind Leahy's best. More's the pity that the marvellous jumping powers of O'Connor are not utilised, and thus prevent [*sic*] those painful surprises and unnecessary frights which Neilson's efforts created amongst the Irish contingent.[15]

Leahy also won the high jump, obtaining two of Ireland's three points, the other honours being taken by Denis Horgan in the shot putt. Were it not for these two experienced athletes, whose skills were honed at home and abroad, Ireland would have been whitewashed. Notably, the decline in Irish athletics that was beginning to make itself felt coincided with a renewal in the fortunes of the GAA, whose main interests were hurling and football.

The athletic highlight of this period in O'Connor's life was undoubtedly the 1905 AAA Championships in Huddersfield, where he took his fifth successive English title. This latest victory

was to the disappointment of English rivals, who were hoping
that O'Connor might have lost some of his "spring" after his marriage! What better way to demonstrate the merits of married life
to would-be doubters than by setting a new English long jump
record of 23' 9½". It was commonly believed in the bachelor
sporting subculture of Victorian England that being single was
conducive to achieving optimum results. O'Connor was quick to
make short shrift of such superstitions.

> The "young married man" has demonstrated to the world that
> he is as springy and active as ever, and his bachelor oppo-
> nents, hailing from America, Scotland, Sweden, England and
> Ireland, who entered in the belief that O'Connor would not
> defend his title owing to his marriage, or that he would not
> "fly" as far as usual, took their beating like real sportsmen and
> were most cordial in their congratulations.[16]

For his efforts O'Connor took home a seven-guinea gold medal and
a perpetual silver trophy worth 35 guineas. Following his victory at
Huddersfield, O'Connor returned to Ireland where he competed in
the annual GAA Championships. There he easily won his favourite
event, the long jump, although he decided against the hop, step
and jump, leaving Con Leahy to regain his title. The GAA event,
held in Cork, was noticeably better organised than in previous
years and the grounds better prepared. This improvement was
probably a result of the fact that the GAA had formed an Athletic
Council that year. The association was also about to go to war with
the IAAA, so the impressive display may have been a concerted
effort to show Irish athletes that track and field events were important to the association and figured in their long-term plans. Quite
unexpectedly, O'Connor found himself drawn into another brew-
ing storm after having a very unpleasant disagreement with one of
the men responsible for orchestrating the GAA's emerging hostile
stance towards the IAAA. Their argument had nothing to do with
athletic politicking but would nevertheless influence O'Connor's
future response to the impending crisis facing Irish athletics.

ଔ

SINCE ITS FORMATION IN 1884, the Gaelic Athletic Association had had a chequered and turbulent history. After an initially promising start, the association underwent countless internal upheavals, leading to the expulsion of its principal founder, Michael Cusack, and the resignation of its first President, Maurice Davin. The association had been torn apart in the early 1890s following its decision to support Charles Stewart Parnell after the Wicklow parliamentarian was named as co-respondent in a high-profile divorce case. Setting itself up in direct confrontation with the Catholic Church, who condemned Parnell's involvement with a married woman, many of the GAA members had been forced to abandon the association. With the death of Archbishop Croke in July 1902, one of the last links to the early years of the GAA was also severed.

By 1901, the GAA had become a shadow of its former self, but an influx of a new generation of officials gave the association a much-needed kick-start. Thanks to the efforts of this new executive, the GAA began to regain much of the ground it had lost in the previous decade. By 1903, it had successfully established four provincial councils and many members from the Gaelic League began to swell its ranks. Though the GAA had initially been set up as a non-political athletic association, it had never been particularly successful at resisting political infiltration. In 1887, the Irish Republican Brotherhood succeeded in gaining control of the GAA for a short time and the association's close affiliation with the struggle for Home Rule in the 1890s underlined its willingness to engage with, and take sides in, political matters. Following the GAA's re-emergence in 1901 as a renewed force, it once again quickly established its political credentials. Two men in particular, Tomas F. Sullivan from Listowel and Pat Nash from Dublin, were responsible for redefining the GAA along clearly political and nationalist lines. Sullivan was a prominent IRB man, who "brought with him in his work for the GAA the assertive separatist ideals of the secret body" and Nash was an active member of Sinn Féin.[17] The first major move came in November 1902 when the Connaught Provincial Council passed a motion suspending "any member of the association who plays or encourages in any way rugby or association football, hockey or any imported game which is calculated to injuriously affect our national pastimes". Not content to merely ban foreign games, at the GAA congress held in January 1903 the GAA introduced a ban on police, soldiers, militiamen and sailors on active service from playing hurling or football under their rules. Although the new rules did not yet affect athletics, a further strain on the relationship between the IAAA and GAA came the same year when the GAA set up its own cycling association to directly rival the ICA. The IAAA and ICA were closely affiliated and often ran their events simultaneously, sharing venues and gate receipts. The GAA had not shown an interest in cycling before 1903, perhaps as its original mission was to preserve the traditional cultural pastimes of Ireland, amongst which cycling clearly did not figure. By attacking the ICA's monopoly on cycling in Ireland, the GAA was indirectly undermining the IAAA.

Despite the tensions between the two associations, their working relationship endured until early 1905 when the GAA announced it was finally going it alone at its annual congress. From that point on, all GAA sports would be held solely under GAA rules, while athletes competing at meetings organised by the British army, navy and police forces were no longer eligible to compete at GAA meetings.[18] As a further insult to the ICA, a motion was passed officially transferring control of cycling to the Athletics Council, underlining the GAA's intention to increase its involvement in cycling.

The 1905 congress effectively drew the battle lines between the GAA and the IAAA and brought to an end a status quo that had existed for 20 years. Later that summer, the ban would receive its first test, bringing the two associations into direct confrontation. Also late in 1905, there was a change of staff at the IAAA, something that boded well for O'Connor. But before his lengthy rift with the IAAA could be healed, he became embroiled in yet another controversy. As the GAA began to put its recent congress rulings into practice, Peter O'Connor's support for the association foundered following the Wicklow GAA Sports in September 1905.

In advance of the Wicklow sports, Matthew Murtagh, secretary of the local GAA club, invited Peter O'Connor to compete at the annual sports. Murtagh had come to Wicklow town to take up a position as principal teacher in Wicklow Boys' National School, when Peter O'Connor's old teacher, Eugene Moriarty, retired. Murtagh was a rather feisty and cantankerous character. He was also a firm supporter of the GAA, active at both local and national level.

On receipt of Murtagh's invitation, O'Connor replied that he would compete if prizes worth £2.10s were guaranteed in each of the jumping events and that he would not be excessively penalised by handicappers. Although O'Connor was always delighted to compete in his old backyard, the prizes that he had won the previous year were not particularly impressive. This year O'Connor wanted to make sure that his trip would not be in vain. Now a married man, with his wife Maggie expecting their first child, he did not want to go traipsing up and down the country without the prospect of bringing something worthwhile back home. Of late, O'Connor's priorities had changed. He could no longer afford to take off for athletics competitions at will.

O'Connor wrote to Murtagh in confidence, presumably expecting some guarantees regarding the prizes in response. Instead he received a rather indignant reply from Murtagh who told him that he had revealed the contents of the letter to the sports committee, who had found his demands unreasonable.

> The committee cannot see that your charge of being badly treated last year is quite true and consider you have not been very complimentary to them or to the town in refusing to compete at their sports unless on exceptional and impossible conditions.

When O'Connor read Murtagh's letter, he was furious. The secretary was clearly relatively inexperienced in organising athletics events, and it was a serious mistake to cause O'Connor to lose face in front of his own people. Over the next days, a barrage of angry correspondence took place between the two, with both men promising to publish the other's correspondence in the local press. O'Connor threatened a "storm" and Murtagh replied that, in a public career, he had weathered countless storms and always came out on top. In the final exchange between the two men, Murtagh goaded O'Connor into action.

> All correspondence goes to press on Thursday evening failing to hear that you have thought better of your hot action. You've more to lose by it than I have. I never try to soar too high therefore will not miss my wings.

Murtagh thought that he had won the battle and, although he may have won the war of words, when O'Connor failed to turn up for the Sports, the GAA man came in for considerable criticism. He had clearly underestimated the extent of O'Connor's popularity in Wicklow, especially since the Annacurra Monster Gaelic Festival of 1901 when his presence ensured that the outstanding debt on the town's statue to the patriot Billy Byrne was wiped clean. The whole controversy could easily have been avoided if Murtagh had exercised some restraint, as O'Connor's request was the norm for top athletes. By accusing O'Connor of professionalism, Murtagh had merely scored a pyrrhic victory.

The absence of O'Connor from the Wicklow Sports was not the only happening that day to create a stir. As athletes came from across the county to sign in for the day's competition, Murtagh turned away an RIC officer, invoking the GAA's controversial rule from the recent congress. The GAA Wicklow Sports was one of the first tests of the association's sectarian ban on soldiers and policemen and Murtagh stood his ground. Although he had claimed in his correspondence to O'Connor that he was used to weathering storms, Murtagh was now attracting more attention than was wise for a man in his position. As the head teacher at the local Boys' National School with both Catholic and Protestant pupils, Murtagh's involvement with the GAA left him vulnerable to attack.

The day after the Sports, the RIC officer who had been turned away put pen to paper and wrote to the Commissioners of the National Board of Education detailing the teacher's role in the affair.

I am a member of the RIC stationed near Wicklow and obtained permission of my Inspector to compete at the Sports. To my astonishment I found that my entry would not be accepted as there is a rule passed by the GAA prohibiting policemen, soldiers, navymen and other persons under government pay from competing and the same rule prevents a miltary band from playing at any sports under the GAA laws. . . . I am reliably informed that Mr Murtagh was the principal agitator in getting such Rules passed. He is one of the trustees of the GAA which is in reality a political organization. I enclose two cuttings from the newspaper *Dublin Sport* showing that Mr Murtagh is a Trustee and a leading member of this association. I am also informed by my brother officers that almost every Sunday throughout the year Mr Murtagh attends meetings of the Association in Dublin, Cork, Limerick, Thurles and other far away places and that he frequently does not return until midday on the Monday following and is then not in a condition to faithfully discharge his official school duties towards the children under his charge. He has I believe a salary as an official of this political organization and I and my brother officers feel it painful that Mr Murtagh should be officially and prominently connected with an association which prevents policemen, soldiers etc. from competing at Sports in this county, all of which are held, through the influence of Mr Murtagh, under GAA rules. The esteemed parish priest of Wicklow is a very easy-going gentleman and he does not take that active interest in looking after the teachers that a younger man would. If Mr Murtagh's connection is not at once severed with the GAA the probability is that a considerable number of children will be withdrawn from the school.[19]

Since the revival of the GAA in 1901, the British government recognised the importance of keeping a close eye on the progress of this nationalist association, and of identifying any political or potentially subversive elements. The Royal Irish Constabulary, who were stationed throughout Ireland, were effectively the eyes and ears of Dublin Castle, constantly sending in reports to headquarters of any kinds of subversive activity. It is most likely that Murtagh's role in the GAA had already come to the RIC's attention, thus explaining how the RIC officer had cuttings detailing his involvement. The RIC reacted immediately, placing the schoolteacher's personal and public life under considerable scrutiny.

The RIC officer's letter was enough in itself to elicit a swift response from the Board of Education but several days later, on 21 September, Peter O'Connor also submitted his own complaint, claiming that Murtagh had misrepresented him in front of his own townspeople. The affair had led to accusations in the local press that he was guilty of professionalism so, predictably, O'Connor had no intention of letting Murtagh get off scot-free. There were few things dearer in life to O'Connor than his good name and hard-earned reputation. Unsurprisingly, O'Connor was very critical in his letter to the Board of Education and questioned whether a man of such a volatile disposition could have the "patience" and "forbearance" required for his calling in life:

> Mr Murtagh may be an excellent teacher but he is of a most cranky and excitable disposition and in matters pertaining to sports football etc. he has if I may express it "lost the head". He imagines he is a veritable king and no one dare express an opinion contrary to his. He appears to me — and I am not alone in my judgement — to be devoting all of his time in the interests of the Gaelic Athletic Association. He is I am informed President of the Wicklow GAA and President or Vice-President of the Irish body of the GAA and is making himself most obnoxious by his pugnacious domineering ways. I am in no way prejudiced against Mr Murtagh but if he persists in his active career as a public man, and will not exercise proper supervision over his excitable temper, an agitation will spring up which will render his sojourn in . . . Wicklow Town intolerable. A military band would not be engaged to play at the same sport, so a civilian one had to be brought from Gorey, and no soldier, policeman or navyman dared compete because Mr Murtagh the shining light of the GAA got rules passed by that association preventing the like.[20]

Following these complaints to the Commissioners of the Board of Education, an investigation was carried out into the various allegations levelled at Murtagh. A request was sent to Rev. Carberry, the parish priest who was then manager of Wicklow Boys' National School, to seek clarification of Murtagh's involvement with the GAA. The RIC officer's assertions that Murtagh had been neglecting his students and was often late after travelling to GAA meetings were red herrings, but there was no denying his active role in the GAA. Since some of his pupils were the sons of militiamen, it was quite possible that they might be withdrawn from the school in protest. Significantly, Murtagh was asked to respond to the accusations with "particular reference" to his supposed support of the recent GAA ban on soldiers and police. To all intents and purposes his career and livelihood were on the line. With his back to the wall, Murtagh denied that he had ever taken part in politics or any political matters and that no pupils had ever been withdrawn from his school on sectarian grounds. Further, he maintained that he wasn't a member of the GAA, having severed his connection "with that body some time ago", and being a "loyal man", he had no sympathy with the recent GAA ban. These claims directly contradicted the plain facts and did not hoodwink the Board of Education, who recommended that Murtagh be censured for his involvement with the GAA and be monitored closely in the near future. Murtagh survived the controversy but this came at a significant cost to himself. He could no longer play any part in the GAA and his recent activity at local and national level came to an end. The GAA had effectively gone to war on the ruling classes in their efforts to stop the gradual Anglicisation of Irish life and culture. The Establishment nonetheless had subtle but effective ways of fighting back, as Murtagh discovered to his cost. He must have had much food for thought in the wake of the 1905 Wicklow GAA Sports. Not only had he managed to fall out with one of Wicklow Town's most popular sons, he had become one of the first casualties in the GAA's newly instituted campaign against Ireland's ruling elite.

Whether O'Connor ever discovered that Murtagh had been censured and forced to cut his ties with the GAA is not known. His experience with the teacher did, however, change his attitude to the GAA. Having grown up in an extremely tolerant family with a Catholic mother and Protestant father, he disliked the GAA's increasing militancy and sectarianism. A traditionally minded Home Ruler, O'Connor probably was not yet fully cognisant of the powerful forces gathering strength in Irish society that would transform Irish politics in the coming years. Cultural nationalism was gradually forging a distinct national identity and associations such as the GAA and the Gaelic League were sowing the seeds of Irish independence.

In April 1906, when it became apparent that the GAA had no intention of backing down from the aggressive stance it had adopted the previous summer, the IAAA had no choice but to ban GAA athletes from its future meetings. Those who had competed in both GAA and IAAA events for years were faced with a stark choice and old allegiances were put to the test. The great loser in the turf war that was about to engulf Irish sport would be athletics itself. As noted already, since 1886 when hurling and football began to gain in popularity, the GAA had shown little interest in athletics, their only real contribution to track and field being the annual championships, whose standards by the mid-1890s were incredibly low.[21] The GAA had stopped its members from competing at IAAA events and it was not clear if the association really intended to invest time, energy and money in track and field sports to ensure the continued development of world-class athletes. It was also believed that these athletes would not be allowed to compete abroad or even at future Olympics, as they would be competing under rules other than those of the association. This kind of isolationism O'Connor saw as the death knell of Irish athletic supremacy and he would oppose it vehemently. Thus, after a number of years arguing with the IAAA following the DMP scandal of 1902, O'Connor now found himself opposed to the GAA. The future of a long and proud Irish athletic tradition was in jeopardy and the time was about to come when new allegiances would have to be forged and old friendships forsaken.

Athens 1906:
The Quest for Olympic Glory

A T THE END OF 1905 Peter O'Connor began to think seriously about retirement. Now 34 years of age, he suspected that his best years of jumping were behind him. Despite his continued dominance in the long jump, underscored by five consecutive AAA Championship titles, there was little chance of him ever improving on his world record or breaking the 25-foot barrier. At the beginning of 1906, there were further fresh grounds for calling it a day when the IAAA and the GAA fell out and dissolved the working arrangement they had maintained since 1888. If he was to continue competing, O'Connor would have to align himself with one of the two associations. So close to the end of his career, the world champion was loathe to become a political pawn in a game of intrigue played out by the IAAA and the GAA. However, as he deliberated over the best course of action to take, news reached him which dispelled any ideas of immediate retirement. While the Irish athletic fraternity were at odds with one another, struggling for supremacy on the domestic scene, preparations for the greatest sporting spectacle of modern times were already well underway in Greece. The fourth modern Olympic Games in Athens would provide the Irishman with the opportunity of a final flourish on the international stage before hanging up his running shoes for the last time.

Up to the 1906 Games it had been decided to hold the Olympics every four years. Thus, after the initial modern Games in

Athens in 1896, Games were held in Paris in 1900 and St Louis in 1904. Though the first Games in Athens were considered a success, the following two, as we have noted, were particularly disappointing. Both Olympics were incorporated into World Trade Fairs and inevitably became sideshows to the main event. Pierre de Coubertin, the founder of the modern Olympic movement, realised that one more disappointment might spell the end to his life's work. The failure of the Paris and St Louis Games to make a significant impact on the collective consciousness of both the media and public presented the Frenchman with a serious problem. Something radical would have to be done to ensure the survival of the modern Olympic movement and establish the Games as a landmark event.

After the initial Games in 1896, King George I of Greece and the Greek cabinet proposed holding future Olympic festivals in Greece. It was only natural, considering the success of the inaugural modern Games, that the Greeks were anxious to hold on to this prestigious showcase event, a cherished part of their country's heritage. As the 1896 Inaugural Games closed, the Greek claim was given the support of the twelve American participants in Athens who praised the "existence of the stadium as a structure so uniquely adapted to its purpose", and noted "the proved ability of Greece to competently administer the Games and, above all, that Greece is the original home of the Olympic Games".[1] The American athletes closed their letter by expressing "the conviction that these Games should never be removed from their native soil". Coubertin, however, was reluctant to see the Olympics return to Athens every four years, as this did not fit in with his international aspirations for the festival. He wanted the modern Olympics to be celebrated in "principal cities all over the world" and that the Games should have an international rather than a national character.[2] As early as 1896 he had been surprised and disappointed by criticism he received in the Greek press, believing that his work in reviving the Olympics had not been fully appreciated. To keep his plans for an International Olympic movement on track, Coubertin suggested a compromise whereby "Pan-Hellenic Games would be held in Athens every four years alternating with the Olympic Games, such that one or the other would be held every two years".[3] So every two years, there would be an international sporting festival, although in time only the Games that were part of the standard cycle of modern Olympics would be afforded official status. Attempts to hold the first of these intermediate games in 1898 were scuppered in early 1897 when Greece and Turkey went to war over control of the island of Crete. Though the war lasted only a month, the political instability engendered by the Greek defeat, as well as the costs incurred in financing the war, meant that another Olympic festival in Athens in 1898 was not feasible. The idea of an intermediate Athens Games was not seriously entertained again until an IOC conference in Paris 1901 when a proposal came from three German IOC members that a second series of Games should be organised in between the regular series of Olympics, to take place in 1906 and 1910. Coubertin did not support the idea of "too frequent Olympic Games" but his voice carried little weight within the IOC at the time. His loss of control over the Paris Olympics had weakened his position as leader of the modern Olympic movement and he found himself increasingly under fire from various quarters as Greek nationalists resented what they viewed as his hijacking of their national institution.

Coubertin's opposition to a further Athens Games principally came from his desire to see the standard four-year cycle work. His chief hopes for the Olympic movement were invested in the next official Games in 1904, the first to be held in America. Though he could not have known it at the time, the Athens Games of 1906 would not only prove a blessing in disguise, but provide just the stop-gap measure required to succeed in strengthening and redirecting the Olympic movement. In any case, having realised that he could not rock the Greeks' conviction that they should permanently host the Olympics, the Athens Games were arranged as a "palliative".[4] The inaugural intermediate games of 1906 would be known as the Intercalated Games. By spring of 1905, thanks to the generosity of a Greek philanthropist, Georgios Averof, the marble Olympic stadium in Athens had been immaculately restored and subsequently the Pan-Hellenic Games were held there as a trial run for the 1906 Games.

When O'Connor heard that the Olympic Games were to break with its quadrennial tradition, he probably considered himself extremely lucky. After missing out on the Paris and St Louis Games, he no doubt thought any chance of competing in an Olympic event had passed him by. Further, owing to the latest rift in Irish athletics it is doubtful whether he would have competed after 1906. Now out of the blue, the opportunity to end his career on a high note, chasing Olympic gold in that most symbolic of places, Olympia, presented itself.

Before any preparations could be made, the question of financing the trip would have to be addressed. As amateurs, the Irish would-be competitors were expected to pay their own way. The costs of travelling the long distance to Greece might mean no Irish participation at the Games, something that would be a further blow to the standing of Irish athletics, already weakened by internal faction fighting. Thus both the IAAA and the GAA decided to send athletes to the Games to represent their respective bodies. Peter O'Connor and Con Leahy would travel to the Games under the auspices of the IAAA, and John Daly, a long-distance runner from Galway, would nominally represent the interests of the GAA. (Daly's participation on behalf of the GAA would later leave that association open to accusations of inconsistency as he was being encouraged to compete against athletes representing other organisations and under rules other than those of the GAA.) As representatives of the IAAA, O'Connor and Leahy both received special blazers with matching green caps that would make their nationality clear to all. O'Connor describes this apparel in some fine detail: "Con and I were supplied with blazers with gold braid around the sides, cuffs, collar and lapel with a gold shamrock on left breast and green caps to match and shamrock on the front." In addition, they each received green flags measuring six feet by four feet, embroidered in gold thread with the words *Erin go Bragh* (Ireland for ever) beneath the symbol of a harp and gold branch.[5] According to O'Connor, Daly was not offered a blazer or flag as the GAA "influenced him to represent them".[6]

O'Connor's and Leahy's Greek trip was financed chiefly by public subscription through the *Irish Field*, a weekly sports newspaper that mainly covered horseracing, cricket, polo, yachting and a host of "West Brit" pastimes. Athletics rarely received more than the briefest of mentions in the news digest section on the front page and the *Irish Field* did not report any GAA events. It was very much an Establishment newspaper and how the two Irish jumpers came to be financed by readers of the *Irish Field* is quite an entertaining story in itself, although participating athletes had to make up any shortfall or additional costs themselves. One Sunday in late February 1906, a lady said to be a close relation of Eamon de Valera, one of the Colls of Bruree, went to a race meeting with the intention of encouraging some of Dublin's leading and most affluent citizens to support and contribute to a fund to send an Irish team to Athens. Whether through good fortune or design, the first person she approached was Boss Croker, one of the most flamboyant and colourful characters in Dublin at that time.

Born in Cork in 1841, Croker's family had emigrated to the United States where he grew up in the rough-and-tumble world of New York street gangs, receiving his education in the Fourth Avenue Tunnel Gang. After using a volunteer firefighting company as the springboard for his political career, he was elected an alderman in 1868, and soon became one of the chief lieutenants of John Kelly, the man who in 1871 succeeded the infamous William M. Tweed as boss of Tammany Hall. Though his political career nearly foundered on a false charge that he had murdered a political opponent in the 1874 campaign for Tammany Hall, Croker took over the Tammany reins from Kelly in 1886, becoming one of the most powerful people in New York until 1901 when he was forced out of office.[7] Croker had a great interest in horse racing and after his time in Tammany Hall, he initially tried to join the racing fraternity in England, bringing his entire stable to Europe. His reputation as a hard-talking, self-serving and somewhat disreputable politician meant that he was shunned in English racing circles and the English Jockey Club issued a barring order preventing him from establishing a stables at Newmarket Heath.[8] He then returned to Ireland, where he lived out the remainder of his life.

Croker was therefore an ideal person to drum up support for Irish athletes. Not only was he well connected to the affluent Irish racing fraternity, but the notion of a renegade team of Irish crack athletes travelling to Athens, independent of the English AAA, no doubt appealed to him after the cold reception he had received in England. Consequently, Croker's response to the lady's request, removing his hat ceremoniously as he did so, could not have been more generous: "Not only will I contribute madam, but I will also collect." With that, he proceeded to solicit contributions from all well-to-do racegoers and promptly returned with his top hat full to the brim with money and a list of all those who contributed.[9]

In the next edition of the *Irish Field*, Croker set up a subscription in the newspaper, donating £10 as his initial contribution and writing:

> I notice that though England and all the Continental countries and America are sending representatives to the Olympian Games, there does not seem to be any intention to organise an Irish team. As the home of great jumpers and weight throwers in particular, it seems strange that Ireland should stand out on such an occasion.

Croker suggested that two or three athletes from the elite such as O'Connor, Leahy, Kiely and Horgan should be sent "to uphold the prowess of Irish athletes at Athens".[10] By the next edition of the magazine, Croker's subscription fund had already reached £40. As it cost £25 for each athlete to be sent to Athens and neither Horgan nor Kiely were willing or able to go, O'Connor and Leahy's participation was now assured. The editor of the *Irish Field* noted that:

> The suggestion thrown out by Croker in these columns last week with reference to having Ireland represented at the Olympian games seems to have the approval of the racing fraternity in particular, for a great many gentlemen identified with that sport have subscribed to the fund necessary to

> defray the expenses of sending a couple of our champion
> jumpers to Athens.

The *Irish Field* listed the name of each person who had subscribed
to the fund, several of whom were aristocrats and establishment
figures. By the time the subscription fund closed, readers of the
magazine had sponsored O'Connor and Leahy to the tune of
£55.10 shillings.

There was intense interest in all sections of the Irish press in
the run-up to the Athens Games, as O'Connor and Leahy were
deemed hot favourites to win honours for Ireland. O'Connor's
unwavering ally at the *Waterford News*, C.P. Redmond, kept its
readers informed of rules, regulations and minutiae regarding the
jumping events. Great hopes were invested in O'Connor and
Leahy and the Irish public were anxious to see a return on their
investment. Now that adequate funds were available to undertake
the trip, preparations could begin in earnest. O'Connor decided to
bring his wife Maggie to Athens, as a kind of second honeymoon.
Although it would mean leaving Edward, their first child, behind
for a few weeks, Maggie would have an opportunity to see her
husband compete against the world's best at first hand. O'Connor
had promised his wife that after the Games he would finally retire
and, perhaps to make him keep his word, she decided to see his
last international performance for herself. So as not to feel alone in
the company of so many men, Margaret invited her close friend
and bridesmaid Bride Power to join her on the adventure.

Some months before Athens, O'Connor had been approached
by the English AAA who invited him to join the British squad at
the Olympics. Leahy likewise had been offered a place on the
squad. The media had been building up the Olympics as a showdown between Britain and America, a clash between the Old and
New World orders. "Experts believe the Games will be in effect a
dual meeting between America and England. . . . The Britons concede the superiority of America in the weights and will devote
their attention to the track events and jumps."[11] As O'Connor and
Leahy were the foremost jumpers of their era in both the long and

high jumps, the AAA was anxious to secure their services. Indeed, no other men in the British Empire stood a better chance of taking gold in their respective events. An Irish sports hack noted that "Ireland claims more than outside rank. For the backbone of the American team is of Irish build, many of its members taking their descent from Irish parentage." The Irish sporting diaspora competing at Athens would be watched no less keenly than O'Connor, Leahy and Daly.

Both O'Connor and Leahy declined the AAA's invitation. This must have come as a blow to the association, yet disappointment probably gave way to incredulity when it was discovered that both athletes intended to compete and the small Irish delegation would share the same passage to Athens as the British contingent. Greek officials had probably informed the British Olympic Council, formed in March 1906, of the Irishmen's intentions at this time to compete solely for Ireland. They were unaware, however, that this was the first Olympics in which only athletes nominated by National Olympic Committees would be allowed to compete. As there was no Irish Olympic Committee in existence, the Greeks would ignore the Irishmen's independent entries and accept the AAA's inclusion of the Irishmen on the British team.

CS

ON SATURDAY 14 APRIL 1906, the Irish contingent, numbering five, set off from Dun Laoghaire, travelling by boat and train to London. Two days later, on Easter Monday, the trip began in earnest as they sailed from London at 9.30 am. It was an extraordinary scenario: three Irish athletes travelling in the company of the British team, intent on representing Ireland only. One wonders what their thoughts on the circumstances were. English AAA officials would by now have learned of their planned defection, which had been widely publicised in Irish newspapers. Nor had the Irishmen applied for a grant from a special fund of £208 that the Greek government had given to the English AAA to fund the British team. In any case, the athletes themselves got on well and

O'Connor, his wife Maggie, Leahy and Daly were included in photographs with the British team on the deck of the ship.

Their impressive itinerary would see them journey by train across continental Europe via Dieppe, Paris, Turin, Brindisi and Bari, then by boat to Corfu and Patras and finally on to Athens. There would be no time for sightseeing, save that which might be accomplished from a moving train. After three days and two nights confined, the athletes were all understandably fatigued. As many had forgotten or neglected to bring adequate food and refreshments for the journey, they were now beginning to feel the pangs of hunger. A British journalist gives an interesting account of this most tiresome part of the journey:

> None of the party was sorry to get to the end of the journey, which, owing to the congested state of the trains, had been a trying one, despite the magnificent scenery witnessed by those who did not have the misfortune to travel in compartments commandeered and turned into temporary dark rooms by energetic press photographers. There were, however, several other more interesting incidents to help break the monotony of the trip, and of these the scrambles for solid and liquid refreshment were by no means the least exciting. Soap, water, towels, and lights were even scarcer than food and drink, and complaints of headaches and stiff limbs were frequent until Brindisi was reached. Every opportunity was seized to get a little exercise, and at Bari some impromptu sprint handicaps were indulged in to the delight and astonishment of an Italian crowd, which cheered the Britishers heartily on their departure.[12]

After being cooped up in trains for several days, the entire company of athletes was relieved to arrive at last in the busy fishing port of Bari. There the *Baron Call*, a "beautifully fitted" vessel, awaited the arrival of the weary travellers. The next leg of the journey provided a welcome reprieve to those who had found the train journey tortuous and claustrophobic and many of the athletes took the opportunity to stretch their limbs and flex their muscles. Several of the British athletes engaged in some light sparring while others "dug in" on the ship's deck for a tug of war contest. Peter and Maggie spent most of their time relaxing on deck, enjoying the afternoon sun and looking very much like newlyweds on honeymoon. As night fell and the *Baron Call* made its way down the Adriatic into the Mediterranean, the company sat down to their first hearty meal since breakfast in London three days before. After supper, plenty of entertainment was provided to keep the company in good spirits. Notable highlights of the evening's diversions were the Scottish half-miler William Andersen's "dramatic" and powerful rendition of "Tam O'Shanter" and the swimmer Paul Radmilovic's rendering of several songs in a splendid baritone voice.

The following morning, several of the athletes failed to put in an appearance at the breakfast table as they were considerably worse for wear from the "rising and falling of the vessel" during the night. To what extent the hopes of the athletes travelling to the Games were compromised by the rigours of the train and sea journey is impossible to calculate. Nonetheless, the conditions of travel were hardly conducive to priming athletes to peak at the Games. Many would have suffered from significant weight loss due to lack of food or seasickness and all individual training regimes had been disrupted. Fortunately, O'Connor, a veteran of transatlantic travel, was at this stage impervious to the trials of the sea and his stomach was well tempered by previous experience.

A welcome chance to set foot on terra firma came as the *Baron Call* paid a fleeting visit to Corfu. There the bemused visitors were welcomed with great pomp and ceremony by the inhabitants of the island. As they stepped ashore they were greeted with a fanfare by a band that had been assembled on the landing quay. Following numerous speeches by local magnates, the group was invited to tea, whereupon G.K. Robertson, one of the British judges, demonstrated at first hand the benefits of a classical education by addressing the locals in ancient Greek, thanking them for their hospitality. Quite how much the locals understood is open to question, because the modern Greek vernacular is quite different to ancient Greek, but the gesture seems to have been appreciated nonetheless.

From Corfu, the *Baron Call* headed for Patras, which they reached early on the Friday morning. As the ship was too large to dock at Patras, the luggage and passengers had to be transferred from the vessel by small boats. Once on shore, the final leg of the trip began, a 180-mile train journey to the Greek capital. On arrival in Athens "again there were scrambles for food at the railway station, men grabbing at anything they could get, such as apples, oranges, figs on strings, brown cakes, hunks of dry bread, and some terrible-looking meat, and paying any price which was asked". The epic journey to Athens was finally at an end.

Once the Irish contingent had found suitable lodgings and dined satisfactorily they could settle down to a much-deserved night's sleep. Most of the visiting athletes to Athens stayed in the "Zappeion", a makeshift hotel that was the precursor to future Olympic villages, but it is likely that O'Connor, Maggie and Miss Power sought out alternative lodgings. Over the next days O'Connor and his wife would explore Athens, the cradle of western civilisation, and visit famous sights of antiquity such as the Acropolis, illuminated by night during the Olympic festival.

ᙇ

BY ROYAL DECREE, AVEROF'S NEWLY refurbished marble Olympic stadium remained closed until the official opening by the King on Sunday 22 April. The organising committee were mindful that many of the participants would probably want to do some training before the commencement of the Games, so the National Gymnasium and the Marathon road were made available for competitors. Though many decided to visit the National Gymnasium and inspect its facilities, not all decided to take advantage of the opportunity to train, preferring instead to conserve their strength and energy. Typically, O'Connor chose to make some practice jumps to judge his form. The exercise backfired, however, when after only a few jumps, he landed awkwardly and sprained his toe. Fortunately, the sprain, though painful, was not serious and he recovered quickly from the setback. With the stadium off-limits O'Connor was probably practising his jumping outside of a proper jumping pit and this may have resulted in his minor injury. He would take it easy for a few days and not tempt fate a second time.

Upon registration, each participant was presented with a souvenir programme of the events that detailed the names and number of participants in each contest, as well as the country they would be representing. The Irishmen, to their dismay, discovered that they were listed as competing for Britain. Before leaving home they had made it clear when sending in their entries that they intended to represent Ireland, but they had been quietly and surreptitiously integrated into the British team. The Irish athletes' presence in Athens was entirely due to the generosity of Irish men and women anxious to see Ireland represented at the Games. Understandably, the three Irishmen felt honour bound to try to amend the situation. Immediately O'Connor set about drafting an appeal to be submitted to the organising committee.

The aspirations of O'Connor, Leahy and Daly to be allowed represent Ireland at Athens may seem naïve to the modern observer. Ireland at that time was of course still a part of the United Kingdom and was governed from Westminster. As such it had neither political autonomy nor an official flag that could be recognised as that of a sovereign Irish state. Their actions, however, were symptomatic of a wider political and cultural struggle to create and assert the notion of a national identity, despite the political union with Britain. It is quite possible the International Jury charged with considering O'Connor's submission viewed the appeal as being more emotive than substantive. Had the Games been held in a country other than Greece, it might have had a better chance of success. Unfortunately for the Irishmen, the Greek and British royal families were related by marriage and, further, both families were in attendance at the Games. Under such circumstances, the appeal was doomed to failure. Nonetheless, O'Connor, a mere managing clerk in a Waterford solicitor's office, would receive a royal audience for his trouble.

On the fifth day of the Olympics, O'Connor had a short interview with Crown Prince George when the International Jury's decision against the appeal was announced. Despite their earnestness, Prince George was not impressed by the Irish athletes' arguments and seems to have taken the matter lightly. His initial reply was short and to the point, and was immediately followed by an additional sarcastic remark. In his opinion, Ireland was not entitled to claim separate representation. "When Ireland has a parliament of its own, you can hoist the flag but not before. Perhaps there will be an Irish parliament by the time the next Games come around." O'Connor was deeply disappointed that the appeal had failed, but he was also particularly annoyed by the tone of the ensuing remark, which he considered in poor taste and unnecessary. Prince George could simply have informed O'Connor that, since Ireland had no Olympic committee of its own, the Irishmen had to compete under the jurisdiction of the British Olympic Council and therefore for Great Britain.

Though in years to come O'Connor recalled Prince George's inadvertently prophetic words with wry amusement, underestimating the Irish people's determination for self-governance, the Prince's decision at the time left the Irish athletes in an awkward predicament. They would be allowed to compete in the Games but only under British colours. Having played their last card, the Irishmen's gamble had failed, bringing an end to what many British commentators perceived as unpatriotic and unsportsmanlike conduct. The likes of O'Connor, Leahy and Daly were not easily discouraged and would not accept defeat without a fight. Few if any could have guessed the lengths they would go to achieve their aim.

CS

ON SUNDAY 22 APRIL, THE GAMES were to be declared officially opened. The citizens of Athens were enormously excited and there was a great atmosphere of festivity in the air, as the Olympic Games were coming home once again to their rightful place.

There was a constant flow of traffic on all roads leading to the city. James E. Sullivan, the American Commissioner to the Olympic Games, captures the sense of excitement and anticipation that seems to have seized Athens:

> It was not rare to see a band of peasants being drawn in a wagon to which was attached a donkey, an ox and a mule. Every street leading to the stadium was thronged with people all good natured and orderly. An excited murmur seemed to be through the city. Occasionally a cheer would be heard. Cabmen were brushing up their carriages in view of their coming afternoon trade and the fancy prices they were going to get. As early as noon the carriages began to roll toward the stadium and drop their human freight about 100 yards from the gate, for only the equipages of the royal family were allowed to cross the bridge of Ilisos, the scene of greatest excitement.[13]

Though thousands began to crowd the entrance to the stadium it still remained closed. When the doors were finally opened, before any spectators could gain entry, thousands of soldiers were marched in to take up positions at the top of the three sides of the stadium. Such measures were taken not so much to ensure security as to accommodate an unusual but significant flaw in the stadium's design. The marble stadium was built between three hills and its open design meant that soldiers had to be posted right along the perimeter of the top of the stadium to prevent gate-crashers from spilling into the Olympic venue. The presence of these soldiers in traditional Greek uniform provided the Greek royal family with an opportunity to showcase to their subjects and the assembled world press their military might. As the British royal family, led by King Edward VII and Queen Alexandra, were also attending the Games, the Greeks were undoubtedly anxious to put on a good show for their British cousins. Whatever the effect the soldiers' presence may have had on the local populace, visitors to Athens were awestruck by the imposing spectacle that awaited them on first entering the stadium.

Here they were stretched shoulder to shoulder, around the upper wall, thousands of them with their peculiar uniforms, their heads showing just against the sky. One can imagine how many of them there must have been when it is known that the upper outer wall of the stadium measures over one third of a mile in circumference.[14]

As soon as the soldiers had taken up their positions in the stadium, the iron gates that had held the large crowds back were removed. Instantly, swarms of people began to heave, pushing and shoving in the sudden lunge towards the stadium. There were four entrances to facilitate the passage of spectators to and from the venue. Two of the points of entry, however, were reserved for holders of tickets in the upper tiers and were accessed by an exclusive marble stairway situated away from the madding crowds. As the stadium quickly filled to capacity, thousands of people who could not get tickets massed on the surrounding hills in the hope of securing a vantage point. Others lined the streets and the bridge leading to the stadium in the hope of catching a glimpse of the royal family as they made their way to the stadium by carriage. For many, particularly those who had travelled great distances, it would be a unique and rare opportunity to see their rulers in the flesh. Standing guard in ceremonious fashion from the bridge of Ilisos to the stadium entrance were the King's personal bodyguards or *evzones*, distinctively dressed in a traditional uniform including "skirts". The ranks of *evzones* stretched from the stadium entrance in two long lines facing one another, leaving between the two lines a lane about ten feet wide through which the royal family passed. Cheers from outside the stadium heralded the approach of the royal carriages and, as King George and his entourage entered the stadium, a crowd of over 56,000 burst into spontaneous applause and cheering. Spectators rose to their feet to get a better look at both the Greek and British royal families while an assembled orchestra struggled to make itself and the Greek national anthem heard amidst the din. Athens at this time had a population of roughly 150,000 people,[15] so over a third of the city's population were present in the stadium, setting the stage for an emotive Olympic celebration, the likes of which had not been seen since the Golden Age of Greece.

The inauguration ceremony lasted some three hours and introduced a new format that would become a model for ensuing Olympic opening ceremonies. Once the King and his guests took up their positions in the royal box and the cheers of the crowd had faded, Crown Prince Constantine stood up to address his father and request that he open the Games officially. As he spoke, the athletes were assembled in columns behind the Prince in groups according to their country. As soon as the King declared the Games open, the athletes paraded before the royal box, one country after another. Significantly, the three Irishmen walked to the rear of the British delegation, O'Connor and Leahy wearing the special green blazers that had been presented to them. Both O'Connor and Leahy must have stood out from the rest of the British athletes with their striking green blazers embossed with gold shamrocks and wearing matching green caps. The English AAA had requested that British athletes wore Union Jacks on the left breast of their blazers. While passing the royal box each group of athletes saluted the presiding monarch and then took up their reserved seats in the left wing of the stadium.

During the parade, the *Hymn of Samara*, the Olympic hymn first performed at Athens in 1896, was sung by four choirs. There then followed a highly successful gymnastics exhibition that was the highlight of the opening ceremony and had been planned long in advance. A group of Danish female gymnasts had been specially invited to the Games by the organising committee and were accommodated during their stay at the royal palace (Queen Alexandra was Danish). When the gymnastics extravaganza was finished, the opening ceremony drew to a close and, following the departure of the royal families, the stadium gradually emptied and the crowds dispersed. Thus what might be considered as the first truly modern Olympic opening ceremony came to an end. In years to come, opening ceremonies would emulate the high level of organisation and choreography first displayed in the 1906 Games. In particular, the Greek idea of parading the athletes of each country in their national colours around the stadium would become a mainstay of Olympic opening ceremonies.

There were no track and field events scheduled until the third official day of competition, so Averof's beautiful marble stadium was left pretty much deserted while the football, tennis, cycling, shooting and some fencing events were contested in different parts of Athens. For those athletes waiting for their events to come round, there were plenty of entertainments: music concerts, presentations of plays and, on several nights, the Acropolis was specially illuminated to celebrate the return of the Games. By the third day, most track and field athletes had recovered from the long journey to Athens and were now getting used to the Greek climate.

The first of the Irish athletes to take part in the Games was John Daly, the long-distance and cross-country runner from Galway, who took part in the five-mile race. Henry Hawtrey of Britain won the event with comparative ease, crossing the finishing line with some 50 yards to spare over the second placed Swede, Johan Svanberg. In a ferocious battle for third place, an exhausted Daly narrowly edged out another young Swede, Edward Dahl, for bronze. In the home straight, as the two surged towards the line, the Galwayman weaved in and out several times effectively denying the nineteen-year-old the chance to overtake him. It was generally accepted that fatigue was the principal cause of Daly's erratic finish, and though his obstruction of Dahl was unintentional, an appeal was lodged which led to his official disqualification from the race the following day.

Despite Daly's disappointment at missing out on bronze, another Irish-born athlete, Martin Sheridan, made his mark on the Games, taking gold for the United States in the discus throw. Sheridan, who was born and grew up in the tiny town of Bohola, County Mayo, had emigrated to America where he became a policeman. He would become the star of the Athens Games, taking five medals in all, two gold and three silver.

Two days later on 27 April, the fifth day of competition, the small Irish contingent returned to the Pan-Athenaic stadium to see O'Connor take part in the long jump, hoping he would have more luck than Daly and take Ireland's first gold at the Games. No track and field events were scheduled to begin before 3.00 pm so as to avoid the hottest part of the day. Owing to the somewhat disjointed nature of international athletics at this time, there was no international agreement as to the required specifications for a jumping pit. Indeed rules, regulations and specifications varied from country to country. The jumping facilities in the stadium were more than adequate, although O'Connor and Leahy had not competed on such a soft cinder track before. Following reports that had circulated after the 1896 Games, specialist jumpers such as O'Connor and Leahy most likely knew what to expect in Athens:

> The take-off board which the Greeks call the line of impetus is five inches wide and is five inches higher than the landing surface of the trench. So that instead of the removal of the semi-circle of turf which causes the foot of a jumper who fouls to dip, the Greeks run upon and spring from a track which is five inches higher than the plane of the landing place. The trench is 40 feet long by 12 feet wide, and is filled to a depth of 20 inches with a mixture of fine sand and sifted earth. Three attempts are allowed to all competitors and three more are assigned to each of the three jumpers who have cleared the greatest distance.[16]

In order to facilitate British and American athletes competing in jumping events, the rules prohibiting jumpers from placing a handkerchief on the bar and a jacket or jersey at the side of the run were waived to agree with British and American custom.[17]

Although 64 athletes were entered in the long jump competition, the two clear favourites for the event were O'Connor and the American Myer Prinstein. Curiously, this was to be the only time that the two would meet in competition. The clash of two such experienced and famous jumpers was eagerly anticipated. O'Connor, as the current world record holder and with the better form in previous years, was the marginal favourite. Yet Prinstein was an experienced Olympian and hardy competitor, with a reputation for coming up big in major events. He came in to the

Athens Games as the reigning Olympic champion, having taken gold in St Louis in 1904, improving on his silver medal at Paris in 1900 behind Kraenzlein.

Despite his rival's impressive Olympic results to date, O'Connor was confident that he would see off the American's challenge. He had been following Prinstein's form in serious competition over the previous five years and had calculated his average at 22' 6". His own average over the same period of time was 23' 10". If he were on form, Prinstein would have to produce something really special to mount a serious challenge.

The running track consisted of very soft, loose cinders which meant that those who jumped first would have a considerable advantage over competitors who came after: the initially smooth track would become cut up and unsuited to sprinting. Less speed in the run-up to the jump would of course have an adverse effect on the height that could be gained and consequently the distance covered. The athletes were to jump in alphabetical order, which meant that O'Connor (38) would only have a slight edge on Prinstein (40) by jumping two places before him. Realistically, both athletes could expect much the same jumping conditions, putting them on an even footing.

As the competitors assembled and waited for the long jump event to begin, O'Connor began "keying" himself up for battle. Keeping a little apart from the other competitors and practising his trademark stretches and exercises, the Irishman blocked out all the distractions around him. Once the judges arrived at the jumping pit, the event could begin. The two principal officials in charge of the event were Matthew Halpin of the US and Perry of Britain. One was to declare the validity of the jumps and the other the distance achieved, while a Greek official held the tape at the take-off point.

As the contest was about to begin, Perry absented himself from the jumping pit, leaving the American Matthew Halpin in sole charge of the event. His departure was unexpected, but probably escaped most people's attention because so many events were beginning simultaneously. In the absence of Perry, Halpin took complete control of the event, acting as the sole judge.

O'Connor probably didn't read too much into Perry's absence, as he was no doubt readying himself for his first jump. Quite possibly, the Englishman had been called away temporarily to assist in another event. As for the remaining judge, he had never seen him before and was unaware that Halpin was in fact the manager of the American team. It didn't take long for alarm bells to ring when he saw his chief rival Prinstein readying himself to jump. With the British judge nowhere in sight, the scheduled jumping order was ignored and Prinstein, who should have jumped fortieth, was allowed to jump third. O'Connor was somewhat taken aback by this unwarranted action but, in spite of the infraction, for the time being he put it to the back of his mind and focused his mind on his first jump.

Once the first jumps were taken, the athletes waited to find out who was in the lead. As was the case at the Athens Games in 1896, however, the distances accomplished by jumpers would not be announced until the end of the competition. This was an unusual and somewhat arcane process, which broke with current practice. The method certainly did not appeal to O'Connor, who was used to knowing what his rivals had achieved as well as his own distances. Otherwise, he would have no idea where he stood in relation to his American rival.

Just before the second round of jumps was due to commence, O'Connor was approached by James B. Connolly, the Irish-American athlete who had taken the first gold medal of the modern Olympic era in 1896 in the hop, step and jump. Ten years on, Connolly had returned to Athens principally as a sports correspondent, although he also was competing in the jumping events. As the two stood talking, Connolly revealed to O'Connor that Halpin was in fact the manager of the American team and then, in quite unequivocal terms, he warned O'Connor that, with Halpin in charge, he would have no chance of winning.[18] Now sensing danger, O'Connor immediately spurred into action and launched a protest, challenging Halpin's authority to be the sole judge. Halpin did not back down an inch, however, and replied in a manner O'Connor deemed offensive, "I am a duly appointed judge and am entitled to act." But O'Connor would not let the matter rest and approached Prince George, appealing to his sense of fair play, requesting him to either remove Halpin or find another judge to help in officiating the competition. For the second time since his arrival in Athens, the Prince, who was President of the International Jury, found himself in an awkward position, thanks to O'Connor. The controversy could not have come at a worse time, since the long jump was one of nine events, the pentathlon, stone throw, 1,500-metre heats, the shot-put, 400-metre heats, two wrestling events and a weightlifting competition being contested simultaneously, each having started at 3.00 pm.

When O'Connor informed Prince George of his complaint, most judges present were probably already involved in officiating other events. As such, he was probably reluctant to interfere with a competition already underway. In addition, the removal of Halpin, apart from creating logistical problems, could be perceived as an admission that certain improprieties may have taken place. Such decisive action would not necessarily bring the matter to a close, since the American delegation would be sure to protest the removal of Halpin without strong evidence of malpractice. The Crown Prince was also anxious to maintain cordial relations with the American visitors and, as President of the Organising Committee, he had sanctioned a donation of $1,500 towards the costs of the American team. Sullivan, the American Commissioner of the team, who was probably the most powerful man in world athletics at the time, was a staunch supporter of the Greek claim to retain Athens as a permanent venue for the Games. If the Greeks were to succeed in re-establishing their right to host the Olympics indefinitely, American support could be vital. In light of the prevailing circumstances, it is quite understandable why Prince George gave Halpin the benefit of the doubt and ignored the troublesome renegade Irishman's latest protest. Predictably, he gave the matter little consideration and ruled in favour of Halpin.

Receiving no satisfaction from the Crown Prince, O'Connor finally caught up with Perry in the company of another British judge and asked him why he had deserted the long jump competition and left Halpin in sole charge. The British judges curtly informed O'Connor that, because of his letter repudiating England, they would not act. By demanding the right to raise an Irish flag and to have the Irish athletes' points accredited to Ireland, O'Connor now found himself stranded, having burnt all his bridges. Although now technically competing under the Union Jack, the British judges washed their hands of him. Returning to the jumping pit in what was becoming an increasingly charged atmosphere, O'Connor got Con Leahy, John Daly and his Irish-American ally, James B. Connolly to take up positions opposite the jumping pit and record the distances of Prinstein's remaining jumps compared with his own.

The competition continued and, in the second round, Prinstein faltered badly and seemed to come down with an ankle injury. Once again O'Connor's second jump was good, and although Halpin still did not announce the distances of the respective athletes, O'Connor was able to gauge from his supporters that he had certainly outdistanced Prinstein's second jump. Fresh controversy erupted in the third round, however, as Halpin declared what was by far O'Connor's biggest jump a foul. The jump had easily surpassed any other effort that day and O'Connor demanded to know why Halpin refused to measure it. Halpin maintained that O'Connor had infringed the rules regarding proper landing, and that he had fallen back in the pit, behind the mark made by his feet. O'Connor fiercely contested the decision:

> My third jump was distinctly ahead of Prinstein's but was declared by Halpin to be a foul and was not measured. I asked how it was a foul as in those days it meant a sprained ankle if your toe went beyond the board take off, and I never fell back after landing, but pitched forward on my hands.[19]

The judge's decision was final, however, and Halpin once again ignored O'Connor's protests. Upon completion of the third round, Halpin consulted with a Greek official and declared that O'Connor, Prinstein and another American, Hugo Friend, had accomplished the best distances and that they each had three more trials. The competition continued with Prinstein performing below par because of the knock he received in the second round. O'Connor knew that he had easily beaten Prinstein's last five jumps but a doubt hung over the first jump. No one had watched the American's first jump carefully, because he had unexpectedly jumped third. Right to the last O'Connor was left totally in the dark, his and Prinstein's fates in Halpin's hands. When the final jumps were complete, the three athletes, the crowd and assembled officials waited for the winners to be announced. The result caused consternation. Myer Prinstein of the United States was first, Peter O'Connor of Great Britain was second, Hugo Friend of the United States third.

Immediately O'Connor demanded to see the distances with which he and Prinstein had been credited. According to Halpin, O'Connor's best jump was a mere 23' 0½", some two inches behind Prinstein's winning first jump of 23' 2½".

> I was enraged and demanded Halpin to state the distance of Prinstein's six jumps, and it showed that his best and winning effort was his first effort and that the distances of all his five others were under 22 feet. If my wife had not been present looking on at this contest, which restrained me, I would have beaten Halpin to a pulp as I was half insane over the injustice.[20]

The American had evidently managed the greatest distance on his first jump, achieving a mark that none of the competitors including O'Connor could match. Not only had he achieved a significant improvement on his recent form, but he had done so on his first jump. O'Connor was convinced that he was the victim of foul play. As he would declare in a written appeal to the International Jury later that evening: "It is a fact unprecedented in the history of jumping for a man to do his best jump first." Further, he questioned Halpin's right to change the jumping order. Surely it was incorrect that an American was allowed to assume the sole duties of judge, measurer and declarer of the distance of Prinstein's winning jump? Peter O'Connor had set out with the intention of winning gold for Ireland in his favourite event, but now he found his Olympic dream in tatters. He had been relegated to second place and to add insult to injury, his two points were credited to Great Britain, and a Union Jack would be flown to mark his silver placing.

∞

THAT FRIDAY HAD PROVED ONE OF frustration and disappointment for O'Connor, but he would yet finish it on a high note. Throughout the day, the Greek crowd had watched the progress of the long jump competition in bemusement as it degenerated time and again into acrimony. Now that the final results were official, there only remained for the flags of the victorious jumpers to be hoisted. The medals would be issued at the closing ceremony on the last day of the Games. The flag-raising was a simple ceremony. Once the relevant flags were hoisted on the three poles to signify the countries that had achieved gold, silver and bronze, the attention of the crowd once again shifted back to the Games still taking place in the stadium. This time, however, the long jump flag-hoisting ceremony would prove to be anything but a formality.

Just after the Union Jack was raised, all eyes turned to a thin lone figure shimmying up a twenty-foot pole in the centre of the infield. When he reached the top, he unfurled a green flag with the words *Erin go Bragh* imprinted upon it and waved it back and forward to a stunned audience. While O'Connor was climbing up the pole, Con Leahy "assisted in the demonstration by keeping fighting guard at the foot of the pole, meantime defying every effort of the officials to prevent the demonstration".[21] Such a scene was unprecedented in the short ten-year history of the modern Olympics. For several minutes all spectators, athletes, officials and soldiers were treated to the spectacle of O'Connor perched twenty feet up a pole, defying Prince George and his visiting cousins, the British royal family. The Irishman's points might well be accredited to Great Britain, but the flying of the Irish flag left none in doubt as to where O'Connor's true allegiances lay.

There were so many conflicting, contradictory and above all inaccurate accounts of this significant moment in O'Connor's career that some 35 years later he set the record straight in a letter to the noted GAA historian, Séamus Ó Ceallaigh:

> When I climbed a pole about 20 feet in height and remained aloft for some time, waving my large flag and Con waving his from the ground underneath the pole, it caused a great sensation. It occurred just as the official hoisted on the Olympic masts the three flags indicating the nationality of the first, second, and third winners of the long jump, the British Union Jack being flown for my being second. It was only the section of the spectators in the seats, near where the jump came off that fully appreciated our demonstration as Irishmen in objecting to the Union Jack being hoisted claiming my being second in the long jump as a win and a point gained for the British team. I had a very excitable temper and was simply furious over the English judges' refusing to officiate as judges because of my letter to the Olympic committee, over the sarcastic remarks of Prince George and over the way I was robbed of victory. I was an accomplished gymnast in my youth and my active climbing of the post excited the spectators who had observed my violent protest to Halpin being sole judge and declaring my best jumps foul.[22]

Despite losing the long jump contest, the small Irish contingent had managed to carry the day, in a symbolic act of defiance to the British royal family. The incident was highly embarrassing to the Greek Crown Prince and it is quite possible that he now regretted his condescending attitude to O'Connor when delivering his judgement. Later that evening, O'Connor scripted the last of his appeals to the Organising Committee challenging Prinstein's first place and the manner in which Halpin had conducted the contest. After his dramatic coup at the flag ceremony, it came as little surprise when the appeal was rejected.

ᘓ

NOW THAT HE WAS BACK ON TERRA FIRMA and his temper had cooled, the realisation that he had failed in his mission to win Olympic gold probably began to sink in. O'Connor was never one to take defeat lightly and he was loathe to end his career second best. All was not lost, however. He still had one realistic chance to prove himself on the Olympic stage, in the hop, step and jump, the event that was a precursor to the modern triple jump. It would give O'Connor another chance to square off against Prinstein. There were two days to relax and put the highs and lows of Friday's events behind him, before throwing his hat into the ring one last time. If O'Connor, Leahy or Daly needed any encouragement to fulfil their Olympic ambitions, it came once again from the Irish-born American athlete Martin Sheridan, who won his second gold medal in the shot-put, adding to his earlier gold in the discus throw.

The following day, the sixth of competition, was relatively low-key, with only two wrestling events being held in the Pan-Athenaic stadium and a smattering of shooting, fencing and swimming events taking place in various parts of Athens. The seventh day was to all intents and purposes a rest day, the highlights of which were an exhibition by Swedish divers, water poloists and life-guards in Neo-Phaliron Bay and a late afternoon staging of Sophocles' *Oedipus Rex* at the Royal Theatre.[23] After two days respite, on 30 April, the eighth day of competition, O'Connor returned with renewed determination to the beautifully crafted marble stadium, seeking to make amends for losing the long jump event.

The hop, step and jump competition was scheduled to begin at 3.00 pm in the Olympic stadium. In addition to O'Connor, Con Leahy, who had been waiting patiently in the wings for his events to come round, would participate and was considered the favourite. Leahy's speciality was the high jump, due to commence later the same afternoon, but he was also an accomplished triple jumper. At the GAA annual Championships in 1904 he had comfortably beaten O'Connor in the hop, step and jump and the following year O'Connor avoided the event. As was expected, Leahy took an early lead in the competition with a jump of 45' 10⅓".

Reports suggest that he could easily have improved on the distance as he was in superb form but the Corkman had some difficulties in hitting the take-off accurately. As the competition progressed, the other competitors struggled to catch Leahy. Thomas Cronan of America could only manage 44' 11½", while Prinstein, still suffering the effects of a sprained ankle, could do no better than 41' 0". O'Connor had begun well with a jump of 45' 3⅓" but in his next four jumps had failed to capitalise on the good start, his next best being 45' 0¾". In the last round, Leahy fouled his jump, leaving O'Connor one last chance to try for first place.

The moment was something of a trip down memory lane for O'Connor as he found himself, in the last great jump of his career, retracing his first athletic steps. As has already been described, as a child he had innocently started his athletics career in Ashtown, County Wicklow with the hop, step and jump, gradually developing and refining a technique that would enable him to successfully clear a grass margin opposite his front door. Now, as he prepared for his final jump and perhaps greatest test in Athens, a child's ambition came to fruition. O'Connor's last effort exceeded all his expectations and catapulted him into first place with a distance of 46' 2⅛". Leahy, though he was probably shell-shocked, must have been delighted for his compatriot. With an Olympic gold to his name, O'Connor's athletics career was finally complete.

∞

THE HOP, STEP AND JUMP had proved a straightforward battle between O'Connor and Leahy with no hint of scandal, but as the two vied with one another for supremacy, fresh controversy involving an American judge was erupting in the 1,500-metre walk. On the first day of track and field events, the American athlete George Bonhag finished fourth in the five-mile race. Five days later, he was equally disappointed to finish sixth in the 1,500-metre race. Anxious not to return home to America without a medal to his name, he looked about for another event to compete in. After approaching and chatting to an experienced Canadian walker,

Donald Linden, he decided to give the 1,500-metre walk a go — an event in which he had never competed. Not thinking that a total novice could prove a serious threat, Linden, half seriously, half jocularly, told him what shoes to wear, how to stride, what the rules were and even encouraged him to enter. Linden would soon regret his generosity because, from the start, "Bonhag was so determined to stay ahead that he began skipping . . . and continued walking so illegally that no honest walker could ever have caught him".[24] At the finishing line, the first two across were Wilkinson of Great Britain and Spiegler of Austria, but they were disqualified for running. When Bonhag crossed the line, however, to Linden's amazement he was not disqualified but awarded first place. The decision caused a considerable scandal as Bonhag's illegal walking throughout the race had not escaped the attention of the Greek officials, who Linden maintained "were pointing to the American's feet and shaking their heads".[25] James B. Connolly later maintained that Halpin "tipped off" Bonhag that it would be safe to "skip the corners", as the "manager's boss, Sullivan, the Spalding agent, was chief judge of walking".[26] As it happened, two of the four appointed judges had ruled Bonhag's form to be illegal. The casting vote fell to the President of the Jury, Prince George, who backed up Sullivan and ruled in Bonhag's favour. The controversy, however, did not end there, and later that evening Linden was informed that the judges had conferred and agreed that Bonhag had broken the rules, and therefore a run-off would be held the following morning at 9.30 am to decide first place. The next day, Linden, the Crown Prince of Greece and other judges waited for Bonhag to show but he did not turn up. In spite of Bonhag's no-show, without any excuse or explanation as to his absence and the judges' clear acknowledgement that he should have been disqualified, the American was still awarded the gold medal.

The Greek inaction regarding the 1,500-metres walk controversy may have been due to political considerations. As the Olympic Games took place in Athens without Coubertin, there was an IOC meeting involving eight of the organisation's 31 members. The meeting was initially intended to discuss the standardisation of rules for future Olympic Games but, as the meeting progressed, some members discussed reorganising the IOC and offering the Greek Crown Prince honorary chairmanship. Such an action would effectively depose Coubertin, who had been elected President for ten years. Even though James E. Sullivan was not a member of the IOC, he was invited to attend the meeting. When the suggestion that Athens might be made a permanent site for future Olympic Games was made, Sullivan and the Swedish delegate, Balck, strongly backed the Greek proposal. As the meeting progressed some members even considered making Sullivan a member of the IOC.[27] Since this vital meeting, which could have changed modern Olympic history, took place behind closed doors, the Greeks no doubt recognised the importance of keeping Sullivan on side. Not only did he support their cause, but should Coubertin be removed, the American might yet become a key figure in the Olympic movement. As events transpired, Coubertin survived the power struggle within the IOC and rejected any moves to bring Sullivan into the Olympic movement. However, the political considerations where Greece was concerned meant that Sullivan was untouchable, his judgements not to be openly or publicly questioned by Greek officials. Whether these backroom political machinations had a bearing on the long jump contest is impossible to ascertain conclusively, but a photograph of Sullivan and Halpin taken in the Pan-Athenaic stadium by Prince George suggests that relations between all three were very cordial.

cs

DESPITE THE DISAPPOINTMENT OF finishing second to O'Connor in the hop, step and jump, Con Leahy had little time to dwell on the matter. Indeed, after only a short pause, his favourite event, the high jump, commenced. Though the hop, step and jump may not have taxed his energy reserves too greatly, as that event only involved six jumps, the high jump would prove to be something of an ordeal. This was principally because the judges had started the contest at 4' 6" and insisted on raising the bar one inch at a time. When the bar reached 5' 6", daylight was rapidly slipping away, so with seven competitors remaining, it was agreed to move the bar one inch at a time. When the competition was halted at 9.00 pm, three hours after it had begun, five competitors remained, amongst them the favourite, Con Leahy, and the talented American Herbert Kerrigan. It must have come as a great relief to Leahy when the competition was finally adjourned as he had been competing for almost six hours without respite.

The hot conditions had taken their toll on the Corkman, and his feet in particular were said to be "roasting from the unfamiliar cinders". In a magnanimous gesture, Leahy was taken in hand by some American athletes, presumably of Irish-American extraction, who brought him back to their hotel (probably the Hotel Gran Bretagne), where they gave him a bath to open the pores on his feet, covered him completely in olive oil, and gave him a bottle of stout as the only refreshment before retiring to rest for the night, where saturated in oil, Leahy "slept the sleep of the just with only a sheet as covering".[28] It was a somewhat unusual step for a highly competitive American team to take when there was still an American left in the competition. (Herbert Kerrigan was, however, a slim prospect for a medal as he was one of several American athletes still recovering from injuries sustained during the American team's transatlantic crossing when a freak wave hit their ship, the *Barbarossa*.)

On resuming the following day at 6.00 am, Leahy was in sparkling form, having benefited immensely from the treatment the previous night. It did not take long for him to display the skills and technique that made him the favourite for the event. With Kerrigan, the only athlete in the field who could mount a serious challenge, clearly off-form, he finally took the gold with relative ease at a height of 5' 9⅞", after an incredible 36 jumps and eleven hours of competition! At the close, Leahy was quite willing to continue and perhaps establish a new Olympic or world record but the officials would not allow him to, and removed the bar.

> The jumping of the different contestants here prove conclu-
> sively that outside of Kerrigan and Leahy, the others knew
> none of the fine points of high jumping. The Greek and the
> Hungarian who figured in the high jump jumped purely with
> strength — with no science — and did remarkably well. One
> of the contestants who cleared 1.75m took off at least 10 feet or
> more from the bar, and who in making his qualifying jump
> slipped at least 18 inches, having no spikes in his shoes.[29]

Despite "a lack of science", the Hungarian Goency managed to out-jump Kerrigan, taking silver for a jump of 5' 8⅞" and the American had to content himself with sharing the bronze with the Greek Diakides, at 5' 7⅞".

The Irishmen were delighted and once again they waved their green flags to signify Ireland's victory, although this time from terra firma. O'Connor was probably very pleased for Leahy after he had snatched gold from him the previous day. He had not origi-nally intended to compete in the hop, step and jump and probably expected to be cheering Con on from the sidelines. Following Con Leahy's victory, the two friends could now return to Ireland with their heads held high and a gold and silver medal each.

Though O'Connor and Leahy's Olympics were now effectively over, John Daly, the third member of the Irish contingent, was still hoping to win a medal at the Games. Daly had come to compete in the five-mile race and the marathon, the most gruelling of Olympic events. He was an experienced international athlete, hav-ing competed for Ireland in Glasgow in 1901 and having taken a silver medal at the St Louis Games in the 3,000-metre steeple-chase. As that event did not appear on the programme of events at the Athens Games, he decided to focus his energies on the long-distance road races. In his first outing in the five-mile race, he had been denied a bronze medal. No doubt, this disappointment made the Galwayman more determined to put in a good showing in the marathon.

There had been great excitement in the local press in the run-up to this event, with the Greeks confidently predicting a local victory. In addition to the glory which a Greek could expect by winning the marathon on home ground, a host of valuable prizes were promised to a local winner. These included a free loaf of bread every day for a year from a baker, three coffees daily for one year at a particular café, a free shave from a barber for life and free lunch for six people every Sunday for one year from a hotelier. Understandably, there was a significant Greek entry in the event, all hoping to follow in the footsteps of Spiridon Louis, who had won the first ever marathon for Greece during the Inaugural Olympics of 1896. The distance from Marathon to the stadium was 41.86 kilometres. To ensure the road was kept clear for the runners, a thousand horsemen were mobilised to patrol the course. In case any of the contestants fell ill or collapsed, medical units were placed every five kilometres and ambulances were on hand to provide immediate relief. Unlike St Louis and Paris, where the event was run in extreme heat, the Greeks scheduled the race to begin at 3.00 pm, thereby avoiding the most uncomfortably hot part of the day, although it could be argued that starting later would have been even better. When the first runners were in sight of the stadium, a cannon would be fired from a hill opposite the stadium to inform the expectant crowd of the contestants' approach. The preparation for this most symbolic Greek event was meticulous, well-thought-out and ahead of its time. The contestants and visitors to Athens were under no illusions: this was the event to win.

On the day of the race, O'Connor and Leahy walked five miles out from Athens hoping to witness another Irish triumph in the making. As the race leader approached, they were disappointed to see that it was not Daly but were equally amazed to see that the lead man had a large shamrock emblazoned across his chest.

> The leading man, Sherring, then unknown to us, carried no flag therefore there was no waving as alleged and we saw there was a huge green shamrock on his white jersey. I ran along the road with him for about 20 yards to enquire his name and nationality. He said, "My name is Sherring. My parents are Irish and I am proud of Ireland."[30]

William Sherring was competing for Canada but clearly identified strongly with his parents' Irish roots. After a public concert to raise funds to send him and another Canadian runner to Athens raised a mere $75, the money was given to Sherring, who was determined to make the trip. Following a tip from a friendly bartender nicknamed "Butch", Sherring bet the $75 on a horse called *Cecile* at odds of 6–1. When the horse coasted home in first place, Sherring had enough money to pay his passage to Greece. Arriving two months early, he got a job as a railway station porter and quietly began his training on the Marathon road.[31] When the day of the race came, Sherring won with comparative ease, leaving the field behind him after 18 miles. On his arrival in the stadium, the Greeks were disappointed to see a foreigner winning the event, but Prince George sportingly ran alongside the athlete.

Daly had started the race well but suffered greatly in the glare of the afternoon sun. After 15 miles his feet began to blister very badly. He had mistakenly chosen leather shoes with special rubber grips on the sole that did not suit the terrain. After 17 miles, he withdrew from the race under doctor's orders as an old ankle injury swelled up again. Daly's Olympic dream was over and he would spend the following three days recovering from what O'Connor noted were the worst injuries he had ever seen in a foot race. The Galwayman reputedly had scarcely an inch of skin left on either foot.[32]

ෆ

SHERRING'S VICTORY IN THE MARATHON was the last scheduled event of the Athens Olympics and it effectively brought the Games to a close, although it was decided to hold a 3,000-metre walk competition on the final morning to appease those who felt hard done by after the farce of the 1,500-metre walk. On the last day, the Pan-Athenaic stadium filled for the final time as the prize-giving took place. Medals and olive wreaths from the sacred site in Olympia were presented to the winners and those who missed out on Olympic medals were presented with souvenir medals. The official proceedings were then brought to a close by King George. Later the same evening a reception was held at the Zappeion. In a final goodbye in a more intimate setting, the King made an impassioned speech that finished with the hope that Greece might have the same pleasure every four years to host a similar festival.

But the next Intercalated Games scheduled for 1910 would never take place, as the Balkan region would prove far too politically unstable. The spectre of the Ottoman Empire still loomed large in Greek minds. The constant threat of the Turks seeking to regain Crete meant that Greece would remain on a permanent military footing over the next few years. Equally, there were social tensions inherent in Greek society in 1906 that were telltale signs of the political unrest that would soon envelop the whole region. At a political demonstration outside the Hotel Gran Bretagne witnessed by numerous foreign athletes and tourists, the Greek army attacked assembled protestors, killing three people and injuring 57. Like many other feudal societies in Europe at the time, cracks were beginning to show in the social fabric and tensions mounting in the lower classes. The Games would not return to Greece in 1910 and it would be another 98 years before the Olympics finally returned to Athens.

From an Irish perspective, the Games proved highly successful. Despite many ups and downs, O'Connor and Leahy together won two golds and two silvers, an impressive tally of 10 points in their near-total domination of the jumping events. The absolute star of the Games was Martin Sheridan, of Irish birth, though he was representing the United States. The Mayoman took five medals, gold in both the shot-put and discus and three silvers in the stone throw, standing high jump and standing long jump, racking up 12 points for the US team. Apart from Sheridan, Sherring's gold in the marathon and Alfred Hearn Healey's silver in the 110-metre hurdles were considered by many to be successes for Ireland. The Irish media portrayed the likes of Sheridan, Sherring and Healey as members of the famed Irish sporting diaspora, referring to them as "the dispossessed Irish at the Games competing under different flags". O'Connor, Leahy, and Sherring's gold medals as well as Healey's silver were credited to Great Britain and constituted 15 of Britain's 26 points in track and field competition. This fact did not escape the attention of the Irish press, who noted that most of Britain's points were made by "sons of the old distressful country".

Curiously, the *Irish Field*, whose subscription fund had enabled O'Connor and Leahy to travel to Athens, did not report their victories at the Games. The by now infamous protest of the Irishmen at Athens certainly would not have been universally appreciated by many unionist subscribers to the *Irish Field*! Perhaps to avoid embarrassment and cover its tracks, no mention whatsoever was made of the Irishmen at Athens.

On a personal level, Peter O'Connor had much to be proud off in his performance at the Games. Not only had he taken home two medals, a gold and a silver, but he had also managed, against the odds, to mount a successful political demonstration against the English Crown, of which he would be proud until the last. Speaking in 1956 at the age of 84, O'Connor recalled clearly the impact that the political protest had at the time.

> The British failed miserably in their efforts to annex any credit for the Irish successes and the flag incident received wide publicity in the world's press and turned the spotlight very much on the Irish political situation at a period when very few dared to raise a protest against the British domination of our country.[33]

Equally, however, he would never forget losing out to Prinstein in the long jump. Indeed, it is impossible to know for sure whether O'Connor was indeed "robbed" of gold in his favourite event. Too many questions remain unanswered. Did Halpin assist Prinstein by declaring O'Connor's best effort invalid? Was Prinstein's first jump measured correctly by Halpin and could the American jumper simply have won fair and square? O'Connor wasn't sure if Prinstein was merely an innocent party in the whole affair, Halpin taking matters into his own hands. He may also have wondered if the British judges purposely left the contest in

Halpin's hands to punish him for his lack of loyalty to the Crown.
James E. Sullivan later tried to underplay Halpin's role in the controversy, endeavouring to quash any notions of impropriety on
the part of his compatriot.

> Prinstein's jump was measured by Mr Perry of England and
> the measuring was witnessed not only by Mr Halpin, but by
> Mr Muller of Germany and Mr Dahl of Sweden. On each side
> of the pit there were boards with the measurements from the
> take-off board and Mr Muller stuck his cane at 7.2 on the out-
> side of the board, when Prinstein's jump was measured as the
> best jump at this time.[34]

This account is somewhat dubious, since it not only contradicts
O'Connor's account of the proceedings but also introduces two
extra witnesses into the equation who are not mentioned in any
other independent source. His assertion that Perry and not Halpin
measured the winning jump is also open to question as the British
judges were "nowhere near the jumping pit, and quite conspicuous in another part of the stadium". John A. Buttery, writing from
Athens for the *Glasgow Daily Record*, offers perhaps the most ob-
jective and non-partisan account of the day's incidents:

> Thus the curious spectacle was afforded of Mr Halpin the
> American athletic manager judging and measuring the long
> jump and deciding between his own man Prinstein and
> O'Connor the Irishman as to what was a foul and what was a
> fair jump. I do not say that O'Connor ought to have won as he
> avers, but to say the least it was scarcely the correct thing that
> the judge should be an acknowledged partisan. Meanwhile the
> eyes of the English judges were glued to a horizontal bar at the
> other end of the arena.

Whether the inaccuracies in Sullivan's account are by accident or
design is open to question. Likewise, his description of the controversial 1,500-metre walk race is highly selective and perfunctory, failing to mention that American Bonhag had never entered
a walking race before and that he did not turn up the following

day for the run-off with the Canadian Linden. In an attempt to dismiss the controversy, commenting that most walking competitions are destined to end in dispute, Sullivan claimed that it "is well-nigh impossible for a jury of men to become a unit when a man's style of walking is questioned".[35]

Just as in the case of the long jump, his account of the 1,500-metre walk does not tell the full story. No doubt as commissioner to the American team in Athens, and President Roosevelt's representative at the Games, he was anxious to avoid any controversy. Sullivan had a reputation for being extremely shrewd, efficient, domineering and autocratic. In 1905, the world's fastest sprinter, Arthur Duffey, was accused of professionalism and, although the charges were considered specious, Sullivan was rumoured to have ruled against Duffey because he refused to wear Spalding spikes.[36] Consequently he was disqualified from amateur athletics. Perhaps the strongest of Sullivan's traits was his ultra-nationalism. By now an institution within the AAU, he effectively controlled American athletics from 1888 to 1914 and is credited with masterminding America's near total domination of track and field in the early Olympics.[37] He had been entrusted by Presidents McKinley and Roosevelt with leading the American drive for international honours at Olympic Games. He evidently took this undertaking so seriously that at times he was willing to bend the rules.

Sullivan was not a stranger to confrontation or controversy and his prime concern was simply to bring as many Olympic champions home as possible, in this way ensuring that American athletes dominated the international stage. Following the final results in Athens he would report directly to Theodore Roosevelt that America had scored 75 points compared to only 39 points by "Great Britain and all her possessions" — a great athletic victory for the US. One suspects that, for Sullivan, the ends justified the means.

In 1910, James B. Connolly, the man who had warned O'Connor that Halpin would prevent him from winning the long jump, openly accused American officials of cheating at Athens. In his explosive article, "The Capitalization of American Athletics", Connolly launched a blistering attack on the American AAU, its all-powerful secretary Sullivan and his protégé Halpin. Connolly claimed that when Sullivan appointed Halpin as manager to the American Olympic team in 1906, Halpin "had never done any-thing which might indicate he could half fill the job" and that he proved himself an "incompetent trainer, a man of impossible manners and a child in travel" even before reaching Athens. Con-nolly also directly implicated Halpin in the scandal surrounding the 1,500-metre walk and alluded to the fiasco surrounding the long jump, describing how Halpin had been accused by "foreign athletes" of "measuring in" Myer Prinstein.[38] The article created such controversy that Sullivan and Halpin had no choice but to sue Connolly for libel, ensuring that the whole affair received maximum publicity and remained in the public consciousness for considerable time. The libel case seems to have been subsequently settled out of court.

Connolly's public exposure of Sullivan and Halpin's shady dealings at Athens also strengthened O'Connor's belief that he may have been the victim of foul play in Greece. This contention became conviction the following year in 1911 when startling news arrived from America. His great rival Myer Prinstein had been disbarred from practising law following an accusation of im-proper conduct by a former client. Over the years, the suspicion that Prinstein's victory in Athens was orchestrated by Halpin be-came an obsession with O'Connor. The lack of concrete proof about the whole affair eventually irritated O'Connor to such a de-gree that in 1925 he determined to travel to the United States and find out once and for all what really happened that fateful day in Athens. Unfortunately, while O'Connor was midway across the Atlantic Prinstein died, taking the truth of what really went on in Greece with him to the grave. O'Connor would never know for sure whether or not he had been robbed of gold in Athens.

એ

THOUGH THE 1906 INTERCALATED GAMES are presently considered unofficial by the International Olympic Committee, owing to a ruling made in 1949, they undoubtedly succeeded in revitalising and refocusing the Olympic movement after the comparative failures of both the Paris and St Louis Games. Perhaps the most important long-term effect of the Athens Games was the manner in which politics entered the Olympic equation for the first time on numerous fronts. Apart from the hands-on role of the Greek monarchy in the running of the event, many other nations sent official delegations headed by commissioners for the first time. The recognition of the potential value of the Olympiads for public relations purposes would not only ensure the survival of the Olympic movement but also its subsequent growth. The downside was that an event which had been originally non-political, amateur and idealistic in nature would become increasingly viewed as a commercial and political vehicle. Importantly, the Irishmen's insistence on their right to represent Ireland and the subsequent raising of the Irish flag was the first overtly political act to take place at an Olympic Games. It is ironic that O'Connor, who always lamented the interference of politics in the Irish domestic athletics scene, should so willingly and deliberately use a sporting moment to make a political statement. At the time he probably gave little thought to his actions, though in years to come, particularly after attending the Berlin Games, he may have reflected on his own contribution to their politicisation.

Retirement

O N HIS TRIUMPHANT RETURN from Athens in 1906, Peter O'Connor contemplated his last season in competitive athletics against the backdrop of the ongoing dispute in athletic circles between the IAAA and GAA. Like many other older athletes who had competed for years at meetings organised by both the GAA and IAAA, he was reluctant to publicly back one organisation over the other. Privately, he disapproved of the GAA's actions. With the growing conflict, Irish athletics was in danger of becoming a political shuttlecock. After O'Connor went to England to defend his AAA long jump title one last time in the company of Con Leahy, at the 1906 annual GAA Championships, both athletes found that the legality of their right to compete was questioned. Consequently, neither O'Connor nor Leahy took part. Any kind of international competition was anathema to the GAA, as its members were in the strictest sense only allowed to compete in events under the association's rules. This isolationist policy would in time do much to strengthen the GAA, especially in the hurling and Gaelic football arenas. But isolationism would prove disastrous for traditional track and field athletics as the cream of sporting talent within the GAA would be channelled into those above-mentioned arenas. In addition, those who wanted to pursue pure athletics under the auspices of the GAA would be denied the chance to compete internationally, a necessity if young athletes wanted to maximise their potential. O'Connor knew that to be the best, one had to measure oneself against the best. This the new GAA rules did not allow.

In early July 1906, O'Connor and Leahy had travelled to Stamford Bridge to defend their long- and high-jump titles respectively. In excellent weather and before 7,000 spectators, the two Irishmen easily prevailed, O'Connor jumping 23' 6½" in the long jump and Leahy jumping 6' in the high jump. O'Connor had now won his sixth successive AAA title, only one less than Denis Horgan, who had seven consecutive 16 lb championships to his name. O'Connor probably believed that Stamford Bridge was his last athletic outing of note. In the wake of Athens, he had once again reasserted his dominance as the greatest long jumper ever produced in the British Isles. Now all that remained was to play out the season in Ireland and decide when to call it a day finally.

Shortly after returning from London, O'Connor unexpectedly found himself called upon to represent Ireland one last time. The annual Ireland–Scotland match was due to take place in Belfast and the IAAA, having declined to pick O'Connor for the team since 1902, wanted to reinstate him at the eleventh hour. This was the twelfth anniversary of the annual event. At the beginning of the series, Irish teams had scored highly, taking a four to zero lead, as the Scots found it difficult to hold their ground even at home. Later, however, the Irish team had become progressively weaker and the Scots had gained the upper hand. The decline in the Irish team's standard was partly because many prominent Irish champion athletes were now approaching the end of their careers and new talent did not seem to be coming up through the ranks. Denis Horgan's departure for America just weeks before was another huge loss to Irish athletics. On the eve of the contest, IAAA officials also learnt that the Scottish team was stronger than they had initially believed.

The Irish showing was also beginning to be affected by political events. The Irish champion hammer-thrower Patrick J. Ryan was dropped from the IAAA selection as he had recently competed at a GAA sports in Ballinasloe. Ryan, who would later win Olympic gold representing the United States, was the first high-profile Irish athlete to effectively choose sides in the growing dispute between the IAAA and GAA, declaring for the latter.

In 1905, Con Leahy had been run extremely close in the long jump by the relatively unknown H.B. Neilson from the University of Aberdeen. Neilson was not expected to be on the Scottish team in 1906 because he had since moved to St Just in Cornwall and was now practising as a doctor. When Irish officials somehow got wind of the fact that Scotland had, at great expense, arranged for Neilson to be secretly drafted into the team to take on Leahy in the long jump, they began to fear a potential whitewash on home ground. The long jump had never been one of Con's strongest events as it had been for his elder brother, Paddy, and the Irish team suspected that, if Neilson had improved since the two last met the previous year, they might lose a contest that was traditionally theirs for the winning. In desperation, the IAAA dispatched an urgent telegram to Waterford requesting O'Connor to travel up to Belfast at cockcrow on the morning of the contest. The invitation was very late in the day but this event meant a lot to O'Connor. Having been excluded from the Irish team since 1902, he grabbed the chance to be reinstated. When he arrived in Belfast it was much to the surprise of all concerned and — as had been hopefully anticipated — his presence caused considerable consternation in the Scottish camp.

It was fortunate that O'Connor showed up, because Leahy proved no match for Neilson, trailing the Scot by three inches. Though fatigued by the early start to his long journey from Waterford that morning, O'Connor won comfortably with a jump of 22' 7½", some 12½" clear of the Scot. Neilson might well have given O'Connor a stiffer challenge, but he found the jumping conditions in Belfast somewhat daunting and was said to be rather afraid of the very ugly springboard loosely inserted in the soil. Irish jumping grounds had changed little in the 12 years in which O'Connor had been competing and were simply a world apart from those he had latterly experienced in Athens. O'Connor continued where he had left off in the 1900 and 1901 Ireland–Scotland meetings, much to the satisfaction of the Irish supporters. The rout of the Scots in the long jump inspired a local wag to compose a limerick specially for the occasion: "There was a young man from St Just, who at

Belfast meant to be 'fust', but upon my honour, one Peter O'Connor, this young man easily bust!"

In spite of the psychological effect of O'Connor's unexpected appearance in Belfast, the Irish team were beaten on home soil for the first time, losing 7–4. Their defeat for a second successive year was by no means insignificant and marked a new low for Irish athletics. In many ways the defeat was a watershed, signalling the end of a golden era. Since the revival of interest in track and field events sparked by Maurice Davin and Michael Cusack, the likes of Peter O'Connor, Con and Pat Leahy, Denis Horgan, Tom Kiely and Walter Newburn, to name but a few, had placed Irish athletics firmly on the world map. Now as an era drew to a close, Irish athletics was about to be left behind. Political infighting and a lack of financial resources would make it very difficult for future generations of Irish men and women to compete on a world stage. Only the Irish sporting diaspora would continue to draw attention to Ireland. Many of these, such as Martin Sheridan and John Flanagan, were Irish by name and birth. However, their primary allegiance lay with the United States and it would be 22 years before Ireland again produced an Olympic gold medallist that it could rightly call its own in the person of Pat O'Callaghan.

ଔ

A FEW WEEKS AFTER HIS LAST appearance for Ireland at Belfast, O'Connor brought his athletics career to a close at a small country sports in St James's Park in Kilkenny. On an overcast day with intermittent showers, O'Connor optimistically tried one last time to cover 25 feet. After his purple patch in the 1901 season, he had never again come close to his established world record of 24' 11¾". The only time he had overcome that magical 25-foot barrier in public had been at Maryborough, County Laois in 1901, although the record was not officially ratified. Now as the curtain came down on his career, O'Connor felt he had one last big effort left in him and trained specially for the Kilkenny sports. When he let it be known that Kilkenny would be his swansong, he also promised to try and set a new world record. It was perhaps somewhat optimistic of O'Connor to think that at 35 he could reproduce his form of five years before. Although he did not set a new world record, he did manage to jump 24' 2", the best attempt he had made in years and an improvement of four inches over his recent best performances. As the day's sports in Kilkenny drew to a close and the prizes were presented, the local St John's brass band played the last lingering tunes of the day and O'Connor's athletics career finally came to an end. His prowess had brought him halfway across the world, west to America and the New World and east to the birthplace of western civilisation in Greece. Now his adventure in the world of athletics finished close to home and at the kind of sports meeting he had participated in at the beginning of his career.

O'Connor may have regretted that he had not achieved an official long jump record over 25 feet but, apart from this small detail, he had much to look back on with pride. The world record which he had set in 1901 still stood and no one looked like coming close to surpassing it in the foreseeable future. He was also holder of the Irish, English and Scottish records in the long jump. His victory at the Buffalo world championships in 1901 and his six successive AAA long jump titles were unparalleled and had made him the most celebrated long jumper in the world. After the trip to Athens he was also the reigning Olympic hop, step and jump champion.

Although he would miss the buzz of the competition, it was time to call it a day. The world of athletics in which he had competed was fast changing. Apart from domestic troubles, further revelations and controversies were beginning to rock international athletics. As we have seen, in 1905 Arthur Duffey, the holder of the world record for the 100-yard sprint, had been expelled by the American AAU for professionalism and his records were expurgated from the record books. Duffey reacted to his suspension by publishing a series of articles and interviews that scandalised the world of athletics. Just as Peter O'Connor had exposed infractions of the amateur code by DMP officials in 1902, now Arthur Duffey exposed the true nature of American amateurism. These revelations not only demolished the myths surrounding amateur sport but underlined the marked differences between the English AAA's and the American AAU's handling of and guardianship of athletics. Duffey was such a celebrated athlete that his voice carried considerable weight on both sides of the Atlantic. In England he had become something of an idol, having won consecutive AAA 100-yard sprint titles between 1900 and 1904. He and O'Connor had been contemporaries for many years, so O'Connor was probably dismayed when he heard that the American sprint legend had been treated so abysmally. For a committed amateur such as O'Connor, Duffey's allegations were bound to be startling.

For the first time since the DMP scandal of 1902, an insider was spilling the beans on the professionalism which was hidden under the guise of amateurism. In a revealing interview with an English sports correspondent, Duffey explained how shady dealings were transacted between athletes and officials:

> Their overtures to crack amateurs are conducted with much caution. You will never find them committing their propositions to writing. Interviews with the athletes are either conducted privately or through the medium of a third person. Furthermore the "expenses" to be allowed are only known to the parties directly involved. If the arrangement became known to the AAA or the public, the consequences might be unpleasant, and that for manifest reasons. Of course I do not feel justified in naming the exact sums which crack amateurs receive under the guise of "expenses". But I may say that they are of an extremely liberal type, and explain how it is possible for an amateur of very moderate personal means, or of no means at all, to travel all over the world in order to take part in contests, and return to the land of his birth with a bank account of a very comfortable nature indeed.[1]

Duffey claimed that ruling bodies such as the AAU and AAA were aware of such abuses, allowing many professionals to compete in their midst, every now and again making scapegoats of certain athletes who had either been careless in covering their tracks or fallen out of favour with officials. Duffey's harshest criticism was nonetheless kept for Sullivan's AAU, claiming that the situation was not nearly as "black" in Britain as in America. Duffey felt there was need for change right across the board and declared, "The time has arrived when every athlete, irrespective of social position, shall be given his chance of getting to the top of the tree." The issue of amateurism and clandestine professionalism was now truly being broached for the first time since Peter O'Connor's isolated outburst in 1902, and Duffey's interviewer lamented that the "opportunity" provided by O'Connor some years before to investigate and perhaps reform amateur athletics had been neglected.

Predictably, Sullivan leapt to the defence of the AAU and tried to play down the import of Duffey's allegations. Experienced in negotiating thorny issues, Sullivan managed to avoid admissions of responsibility or accountability on the part of the AAU while tacitly acknowledging that international athletics was now at an important crossroads:

> Things have now come to such a pass in athletics that there must be a new working arrangement between the Old and New countries. So long as America accepts English athletes and vice versa, we should have some control over them. The officials of both countries should realise that there have been abuses in athletics, and that the sport is now in a critical condition.[2]

Through Duffey's revelations, it became clear to the athletes and the sporting public that for many years America had been practising a different sort of amateurism to that which it preached. Since the early 1890s, the American athletics establishment had effectively been promoting and using professional models to nurture and develop its sporting talent, while simultaneously "claiming amateurism to the world". Though abuses of the amateur code also undoubtedly existed in Britain and Ireland, they were probably on a smaller scale than in the United States and mostly concerned the issue of expenses. The nineteenth-century invention of pure "amateurism", which was prevalent in Britain, never succeeded in taking root in American culture. British amateurism had been devised to prevent the working classes from competing in athletic events. The United States was too democratic for such an imperial elitism to ever take hold.[3] From an early stage both Ivy League universities and later New York sports clubs quickly adopted a professional model in their approach to athletics. Since 1896 American athletes had proved how successful this method was, the American team growing in strength at each Olympics.

Now at the end of his career, in the wake of Duffey's revelations, O'Connor could fully understand how it was that America had become such a dominant force in world athletics. Not for a moment regretting his own strict adherence to the amateur code, he may well have wondered how much earning potential he might have had at the peak of his fame had he adopted the American way. His amateur status had not made him rich but he could retire knowing that he had triumphed — more often than not against the odds — without sacrificing his idealism.

଄

NOW THAT PETER O'CONNOR HAD finally decided to call it a day, he settled down to life in Waterford with Maggie in Sweet Briar Cottage. It was high time he turned his attention to rearing his family and concentrating on his career. A visiting Australian priest, Rev. T.A. Fitzgerald, who came to interview him for the Australian *Freeman's Journal*, portrays the couple's simple married life, describing their homely cottage as "standing in a spacious kitchen garden where every kind of fruit and vegetable seems to grow, and where the champion keeps his muscles in order with the help of the hoe and spade". Throughout his life O'Connor was a keen gardener, prizing above all else his apples, pears and tomatoes. The interior of the house resembled a jeweller's shop, with all sorts of trophies glistening in cases, on shelves and on the mantelpiece. Prime exhibits amongst these were the wedding belt of gold medals that O'Connor had given to Maggie on their wedding day and the valuable AAA trophy that he had just won for the sixth year in succession. Maggie and Peter took particular pride in their young son Eddie, born in December 1905, whom Fitzgerald noted was "a baby athlete who has inherited the paternal accomplishments and makes creditable attempts to jump out of the perambulator". Life for Peter and Maggie was certainly quite idyllic at this moment in their married life.

On his return from Athens, Peter O'Connor had at last been apprenticed to become a solicitor and was registered by the Incorporated Law Society of Ireland. A time of new beginnings, the only possible threat that Maggie saw to their happy lifestyle was her suspicion that Peter might be tempted to compete for just one more season. O'Connor was particularly reluctant to give up the English Championships title he had won for the previous six consecutive years and he had taken a particular shine to the perpetual trophy that the AAA sent over to him each year, valued at 35 guineas, and was reluctant to part with it. Suspecting that his attachment to this title and trophy might lure him out of retirement, and determined that he should quit with his reputation and records intact, Maggie decided to take matters into her own hands. Late in November 1906, she wrote to the Lord Chief Justice of England, Lord Alverstone, who presented the prizes at the annual AAA sports, in the hope that he might intercede with the AAA on her husband's behalf and award him the trophy as a mark of recognition of his six consecutive titles. Maggie was even willing to contribute the sum of £10 towards the costs of purchasing a new trophy. Quite what Lord Alverstone made of this most unusual request is not known but Maggie received a reply from one of his secretaries just over a week later. Evidently her proposal was "quite impossible". The cups were all perpetual trophies presented by various donors and could under no circumstances be retained by the winners.

Maggie's attempt to obtain the cup may also have been rejected for obvious political reasons. After her husband's protest at Athens, which she herself witnessed, it was highly unlikely that the AAA would consent to awarding O'Connor such a valuable perpetual trophy. Equally, Lord Alverstone, who was one of the most powerful men in England and a pillar of British society, would almost certainly have disapproved of O'Connor's spirited and by now infamous protest against the Crown in Athens.[4] Maggie's worries that the 1907 AAA Championship would prove too great a temptation for O'Connor were unfounded. The following July, the prized long jump trophy was simply sent back to the offices of the AAA. O'Connor's name appeared on the programme as holder of the event but his name did not figure amongst the participants. In his absence, for the first time in six years, the English long jump title was surprisingly won by Denis Murray, the Irish sprinter who had no track record in long jumping.

O'Connor had retired from active competition, but his interest in athletics did not diminish and he soon began coaching a promising Waterford athlete called Percy Kirwan from nearby Kilmacthomas. In 1906 Percy and his brother Rody had played on the Kerry Senior Football selection in the Railway Shield at Jones's Road in Dublin. In 1908 Percy would become the star of the Papal Games in Rome when as part of a GAA team he won the 100 yards, 200 yards and the long jump, before receiving a personal congratulations from Pope Pius X. Percy and Rody would become two of O'Connor's closest friends and staunchest allies in the years to come.

11

The GAA/IAAA Dispute in 1909

IN THE THREE YEARS SINCE O'CONNOR had withdrawn from competitive athletics he had been keeping a keen eye on the dispute between the IAAA and GAA. Though he was previously reluctant to become openly involved, by December 1909 he felt the need to intervene. Following the publication of a letter by an anonymous GAA member in the *Irish Daily Independent* on 2 December, the dispute was once again thrust into the public domain. The correspondence that the newspaper published in the ensuing weeks provides a fascinating insight into the extent to which the various factions were divided. Copious amounts of letters streamed into the offices of the *Irish Daily Independent* from all parties involved in the conflict as supporters of the GAA, IAAA and ICA sought to defend the actions of their respective organisations. At times the debate descended into farce as over-zealous and not so well-informed contributors overstepped the mark and let their passions override reason. In particular, several GAA supporters struggled to defend their association from accusations that it had become increasingly political in nature. In such attempts to deny the obvious, the key issues often became confused:

> The kernel of the dispute is in the answer to the question — Is Ireland a province of England or is Ireland a distinct nationality? It is alleged that the IAAA is only a branch of an English body. In proof of this it is pointed out that at the recent Olympic Games the IAAA supplied its athletes to England and allowed them to be entered as Britishers. If these allegations are

true it is easy to understand the attitude of the GAA. Of course the GAA is non-political and the meaning of that is that it takes no sides in the discussion among Irish nationalists — Parnellite, Dillonite, Healyite or Sinn Féiner. But it does take sides against any man or body of men that wears the British label. No English athletic body would allow its members to be called Irish or to represent Ireland. The rule about soldiers is intelligible and it is the only consistent attitude for an Irish national body to take up. Any conference between the rival bodies must suppose this as fundamental.[1]

Though "Gael", an anonymous contributor to the *Independent* debate, might be interpreted by some as being inaccurate, contradictory and unrepresentative of the GAA's official stance, it could be argued that certain inconsistencies in his outlook did reflect idiosyncrasies present in the GAA at the time. His somewhat convoluted definition of what "non-political" signifies is particularly problematic when one considers the GAA's recent ban on forces of the Crown. Clearly the GAA's increasing political function was at odds with the original mission statement in its constitution. The motions passed at the 1905 convention, which were the source of the controversy, were undeniably political in nature.

Apart from the GAA's political reasons for wanting to break its truce with the IAAA, there were also economic factors at work, a point which was not lost on many observers, especially supporters of the Irish Cycling Association. Cycling was a relatively new and modern sport and though it clearly belonged to the "foreign games" category, by 1905 the GAA's attitude to the sport had changed and they made moves to incorporate it into their association. The GAA's shift in attitude to cycling was influenced not just by a desire to weaken the ICA and the IAAA but also probably by economic concerns. Cycling was an increasingly popular sport in Ireland at the time and its inclusion at an athletics meeting was guaranteed to pull in a good crowd.

As an avowed nationalist, O'Connor may have sympathised with many of the long-term objectives of the GAA, such as safeguarding the national pastimes and contributing to the growth of a national consciousness. However, as we have seen from the Murtagh affair in 1905, he did not approve of the methods of exclusion and isolationism being employed by the GAA, viewing them as unnecessary and damaging to athletics. As the dispute raged in the *Irish Daily Independent*, O'Connor sought out Maurice Davin, the first President of the GAA, to ask his help. Davin had presided over a similar dispute in 1885 between the two associations, which led to a truce that lasted twenty years. An account of this meeting was published in the *Independent* on 13 December 1909 and O'Connor was now seen to have thrown his hat into the ring.

> I made up my mind not to take part again in this regrettable athletic dispute and I only do so now in the hope of effecting an amicable settlement, which I think is possible as a result of a chance interview with my old and esteemed friend, Mr Maurice Davin of Deerpark, Carrick-on-Suir, the "Grand Old Man" of athletics, whose name, fame and records and those of his athletic brothers in the "seventies" and "eighties" are known to sportsmen in every part of the civilized globe. Having to go on legal business to Carrick-on-Suir on the 10th inst. I called to see him. I found him in his beautiful home by the silvery Suir, looking hale and hearty and as athletic and robust as he was twenty years ago. Attired in the old style of knee breeches, erect and manly and with his snow-white hair and beard, he looked as fine and handsome a picture of a typical old Irish gentleman as I ever beheld. I asked him would he act the "strong" man referred to in one of your correspondent's letters and offer his services to try and settle the dispute. With sad and dejected look he said he had very strong reasons for not interfering again in the management of the GAA and that he wished to live in peace and friendship with all true sportsmen for the rest of his life. He showed me, in his valuable scrap album, dozens of letters which were published in the daily newspapers about the athletic dispute which occurred in the year 1885. It struck me as remarkable that the arguments then used by those anxious to have peace were almost identical with the arguments now used to achieve the same object.[2]

An important result of O'Connor's meeting with Davin was the latter's explanation of how the original dispute was resolved through the intervention of Archbishop Croke as peacemaker. At the height of the dispute, Croke had written to the GAA calling for an end to the feud. This had an immediate effect. The extent of Croke's role had not been publicly known before. Now, with the dispute renewed some twenty years later, Davin and O'Connor hoped the publication of Croke's letter might once again effect a truce. Thus, Davin entrusted the letter to O'Connor and gave him his blessing to publish it.

> "I cannot see my way to preside at a Conference between repre-
> sentatives of the two associations; but here" said he, pointing to
> a letter in his album, "if that is published I believe it will have
> the same effect as in 1885 and again settle the unfortunate ath-
> letic dispute between brother Irishmen once and for all".

Both Davin and O'Connor hoped that Croke's letter would bring the warring factions to the peace table. But the current GAA had changed and developed since 1885 and was now a much stronger organisation than at the time of the original dispute. With the members of the association involved at that time all now deceased or retired, Croke's twenty-year-old letter had little chance of convincing a new generation of GAA leadership holding militant and trenchant nationalistic views.

In the event, the publication of Croke's letter did not make as big an impact as O'Connor and Davin hoped. The *Independent* had not provided a healthy forum for initiating dialogue between warring factions. Constructive debate was for the most part eclipsed by insults and accusations directed at the opposing side. The fact that many contributors hid behind *noms de plume* meant that vitriolic opinions could be expressed at will under the cloak of anonymity. As a result, it was often unclear which of the contributors were expressing their own opinions or that of their chosen association. Passions and tempers were running high as a P. Harding, a well-known athlete and official of the IAAA, testified to when writing to O'Connor:

> I knew all about that letter of Dr Croke's and I intended to ask Maurice about it when the blatherin' shites had exhausted themselves. It was too good to keep quiet. It had to come out somehow, and as you say it must have caused a flutter in the henhouse. Why the blazes don't the correspondents stick to the point? I wrote under the *nom de plume* of facto and I'll stick to everything I said. [3]

It was now clear that the *Independent* correspondence was doing more harm than good and O'Connor felt that further action and more proactive measures were necessary. When O'Connor and Davin first met in Carrick-on-Suir, O'Connor had suggested approaching the then Archbishop of Cashel to intervene in the dispute. Anticipating that Croke's letter might fail to bring the two associations to book, O'Connor began drafting a letter to be sent to the new Archbishop. As Croke's successor to the See of Cashel, Archbishop Fennelly had been approached by the GAA late in November 1902 and invited to become patron of the Association. Dr Fennelly had duly accepted, giving the new executive his blessing. Peter O'Connor was hopeful that the Archbishop might be just the "strong man" required to end the hostilities that had riven Irish athletics. As he set about formulating his letter, O'Connor remained in frequent contact with Davin, who secretly acted as editor, making suggestions and amendments to the document. Though Davin had repeatedly claimed that he did not wish to interfere in the running of the GAA again, he was more than willing to offer guidance and advice behind the scenes:

> That letter is all right, but if you have not sent it on I think you had better wait for a little time. Your letter to the *Independent* will have more effect than you think. Most of the letters of the *Independent* since (I have not seen this day's paper yet) were written before yours appeared. F.B. Dineen called on the Archbishop when they were working up the team of athletes for Rome. I don't think he tried to help them much in that business. The Archbishop knew all about the dispute in the old times. Most likely he is aware of the present state of things in the athletic line and may have his own reasons for not inter-

fering. I think I would understand some of them. If you went with a deputation of GAA athletes to the Archbishop and stated your views exactly as you have put them in the letter I think it would have more effect, and you would know better what to do afterwards for I think you will not let the matter rest now that you have taken it up.[4]

Dr Fennelly was known to be more interested in educational and farming matters than in sport. Though a well-liked, humorous and down-to-earth man, it was doubtful whether any intervention on his part would really influence the GAA. Unlike Croke, Fennelly did not involve himself in high-profile political matters and lacked the commanding presence on the national scene that his predecessor enjoyed. Croke's open support of the Land League and tenant farmers during the Land War of the 1870s had earned him unqualified admiration and respect from Irish nationalists. Thus, his 1885 letter appealing to the two associations to bury their grievances had had an immediate impact then and that conflict was resolved. In 1909, however, there was no second truce. Croke, who had died in 1902, was only a distant memory.

Three days after Croke's letter appeared in the *Independent*, O'Connor dispatched his letter to Archbishop Fennelly in Cashel. In it, he draws attention to the Archbishop's role as patron of the GAA and reminds him of how quickly and effectively Croke's intervention in 1885 had brought about a truce. Then he provides an interesting analysis of the ramifications of the GAA's boycotting rules:

> The effect of the rules according to my experience of them in theory and practice is that if an Irishman takes any part in foreign games, such as Rugby or Association Football, Cricket, Hockey, Golf, Rowing in a boat, Lawn Tennis, or base-ball (Cycling, a foreign game, is excepted because the GAA makes financial profit out of it), or competes against policemen, soldiers, navy-men or pensioners, or at a sports where a military band plays or at a sports held under rules of other athletic associations, in or outside of Ireland, he (such Irishman) becomes ipso facto according to the GAA diagnosis, a West-

Briton and Shoneen, and is not allowed to compete in Gaelic Football or Hurling or at Athletic sports under their rules. Gaelic Football and Hurling are excellent though very vigorous games, but there are thousands of young men in Ireland today who are physically unfit to take part in them or prefer cricket or some other gentler game to suit their constitutions, and there are also thousands of others who prefer to take part in other less vigorous games, particularly during the summer season, or who deliberately refuse to take part in GAA games by reason of the intolerant and coercive measures [taken to] compel them to do so.[5]

O'Connor makes no bones about the fact that cycling's profitability was the principal reason behind the GAA's recent hostility to the IAAA and ICA. Although economic factors may indeed have given some impetus to the GAA's attempts to take over cycling and undermine the ICA, O'Connor's assertion that it was the association's principal motive shows a lack of appreciation of the wider national scene at the time. The association's role and influence in Irish life was far more complex and far-reaching than that played by the IAAA and ICA. The latter two associations had tentative unionist affiliations but, unlike the GAA, were not actively political. Some nationalists nonetheless viewed the two associations as instruments of Anglicisation. O'Connor probably saw them as essentially non-political sporting bodies. By attacking the IAAA and the ICA, Irish athletics itself would be the first to suffer and that was O'Connor's primary concern. In his mind, the issue was black and white. If the dispute could not be resolved, the consequences for athletics in the long term would be grave.

The GAA has made a supreme effort since 1906 to wipe out the IAAA and the ICA, but it has signally failed. As a result of this unfortunate struggle, the Athletes and Cyclists of Ireland have been the real sufferers, though in no way [responsible for or] concerned with the quarrel. I feel that if your Lordship's views coincide with the late Dr Croke's and that you can see your way to communicate with the GAA privately or write a letter to the *Independent* expressing your views and suggesting

that the GAA should, graciously, in the interest of good sport
and healthy competition, withdraw their objectionable rules,
that the gentlemen controlling it, in deference to your Lordship's and the late Dr Croke's wishes, will instantly do so.

What Archbishop Fennelly made of O'Connor's letter is not known.
Nor is it known whether he decided to act on O'Connor's request
and made any attempts to act as peacemaker. If he did make discreet efforts, they were to no avail, as the GAA made no immediate
moves to rescind the bans introduced in the first years of the twentieth century. Indeed these would endure until well after the formation of the Irish Free State and Republic. Significantly, it would take
over 96 years for the 1905 ban, which had caused all the trouble, to
be removed from the GAA's constitution.

Following O'Connor's disappointing failure to facilitate a reconciliation between the IAAA and GAA, he removed himself
from the spotlight and decided to play no further role in the politics behind athletics. In the course of the following years, he
would watch with regret as Irish athletics began to founder and
the IAAA quickly began to lose ground to the GAA. It would
have taken a strong personality with an impressive national
standing to unite Irish athletics in 1909 and, considering the powerful forces and disparate elements vying for supremacy in Irish
society at the time, it is doubtful if there really was any one person who could have brought about a truce.

12

Family and Career (1910–1931)

IN 1906 PETER O'CONNOR HAD BEGUN his apprenticeship in order to qualify as a solicitor. His employer, Daniel Dunford, was coming close to retirement age, so it was a sensible move. In 1908, O'Connor sat and passed the preliminary examination for the Incorporated Law Society and the following year in July of 1909 he also passed the intermediary exam. O'Connor's aspirations to move up in his profession were most likely spurred on by the birth of his fourth son Walter in 1910. As Maggie had been pregnant every second year since their marriage, their family responsibilities were increasing rapidly. At the rate his family was growing, the income of a solicitor was an attractive prospect. Though still some way off from completing his final exams at Blackhall Place, O'Connor's future practising law in Waterford city seemed secure. After arriving in Waterford a relative stranger with next to nothing, he now had much to look back on with pride. He had married well and his and Maggie's home, Sweet Briar Cottage, was in one of the more affluent parts of Waterford. Dunford frequently intimated that in the future he intended to reward O'Connor's years of devoted service by leaving him the office on his death, although he had not yet committed this promise to paper. There could be no better way of proving old James Halley wrong, when he deemed O'Connor an unsuitable match for his daughter Maggie, than by finally becoming a fully fledged solicitor and building up and then taking over one of Waterford city's most respected legal practices.

Late in the summer of 1911, Maggie gave birth to their first daughter, Margaret Mary, her fifth child in seven years. As Maggie was worn out from so many pregnancies and somewhat pale and listless, O'Connor decided to send Jimmie and Peter (Petie), now 5½ and 4 years old, to their O'Brien grandparents in Wicklow for a prolonged holiday. Eddie, the eldest, was a quiet sort and serious by nature compared to his two more boisterous younger brothers, so he was allowed stay on at Sweet Briar Cottage with the baby and toddler Walter while their mother recuperated. By 3 October Maggie had recovered sufficiently to allow the couple to go on a rare shopping jaunt to Dublin for the weekend. On the return home to Waterford they passed through Wicklow to visit the grandparents and collect Jimmie and Peter.

In 1912, O'Connor sat his final law exams. The results were published on 1 February 1912 and, of the 17 candidates who passed, O'Connor finished ninth in the pecking order. It was a landmark occasion in his professional life. He had at last risen through the legal ranks, overcoming his lack of a secondary or university education. However, O'Connor's wages were not increased significantly upon his qualification, principally because Dunford had promised him that he would inherit the practice upon his death. Since O'Connor had taken his first exams in 1908, Dunford had more or less left the running of the office to O'Connor, calling only infrequently to the office. By 1912, Dunford was already in his seventies and quite content to live off the income which the firm provided under O'Connor's control. Because of Dunford's age, O'Connor did not press him for the partnership which he undoubtedly believed would come in due course. At this stage he was Dunford's personal assistant.

Now that he had made this new step in his life, O'Connor set about obtaining a new home that could accommodate his large household. He would not choose just any large house, however, but one commensurate with his new status as a qualified solicitor. The year 1913 saw the birth of another son, Arthur. Now with six children, two parents, a housekeeper and a maid in the house, it was impossible to stay in Sweet Briar Cottage any longer. That

September an ideal property came on the market. The house, called "Upton", belonged to a Colonel Robert S. Watson and was an excellently designed and impressive three-storey Georgian house situated in Newtown, a stone's throw from Sweet Briar Cottage. The house had six large bedrooms, a garden with fruit and vegetables and a stables with a loft suitable for pigeons. It was just the property O'Connor was looking for, a spacious and imposing residence with solid granite steps leading up to the front door. Hastily Peter and Maggie put Sweet Briar Cottage up for sale, eventually selling it to an army man, Commandant Power, for 310 guineas. With the transaction done, they moved to Upton. O'Connor was thrilled with his new garden, documenting meticulously its contents which included 28 apple trees, 45 gooseberry bushes, 17 currant trees and 32 pear trees against the garden wall. In some respects, Upton, with its beautiful orchard and situated so close to the River Suir, was similar to the old Connor family homestead at Dunbur, though Upton was undoubtedly a more grandiose residence, prominently situated in one of Waterford city's wealthiest areas. As the family moved the short distance from the small but homely Sweet Briar Cottage to Upton, there was no doubt that O'Connor had truly arrived.

ෆ

ON 28 JUNE 1914 ARCHDUKE FERDINAND, the heir to the Austro-Hungarian Empire, and his wife were assassinated. The Great War followed. Though many Irishmen enlisted in the British army, heeding Redmond's call to arms, the War had little impact on O'Connor's life. His prime concern at this time was his parents. In August 1914 his mother, Mary O'Brien, died at the age of 72 and was buried in Glenealy Catholic Cemetery just outside Wicklow town. With her death, O'Connor's youngest sister Evelyn, who had been caring for her mother, entered convent life. The same year, Edward O'Connor retired as overseer of the waterworks and moved back to the family house at Kilmantin Hill.

In March 1915 the family had a minor health crisis when Petie contracted scarlatina and had to be taken to the fever hospital. Within a week Jimmie also came down with the illness and was likewise packed off to hospital. By the time the two boys returned home late in April, O'Connor could report that Jimmie looked "fat and blooming", but Petie was "something of a sad wreck". Just weeks after the return of the boys, Maggie gave birth to another daughter on 18 May, Mary Josephine. As Petie took several months to recover from his ordeal, Maggie had her hands full, with two sick boys and yet another new baby daughter. Now that some of their children were of school-going age, Maggie and Peter decided to send their sons to Waterpark College, a few hundred yards from Upton, while the girls would in time be sent to the local Ursuline convent.

The Easter Rising of 1916 took much of Ireland, including Waterford, by surprise. Dublin was the only place a full-scale insurrection took place and consequently this latest push for Irish independence was destined to fail. Within a few days, the British army defeated the insurgents, although there was considerable destruction to Dublin city centre as well as numerous civilian casualties. Unsurprisingly, there was little or no reaction in Waterford city or county, with the county council publicly condemning the Rising. Waterford was still very much a bastion of Home Rule, thanks to John Redmond MP's influence and thus maintained close links with the British Crown. O'Connor was probably as stunned by the events of Easter 1916 as most other Irishmen but as Maggie was expecting their eighth child he already had a lot on his mind. Kathleen Gertrude was born on 16 September 1916.

On the economic front, the Great War brought affluence to many Irish farmers, since their produce was badly needed in war-time Britain. This had a positive effect on the Irish economy in the short term and, in 1915, O'Connor had taken on another clerk at £2 5 shillings a week. These years were essentially a quiet period in O'Connor's life, dedicated for the most part to raising his family and building up Dunford's practice. With such responsibility, O'Connor could not have been actively involved in any political movement. In any case, he had always been a Home Ruler of the Redmondite school. As the aftermath of the Great War would soon show, however, Redmond and the Home Rule movement were becoming redundant. Too many concessions had to be made to northern unionists in exchange for Home Rule. The northern counties and partition would prove to be too great a psychological stumbling block for many Irish nationalists anxious for independence. Also, in the wake of the 1916 Easter Rising, a growing militancy in Irish nationalism began to make itself felt. The summary court-martials and executions of most of the Rising's leaders contributed to this. The British government's swift and ruthless response to the Rising, and their attempts towards the end of the War to introduce military conscription into Ireland, were almost universally condemned. The Home Rule Bill successfully negotiated by Redmond and passed by the Westminster parliament in 1914 was by now outdated and insufficient to placate the new wave of Irish nationalism. When Redmond died in 1918, the Home Rule cause that he and Parnell had fostered and championed had become obsolete. There was now little faith amongst the Irish populace that real political autonomy could be achieved through parliamentary means. A new generation of Irish nationalists and republicans were about to take centre stage and Ireland entered an uncertain period of turbulence, struggle and change.

cs

WHEN O'CONNOR FIRST CAME TO work for Daniel Dunford in Waterford in late 1898, his employer asked him to sign a document stating that, should he become a solicitor, he would never set up a practice in opposition to his own office in Waterford. In such a way Dunford safeguarded his own interests, making it impossible for his employee to strike out on his own. O'Connor would be tied to Dunford's practice for as long as he remained in Waterford. O'Connor could not have realistically refused to enter into such an agreement with Dunford and at the time he probably did not give the matter too much consideration. In the many years in which O'Connor had worked for Dunford, O'Connor had done much to build up his employer's practice, effectively running the firm since qualifying as a solicitor himself.

> I had been twenty years as his assistant, and as a result of my management I increased his business, and made it a very prof-itable one. When I entered his employment he paid me a sal-ary of £300 per year but after my marriage many years afterwards I found it difficult to keep out of debt notwith-standing strict economy. I never had any disagreement with him during our long connection of 20 years, the last 12 of which he rarely visited the office. The accounts were audited each year, and he saw that I had increased his business and was making substantial profits for him. He frequently told me he had made his will and had left me the offices and the busi-nesses and all debts due to him by clients.[1]

Dunford had not given O'Connor a written undertaking that he would leave him his business upon his death. O'Connor took Dunford at his word and may have thought it imprudent and somewhat impertinent to seek a written assurance from his em-ployer of over 20 years. The contract did, however, leave him in a somewhat vulnerable position. Towards the end of 1919, O'Connor, with Maggie's encouragement, decided to seek some solid assurances from Dunford regarding the future. Maggie was pregnant once again, expecting their ninth child, Agnes Joan, who would enter the world on 17 June 1920, so at last O'Connor ap-proached Dunford and asked him for a partnership. He pointed out to his employer how he had worked up the firm's business, resulting in a big increase in the practice's income and capital. De-spite the growing success of the practice, O'Connor's salary had not changed since he started work there. O'Connor now had a wife and nine children to support and no doubt felt he was due a raise after 20 years of loyal service. Dunford listened attentively to O'Connor's arguments and seemed at first "inclined to agree" with O'Connor's request. He requested some time to think about the matter and promised to give O'Connor a decision in a few days.

When the two men next met, far from fulfilling O'Connor's expectations and acceding to his request, Dunford delivered an unexpected and shattering blow. He had evidently consulted a close friend, a parish priest from Cahir, County Tipperary, who had been living in Waterford city for 20 years. After his consultations with the priest, Dunford's attitude to O'Connor changed and he refused to give him a partnership. O'Connor was curtly informed that a young solicitor who was a friend of the priest's was anxious to purchase the practice. O'Connor could scarcely believe his ears when Dunford informed him of his decision. This had gone against everything his employer had promised over the previous 12 years. O'Connor's world stood in ruins, thanks to a meddlesome priest who was looking for a soft landing for a personal friend. Dunford was 80 years old and, as such, may have been easily led. Nonetheless, O'Connor was shattered that Dunford was reneging on his promise. Extremely distressed, he lost his temper, handed over the keys of the office and returned home to Upton, where he remained "well nigh broken hearted for a week". This crisis could easily have signalled an ignominious end to O'Connor's legal career in Waterford had it not been for one of his clients, noted both for her persistence and formidable temperament. This was the kind of client the elderly Dunford had only been too happy to let O'Connor deal with in the past.

Over the course of the following days, business in the office slowed to a trickle and was in danger of grinding to a halt. There were still clerks working in the office but there were no key decision-makers. It was during this period of O'Connor's self-imposed exile that Miss Annie May Sadleir visited the office to see him and became increasingly annoyed at his absence. The clerks in the office had no idea where O'Connor was, since they were oblivious to the rift between Dunford and his second-in-command. Her pressing business with Dunford's firm concerned the sale of her family's ancestral home, Cregg House in Tipperary. Due to the increasingly uncertain political climate in Ireland at the time, Miss Sadleir was anxious that she and her two sisters, Augusta and Louisa, should sell the property and move back to England. In

1919, the Irish Republican Army had begun to escalate its war against the British establishment, gathering intelligence and orchestrating attacks on the RIC countrywide. Annie May's sisters had been reluctant, like many other Anglo-Irish families, to sell up and move away. Peter O'Connor had been able to convince her two sisters to sell the family property and assure them that they would benefit considerably from a successful auction. He had dispelled any doubts that Miss Sadleir's sisters had when he suggested dividing the trust funds between the three of them so that each could feel "genuine pleasure and a feeling of independence in having a large sum of money of their own at their disposal". If O'Connor was not involved in the sale, the auction might fall through or the sisters' best interests might be poorly represented.[2]

When, after her second visit to the office, there was still no sign of O'Connor or any explanation for his absence, Miss Sadleir went to Upton where she finally caught up with him. There she learned about his disagreement with Dunford and that he had effectively quit the office. Determined to have her own way, Miss Sadleir went to visit Daniel Dunford at his private residence and insisted that O'Connor should have full charge of her auction. According to O'Connor, Dunford was always "rather timid and frightened" of Miss Sadleir, who was a very demanding client. In order to avoid her wrath, Dunford wrote to O'Connor empowering him to take full charge of the auction. On the first day of the sale of Cregg House, Dunford turned up in the company of Fr O'Donnell to inspect the sale, although he gave O'Connor "no recognition". No doubt annoyed by his behaviour, Miss Sadleir extended the same courtesy to Dunford, completely ignoring the elderly solicitor and his companion. As O'Connor would later recall: "It was one of the most successful sales in the South of Ireland. Since then there are hundreds of lovely mansions in Ireland vacated by the owners, who went to reside in England, which are now 'White Elephants', and cannot be sold."

Immediately after the auction, O'Connor received an ultimatum from Dunford. He was given notice to quit unless he undertook to buy the practice for the princely sum of £5,000. According to O'Connor, no solicitor in Ireland would have paid such a sum for Dunford's practice; the business was not worth half that. Nonetheless he had little choice but to take the offer seriously. Since he had voluntarily signed an agreement that he would never start up in opposition to Dunford in Waterford city, his only other option was to leave Waterford "and start as a perfect stranger in some other town or city". The notion of uprooting his wife and large family to start afresh was inconceivable for a man who was then almost 50 years old. Eventually after much coaxing from his wife and her brother and sisters, O'Connor most reluctantly agreed to taking over the practice on Dunford's terms. The fact that Peter and Maggie had to raise the sum of £5,000 in the bank at 6 per cent interest meant that times would be leaner for their family in the coming years, something they had not previously expected. (As a parting shot, emphasising the extent to which their working and personal relationship had deteriorated, Dunford insisted that O'Connor get none of the costs gained from the sale of Cregg.)

So it was that, in circumstances that he least expected, Peter O'Connor finally made the transition from paid assistant to self-employed businessman. Despite the bitterness he may well have felt towards Dunford, he must nonetheless have felt a great deal of satisfaction when the offices of Peter O'Connor & Son opened for the first time. With so many sons in the family O'Connor could well expect that at least one of them would eventually follow him into the business! The office was hard won but the name Peter O'Connor & Son would become a permanent fixture of the Waterford city streetscape.

◌ঝ

AS AN IMPORTANT CHAPTER IN O'Connor's life opened, the death of his father on 28 March 1921 signalled the close of his family's long association with Wicklow town, dating from the Battle of the Boyne in 1690. Edward O'Connor passed away peacefully at his last residence in Newstreet and was buried in the Protestant church graveyard at Church Hill. The O'Connor family's time in Wicklow was at an end.

A few months later, on 23 July 1921, an American, Edward (Ned) Gourdin, sensationally broke O'Connor's long jump world record, setting a new distance of 25' 3". O'Connor's world record had stood for almost 20 years and was the first official record recognised by the International Amateur Athletic Federation when it was formed in 1913. Gourdin, the man who had at last surpassed O'Connor's mark, was an African-American, studying law at Harvard University. When O'Connor heard the news, James B. Connolly would report that the Irishman was not particularly disappointed but was more surprised that the record had not been broken earlier. Before Gourdin, the closest anyone had come to jumping farther was at the 1912 Stockholm Olympics when O'Connor witnessed another American, Albert Gutterson, come within half an inch of his Ballsbridge world record. Gourdin's breakthrough finally brought to an end the glorious golden era of Irish jumping that had started with Pat Davin in the 1880s; but it ushered in a new golden era, when African-American athletes would begin to dominate international athletics.

Following a truce in July 1921 between the British government and the IRA, an Irish delegation visited London, returning home with a proposed settlement to put to the Irish people. The terms of the Treaty would lead to the formation of the 26-county Irish Free State, and the six-county Northern Ireland. Partition was not an ideal solution and was a compromise that many Republicans could not accept. On 18 June 1922 the Irish population voted overwhelmingly to accept the Treaty. Just ten days later, Civil War erupted.

In 1922 there was much excitement in Irish sporting circles as a new athletics association was formed, the National Athletic and Cycling Association of Ireland (NACA). The new association merged the IAAA and GAA athletics interests and promised to bring to an end the divisions that had existed in Irish athletics since 1905. As a modern version of the Tailteann Games was being proposed for that summer, it seemed that the fortunes of athletics might again be on the rise. The idea that had been mooted for over three decades looked certain to become a reality, but this was put paid to by the Civil War. As soon as Republican and Free State troops began fighting, any thoughts of a revival of the ancient Celtic sports festival had to be shelved.

Just as had been the case during the struggle for independence, life throughout the fledgling Free State was disrupted. In Waterford there was considerable military activity in early July when Free State troops tried to enter the city, which was controlled from Ballybricken by Republicans. With the bridge raised, the Free State troops set up a sixteen-pound field gun on Misery Hill on the other side of the Suir and shelled Republican positions on the quayside. Under cover of fire, Free State soldiers crossed the river in small boats and quickly took control of the city.[3] During this time, Peter and Maggie kept the children at home because it was considered too dangerous to venture out. However, a lone sniper targeted Upton from across the river, lodging bullets in the back wall of the house and narrowly missing a window. There could be no doubt as to the seriousness of this latest conflict. In May 1923, after almost a year's fighting, Eamon de Valera's Republicans conceded defeat to the Free State government led by W.T. Cosgrave. The effects of the Civil War would be felt for many years to come.

Now that peace and some semblance of stability had been restored, the issue of the Tailteann Games was brought up once again in 1924. Its revival was something that would appeal to all Irishmen and women and O'Connor enthusiastically gave his support to the idea, although he pointed out that Irish athletes would stand little chance of achieving any notable successes "through want of competition and encouragement" in the previous fifteen years:

> I have read from time to time in the sporting pages of the newspapers the correspondence and discussions as to the feasibility of holding the Tailteann Games this summer. I am strongly in favour of their being held. They were not held last summer and very properly so, for obvious reasons. Our athletes will do the best they can and pessimists may be agreeably disappointed when they cheer some of them, perhaps to

victory. My own personal view is that it is worth holding the Tailteann Games this summer if only to show our athletes what other athletes are capable of doing as a result of systematic and scientific training.[4]

Over the course of the next eight years, O'Connor became a staunch supporter of the 1924, 1928 and 1932 Tailteann festivals. He would help promote each festival and attend the extravagant and spectacular opening ceremonies in Croke Park, at the forefront of veteran athletes leading out the competitors.

O'Connor travelled to all the Olympic Games after the Great War but the most memorable of the 1920s was undoubtedly Amsterdam in 1928. There, for the first time since the formation of the Irish Free State in 1922, Ireland won a medal when Dr Pat O'Callaghan took gold in the hammer. With O'Callaghan's victory, for the first time since Athens in 1906, an Irish flag, this time the tricolour, was raised at the Olympics. It had been a long time since an Irish athlete had made his mark on an Olympic stage and in a throwing event, which had previously been an Irish speciality. Another athlete whom O'Connor followed closely in Amsterdam was his cousin Norman Judd, who was representing Ireland in the water polo competition. Ireland only ever entered such a team event in two Olympics, Paris in 1924 and Amsterdam in 1928. Though they failed to win a medal, O'Connor must have been proud to see his cousin representing Ireland. A common love of sport now brought him back in touch with his Dublin cousins. Despite their age gap, a friendship of considerable trust and mutual respect soon developed between Norman and Peter.

ೞ

BY THE EARLY 1930S, the offices of Peter O'Connor & Son had been operating for ten years. In January 1930 Daniel Dunford died aged 91. O'Connor had optimistically expected that his former employer might leave him some testimonial in his will for all of his years' service. There was nothing, however, and O'Connor probably wondered if the old solicitor had ever really intended to leave him the practice when he died. In the time since O'Connor had taken over the office, Ireland had changed dramatically. The turbulent last decade had witnessed a successful War of Independence, followed almost immediately by a divisive Civil War and then an uneasy peace. In those years of upheaval, O'Connor quietly continued to build up his business and the practice had gone from strength to strength. For him the 1920s had been a period of consolidation and growth. His perseverance and success was recognised in 1930 when he was made a member of the Waterford Chamber of Commerce. Two of his sons had followed in his footsteps and studied law, one of whom had qualified and now joined him full-time in the office.

At this time also, O'Connor had become involved in perhaps the most high-profile legal case of his career, an alleged murder case that captured the attention of the nation and became known as the Mystery of the Missing Postman. This case concerned the mysterious disappearance of Laurence Griffin at Stradbally, County Waterford on Christmas night 1929. That day, the postman left home at 11.00 am to deliver letters in Kilmacthomas and Stradbally, some six miles away. His wife expected that her husband of 22 years would be home by 10.00 or 11.00 pm that night — but he never returned. Griffin had served in the British army during the Great War from August 1914 to mid-1916, at which date his period as a reservist expired. From 1913 until his disappearance in 1929, apart from his war service, he had been employed by the post office. Griffin was reportedly last seen alive in Stradbally that evening at 7.00 pm in Whelan's pub. When he failed to return, a massive investigation was launched. Griffin's bicycle and leggings were found on the road from Stradbally to Kilmacthomas, which led his wife and the police to suspect that he was dead.

Ten people were eventually charged in court with his alleged murder and with disposing of the body to prevent an inquest. The case attracted huge media attention as two of the accused were civic guards stationed in Stradbally. In the proceedings the state was represented by Mr Finley, barrister-at-law. A Mr M.J. Connolly BL defended seven of the accused and was instructed by

Peter O'Connor. The case was heard at a special court and later at the district court on and off in 1930, from 25 January to 5 March. The accused were remanded from week to week over this period and spent their time in Waterford Jail. Proceedings were dragged out by the fact that, despite extensive searches, no body had been found. In the absence of a body, it was impossible to know whether he died accidentally or as a result of foul play.[5]

Because of the huge media attention that this case attracted, and the fact that two guards were suspects in the affair, General Eoin O'Duffy, the chief Commissioner of the Garda Síochána, came down to Waterford to take control of the inquiry into Griffin's disappearance. The case continued to dominate national headlines for the six weeks in which the prisoners were remanded in custody, an unusual step considering that there was no hard evidence against any of the accused. Eventually, for lack of evidence and the absence of a body, the case was dismissed.

The following July, five actions for libel were heard by Justice Hanna and a jury against the *Waterford News*, arising out of an article describing the mysterious events at Stradbally. During the course of these proceedings, one of the defendants was cross-examined and said that she had been in constant communication with her solicitor, Peter O'Connor, when in jail. The article only came to her attention when O'Connor had brought it in to her. When the defendants were eventually released from jail, O'Connor successfully pursued a libel case against both the *Waterford News* and the *Cork Examiner* on behalf of five of the acquitted defendants. Eighteen months later, Mrs Griffin applied through the courts for access to her husband's pension, which was granted. To this day Laurence Griffin's disappearance has never been accounted for.

The unsolved mystery was the most extraordinary and perplexing legal case that Peter O'Connor ever worked on. Over the years, during many late-night fireside chats, he would muse about it. The case was also memorable in that it provided the first opportunity for O'Connor to further his acquaintance with General Eoin O'Duffy, who was about to play a vital role in Irish athletics in the coming years.

A New Beginning for Irish Athletics

AFTER PETER O'CONNOR'S ATTEMPTS to act as a peace-broker between the IAAA and GAA in 1909, for over two decades he steered clear of the politics behind athletics in Ireland. In those years O'Connor remained an enthusiastic supporter of athletic events up and down the country, and he particularly championed the Tailteann festivals. At the beginning of the 1930s he was once again drawn into the Irish athletics scene. The principal catalyst for this was General Eoin O'Duffy, a highly colourful and charismatic figure in Irish public life. O'Duffy's emergence as the official spokesperson for Irish athletics after taking over the NACA presidency in January 1931 promised a revitalising influence in the sport, something O'Connor held dear. Irish athletics was also facing its biggest crisis since the birth of the NACA in the wake of the formation of the Irish Free State: how to avoid a "partition" of the association following the emergence of a new Northern athletic body that was affiliated to the English AAA. As it was the question of partition that had effectively caused the Civil War between 1922 and 1923, the issue was extremely delicate and needed to be handled with considerable care and tact. O'Duffy was then Commissioner of the Garda Síochána and had considerable experience in political matters. A well-known and powerful figure within the Irish political spectrum, many hoped that he might be able to bring about a settlement.

From the very first moment that Eoin O'Duffy's tenure at the NACA began, he set about giving a kickstart to Irish athletics. In his opening keynote speech at the 1931 NACA congress, he put forward an ambitious and far-reaching agenda aimed at restoring interest in athletics. He proposed holdings meetings throughout the country and involving local politicians, senators, clergy and Gardaí. He hoped that these meetings would encourage athletes and raise finances to clear off the NACA's debt and provide funds to send a team to the forthcoming Los Angeles Olympics.[1] O'Duffy had a particular interest in seeing Ireland make its mark at the Olympics. As early as 1922, when he was Chief of Staff of the National Army, O'Duffy had summoned J.J. Keane, then chairman of the GAA athletic council, and requested that he would without delay "devote himself to the unification of the various athletic bodies in Ireland and, of greater importance, he was to ensure that Ireland, as an independent nation, would be adequately represented" at the Paris Games in 1924.[2] O'Duffy's interest in athletics was passionate rather than political and it was this pure, unadulterated love of sport that clearly struck O'Connor, who would later declare that O'Duffy was the greatest lover of sport that he had ever known. O'Duffy was also proactive in involving high-profile veteran athletes such as O'Connor and Kiely in get-togethers and meetings to support fundraising ventures.

Within only two months of O'Duffy's presidency, Irish athletics celebrated a notable first as Tim Smythe won an international cross-country race at Baldoyle racecourse, finishing 100 metres ahead of an international field. That night O'Duffy spoke at a banquet to celebrate the fine victory, which was attended by President Cosgrave and several government ministers.[3] A key player in the Cosgrave pro-Treaty regime, the new NACA President had connections and influence at the highest level. Under Michael Collins, O'Duffy had been Chief of Staff of the IRA in 1921. After the Treaty, he progressed to Chief of Staff of the National Army in 1922 before becoming Commissioner of the Garda Síochána in 1923, a position he still maintained. With such close links to the Government of the day, the future of Irish athletics seemed to be in safe hands. It was immediately clear to veteran athletes such as O'Connor that O'Duffy could be just the man to put athletics back on the map.

By the annual congress at the end of January 1932, the NACA's debt of £800 was wiped out and the association had some £2000 in the coffers, thanks to fundraising campaigns. O'Duffy then revealed his vision for the revival of Irish athletics, even suggesting that Ireland could hold an Olympics if a suitable stadium was built, although such an undertaking should not be inititated until steps had been taken to nurture the athletic talent of the nation by investing in school grounds and sports centres.[4] In just over a year O'Duffy had left his mark on Irish athletics, the NACA was out of debt and an end to the dispute regarding the Northern counties looked likely.

However, two months after the 1932 annual congress, Irish athletics was once again in crisis as, following criticism in the *Irish Press* and from the previous President of the NACA, Dr E. O'Sullivan, O'Duffy sensationally resigned from all of the sports bodies of which he was a member. After such a successful start to his term as President of the NACA, O'Duffy's sudden resignation rocked Irish athletics. So close to the Los Angeles Olympics, his departure also seriously undermined any hopes that Ireland might be able to clarify its position in relation to Irish representation when IOC delegates met for the Olympic Congress in Los Angeles. Now more than ever, Irish athletics needed a negotiator who had influence at the highest level, someone with enough charm and charisma to foil British attempts to have Northern Irish athletes assimilated into the British team. The stakes were high and O'Duffy as President of the Olympic Council had been expected to fight Ireland's cause. With him out of the picture, Ireland's chances of success would be greatly reduced.

Another reason the prospect of O'Duffy's departure was so sorely felt by the likes of Peter O'Connor and Tom Kiely was because he was undoubtedly the most important figure in Irish sport. At the time of his shock resignation, apart from his roles in the NACA and the Olympic Council, O'Duffy was a member of the central council of the GAA and the Tailteann Council, Treas-

urer of the GAA Ulster Council and Vice President of both the
Boxing Council and the Central Handball Council. A key player in
both the GAA and NACA, his influence permeated through the
ranks of Irish sport, leaving him in a unique position to unite
sporting factions that were traditionally opposed to each other.
O'Duffy was just the kind of "strong man" who might have been
able to heal the rifts between the GAA and IAAA in 1909. Since
that dispute, Irish athletics had gone through the doldrums while
the GAA had prospered. In the short time O'Duffy held the
NACA presidency, he had begun to redress the imbalance between Gaelic sports and traditional track and field athletics. Now
all the ground that had been gained stood to be lost. It is little
wonder that veteran athletes such as O'Connor, Kiely and others
rallied to defend O'Duffy. The temperamental general with the
seeming Midas touch was the lynchpin vital to the recovery of
Irish athletics.

The following day in the *Irish Independent* O'Connor expressed
genuine sorrow at the news of O'Duffy's resignation, though he
professed to understand his reason for doing so. Perhaps more
serious than the *Irish Press* attack was the criticism of Dr
O'Sullivan, whose opinions still carried a lot of weight both
within and outside the association. Thus it was clear to O'Connor
that O'Duffy "had no option but to do as he has done". Nonetheless he regretted the general's swift response and expressed the
hope that he would not as yet return the subscriptions worth
£1,500 that he had already collected on behalf of Irish athletics.
Most significantly, O'Connor called on O'Sullivan to follow the
"sportsmanlike example of the *Irish Press* and withdraw his opposition to the honorable settlement" that O'Duffy had negotiated to
solve the Northern question and restore the unity of Irish athletics. O'Connor's support and praise were unequivocal and calculated to minimise the damage caused by the former President of
the NACA and the newspaper.

> Through his great tact, organising ability, and pleasing per-
> sonality, he has caused a wonderful revival of sport in all its
> many branches which is good for our youth and for our coun-

try. His has been a very heavy and laborious task. He has un-
selfishly devoted his leisure hours and freely given his organising ability and talents to fostering and encouraging the
physical development of our youth, and, in my opinion no
Irishman could undertake a greater or nobler work. Let us all
hope he may see his way to continue his good work.[5]

Tom Kiely likewise fiercely defended O'Duffy, remarking that he
was the "most important and influential figure in Irish athletics
since Maurice Davin died". The views of the *Irish Press*, Kiely felt,
were unrepresentative of any large or important section of Gaels.
Perhaps influenced by this public show of solidarity from distinguished and respected veterans, O'Duffy withdrew his resignation, thereby ensuring that a forceful negotiator would represent
Irish interests when the IOC met in Los Angeles.

In the wake of the Irish Civil War, great tensions permeated
Irish political life as disparate pro-treaty and anti-treaty elements
strove for supremacy. Following a change of government early in
1932, Eamon de Valera's anti-treaty Fianna Fáil assumed power.
The new President initially used his power responsibly resisting
any temptation to punish those in the previous administration
responsible for keeping him in the political wilderness since the
onset of the Civil War. The handover of power was remarkably
smooth, considering the bloody and divisive conflict of 1922–23.
Rumours that the Army might stage a coup proved to be without
foundation and the Irish Free State's first true test of democracy
was passed with flying colours. Though no heads rolled in the old
administration as de Valera took over the reins in January 1932,
early the following year General O'Duffy would become the first
high-profile casualty of the old regime. Considered too risky to
remove O'Duffy in 1932, de Valera bided his time before disposing of O'Duffy's services.

It is quite possible that the *Irish Press*'s attack on O'Duffy in
January 1932 may have been politically motivated and an early
attempt to destabilise one who had been such a key figure in Cosgrave's regime. The *Irish Press* had been founded by de Valera in
early 1931 and was an ideal medium for his new party's propa-

ganda. Peter O'Connor's later antipathy towards "Dev" possibly
dated from this time. Before the newspaper's attack on O'Duffy, it
seemed that a resolution to the Northern athletics question was
within reach. Sport was O'Connor's first love and he probably did
not care to see outside political considerations once again interfering in the athletics world he loved so dearly. He certainly did not
want to see the current crisis take the same route as national
politics:

> The athletic platform of sport has been, and I hope shall al-
> ways be, kept clear of religion and politics so that all genuine
> lovers of sport could meet in friendly intercourse. This is nec-
> essary as athletics and sport are world-wide and, therefore, in-
> ternational. We do not wish or desire them to be purely
> provincial.[6]

By 20 March 1932, when an emergency meeting of the NACA was
held, O'Duffy agreed to retain his presidency of the association
and do Ireland's bidding at the Olympic congress in Los Angeles.
Immediate disaster had been averted and hope was restored.
O'Duffy had, however, shown the first signs of his volatility and
would yet prove to be something of a loose cannon.

∞

IN AUGUST OF 1932, THE OLYMPIC GAMES was set to return to
America for only the second time since St Louis in 1904. The tenth
modern Olympics Games was to be held in Los Angeles, California, the sunshine state.

For Peter O'Connor, who had by this time been to America
many times, this would prove the most memorable visit he had
undertaken since his historic first trip in 1901. The Los Angeles
Games were particularly special for O'Connor as he was not going
just as a spectator this time but in an official capacity, first as a
judge and second as an NACA delegate to the International Amateur Athletic Federation Conference. Knowing that he would once
again be taking an active role at an Olympics must have been

deeply gratifying for him. He had been to every Games since Athens in 1906 but this was the first time he had been asked to officiate.

On 10 July 1932, the Irish contingent, led by General O'Duffy, and including O'Connor and the Kirwan brothers, left Cobh for America on the *SS Baltic*. The four track and field athletes — hurdler Bob Tisdall, hammer-thrower Pat O'Callaghan, steeplechaser Michael Murphy and triple jumper Eamon Fitzgerald — had left Cobh a week before to become acclimatised to the Californian sun and atmosphere before they took part in the Games. The remainder of O'Duffy's team were made up of Irish boxers: J. Murphy, light heavyweight European champion; J. Flood, Irish lightweight champion; Ernie Smith, Irish welterweight champion; and P. Hughes, Irish bantamweight champion.

Everybody on board the liner took a shine to the four Dublin boxers and O'Connor particularly enjoyed their company. The boxers were a "distinct acquisition to the party".

> Their accomplishments, especially from the humorous angle, constituted them the life and soul of whatever merriment was organised. Their quaint Dublin accent, their fund of comic numbers, their wit and repartee, made them quite an entertainment troupe in themselves. They were great favourites throughout the voyage and as dancers they gave first to nobody.[7]

Excellent catering arrangements had been made for the comfort of the Irish contingent during the trip across as special two-berth accommodation was provided for each member and facilities included first-class swimming baths and gymnasiums. O'Connor loved life on board a luxury liner and could not praise the voyage across enough. His trip this time was certainly much different to his first visit in 1901. Now above deck and in the lap of luxury, he delighted in the "complete restfulness of body, and the mental exhilaration induced by the bracing fresh open air, which is entirely free from microbial infection". Nor did the Irishmen miss home cooking during the crossing, the food being so plentiful and of such a high standard that some of the boxers had trouble controlling their appetites.

> Naturally the question of food would be a consideration in the case of a body of competitors who were out to seek world honours, and in reply to a query in this connection O'Connor said the dietary was beyond compare. In fact he continued with a humorous twinkle, our great trouble was to keep the boxers from putting on weight beyond the standard at which they had entered in their several events. As a matter of fact, Mr Flood put on a stone extra, and he had some trouble in reducing. However, said Mr O'Connor with a reminiscent laugh, he achieved it in the end.[8]

On the journey across the veteran Irish athletes enthusiastically set about forming a sports committee, organising a range of sporting diversions from athletic events to deck tennis, quoits and ping pong. There was also plenty of nighttime entertainment and once again the Irishmen were to the fore and, when it came to Irish humour, "the general talent displayed was of the very highest standard, while the comedy of the four Dublin boxers was inimitable". O'Duffy used the trip to fine-tune his oratorical skills, making several speeches, "delivered with great brilliance and clarity of enunciation", his final speech at the conclusion of the programme being "a masterpiece of wit and oratory" — according to O'Connor!

After a thoroughly relaxing and smooth crossing, the *Baltic* approached its landing berth in New York where a huge reception committee was eagerly awaiting their arrival shoreside. The New York Irish-American community, city dignitaries and police had an unforgettable welcome in store for them.

> Long before we landed, we could see thousands of people assembled in the vicinity of the ship's berthage. When we got to within hearing distance, their cheering and their shouts of "céad míle fáilte" at once proclaimed them to be Irish. As the first members of the party from Ireland appeared at the head of the gangway preliminary to their stepping ashore, cheer upon

cheer rent the air. Everyone wanted to shake hands with all of us at the one time, and questions about the welfare of the "old country" were hurled at us with amazing speed and volubility. The rousing nature of our reception will never leave my memory. Photographers got special permission to enter the ship and photograph the party of Irishmen. I have rarely had to face such batteries of cameras as on this occasion.[9]

Eventually they succeeded in making their way through the admiring and enthusiastic crowd to a fleet of NYPD cars which had been placed at their disposal and shuttled them across New York city in double-quick time. O'Connor noted that this VIP treatment was a special compliment to O'Duffy as Commissioner of the Garda Síochána. The huge proportion of Irish-Americans and former Irish sportsmen in the NYPD and police forces across America meant that wherever the Irish contingent led by O'Duffy went they received incredible hospitality.

In 1932, the American economy was still trying to recover from the Wall Street crash of 1929, which had triggered the Depression. Prohibition outlawed the sale of alcohol and gangsters were enjoying their heyday. Everywhere O'Connor went he observed that Irishmen seemed to be policing the nation. In the 31 years since his first visit, O'Connor would now see at first-hand how far the Irish-American community had progressed and the extent to which they had successfully integrated into American society and prospered. O'Connor met many Irishmen and women who had started from scratch in America and had now made good, in particular many old friends he had known through athletics who were now well up the hierarchy of various police forces. Athletics had proved a window of opportunity for many of the Irish sporting diaspora, enabling them to carve out careers in American police forces. In contrast to his American adventure in 1901, when O'Connor was, often to his detriment, very much the centre of attention, this time as an official he would be able to delight in all the trappings of stardom unique to the Olympic experience.

Once whisked away to the accompaniment of thunderous cheering, the first stop of the Irish contingent was the headquarters of the NYPD, where the team was shown around and entertained. There followed a magnificent reception and banquet for over 100 guests at the New York Athletic Club. Amongst the many prominent figures from New York's Irish community who attended were Liam O'Shea, sports editor of the Irish-American paper, *The Advocate*, an old friend of O'Connor's; Wedger Meagher, sports editor of *The Echo*; the President of the NYAC, Cunningham; and two brothers of Martin Sheridan, the hero of the 1906 Athens Games. Like their famous brother from Bohola, County Mayo, the two had emigrated and one was now a leading New York solicitor and the other a captain of police. After the banquet, the Irishmen were given a three-hour whistle-stop tour of New York's most important landmarks and places of historical interest.

That evening at 6.00 pm, their last stop was the Pennsylvanian railroad station where they commenced the long four-day transcontinental journey to Los Angeles. They did not make the journey unbroken, however:

> . . . once more the thoughtfulness and foresight of General
> O'Duffy who was with us all the time manifested itself. In the
> interests of the competitors and fearing that such a wearisome
> journey would tend to render them tired or unfit, General
> O'Duffy arranged for certain breaks on the way.

Thus the Irish contingent stopped en route, spending nights in Chicago and Denver as well as a short five-hour break in Salt Lake City. In each place, O'Duffy had arranged overnight accommodation and, as in New York, motor car transport was provided free for sightseeing. Wherever they stopped, O'Connor and the Kirwan brothers met many veteran Irish athletes, the majority of whom had become policemen. On one occasion, an old Irish friend "in the know" brought them to a speakeasy for a drink, something Percy Kirwan remembered with amusement years later.

The party eventually reached Los Angeles after almost a week's travel from New York. The reception they got in the Californian city was on a par with that in New York. Wherever they went the Irishmen were treated like heroes. People of Irish descent came out in their thousands to welcome the champions of the land that they and their forefathers had been forced to leave.

> Fully ten thousand people turned out to meet us on our arrival. They were accompanied by bands and banners. For over an hour the Irish travellers were unable to leave the precincts of the railroad station. Eventually, however, after a brief interval of introspection, a passage was forced for us to the entrance to the station, where we found the Mayor of Los Angeles, presidents of the different Irish athletic societies and the Chief of Police of Los Angeles. . . . The thousands of people who were unable to gain entrance to the railway station insisted on shaking hands and having a word or two with each member of the contingent before releasing them. The proceedings here wound up with a splendid oration from General O'Duffy, who for the time became the hero of the hour.[10]

ೞ

LOS ANGELES PROMISED TO BE the most high-profile venue for any Olympic Games to date and, as home to the Hollywood movie industry, images of the Games would be immortalised on celluloid and replayed in newsreels right across the world. Six months before they were due to start, a doubt hung over whether they would take place at all. A magnificent stadium awaited American and international competitors but the effects of the Great Depression meant that many foreign countries were slow in committing teams to making the long and expensive journey to LA. Many tickets for the Games remained unsold and it was feared that the stadium might remain relatively empty during the event. The intervention of several Hollywood movie stars — Douglas Fairbanks Jr, Charlie Chaplin, Marlene Dietrich and Mary Pickford — saw ticket sales rise as they and other stars undertook to entertain the crowds. The modern Olympics was about to experience more glitz and glamour than it had ever known as international sports stars rubbed shoulders with film stars and celebrities. In the end, some 1,408 male and female athletes from over 37 countries *did* make the journey to contest 116 events.

Now that their roller coaster trip was at an end, the Irish team met up with the other Irish athletes already stationed in the Olympic village. This was not the first time that a designated residence had been provided for visiting athletes. That honour fell to the Zappeion at Athens in 1906. The Olympic village at Los Angeles did, however, eclipse anything that had previously been provided for competitors. The purpose-built village that was constructed at LA would become the model for all subsequent Olympic villages.

Built on 321 acres on hills overlooking Los Angeles, some eight miles of streets had been laid down to accommodate over 500 portable two-bedroom bungalows. Security in the village was provided by gauchos on horseback, who also did many impromptu exhibitions. The makeshift city that had been built to house the male competitors and officials at the Games was designed to be self-sufficient and housed a hospital, post office, library and several restaurants. (Female competitors were housed in various hotels.) In this "miniature temporary city of Olympia", the facilities and food were the very best. As an official at the Games, O'Connor had the chance to stay in the Olympic village and he marvelled at the care and attention lavished on the layout. As a keen gardener, he was distinctly amazed that "the grass in the vast enclosure was always green and neatly trimmed as a tennis court . . . thanks to underground pipes that enabled sprays to irrigate the lawns". At a time when the world was still in the grip of the Great Depression, the seemingly utopian Olympic village and the massive Coliseum stadium with a capacity of 105,000 were in stark contrast to the prevailing economic reality of life in America in the early 1930s. The facilities provided were the best O'Connor had ever seen and enhanced the athletes' capabilities. As judges, he and Percy Kirwan had the opportunity to inspect first-hand the LA track, and see at close quarters an entirely different breed of athlete to that of his day. Subsequently, in a letter to Denis Power, O'Connor commented that in LA:

> The ground was a veritable springboard, built on cotton fibre, and had we such facilities and training in our day, existing records would be small compared with what I believe we could have done on such grounds and [with] proper training. We were in the old days just like cart horses as compared with present day athletes who with scientific training are like race horses.[11]

When Bob Tisdall and Pat O'Callaghan took to the Coliseum Stadium on 1 August 1932, both Irish athletes were determined to bring home gold but neither could have imagined the drama that would unfold. On the opening day of competition, Bob Tisdall had shown that he was a serious contender for gold, winning his first heat in the 440-metre hurdles in a time of 54.8 seconds. Two hours later, he comfortably dominated the semi-finals, clocking 52.8 seconds. When Tisdall turned up for the final the following Monday at 3.00 pm, Pat O'Callaghan, the reigning Olympic hammer champion, was about to contest the final of the hammer. O'Callaghan was in second place behind a Finn, Porhola. Tisdall's fate would be decided first and in the 440-metre hurdles he lined out against a Swede, Areshoug, an Italian, Facelli, Taylor and Hardin of the US and the defending British champion Lord Burghey. Tisdall got an excellent start and was well ahead of the field as he approached the final hurdle. Disaster almost struck at the last when, being extra careful, he bundled over it. After faltering momentarily, Tisdall quickly regained his composure and coasted home just ahead of the two Americans to take gold. His time of 51.7 seconds was a new Olympic and world record but, as he had knocked over a hurdle, the rules of the time dictated that the Olympic record went to the second placed Hardin, who finished in 51.9 seconds. Ireland had taken its first gold at the Games but yet more excitement was about to come as Pat O'Callaghan attempted his second successive Olympic title. The Corkman had unfortunately worn the wrong shoes for the occasion and his throwing was consequently affected. In between throws, he hastened to an equipment room, desperately trying to pare down the spikes on his shoes that were interfering with his throwing pattern. When Tisdall realised what was going on, he immediately came to O'Callaghan's aid and busily set about trying to remove the spikes. O'Callaghan was still trailing Porhola when he stepped up for his final throw — everything was down to his last effort. He later said that after seeing Tisdall's victory, "I felt then I would be a very poor Irishman if in the circumstances I did not rise to the occasion." Though he had not managed to remove all of the spikes in his shoes, O'Callaghan made one last superhuman try and saw his hammer sail over 5′ 5″ past the Finn's leading mark. The throw under incredible pressure was the stuff of legend, as Tisdall later recalled:

> There was pandemonium in the stadium. Speech was impossible for almost five minutes, and the few who did not appear to be Irish were shouting, if not for the significance of the achievement, for the manner of its doing. It was indeed a great achievement for Ireland.

For O'Connor, Pat O'Callaghan was "unquestionably the most outstanding and most popular figure in LA". The manner in which he defended his Olympic hammer title on his last throw caused the 105,000 spectators in the stadium to practically "rise at him as one man when he achieved this great feat". O'Connor was no less impressed by Bob Tisdall, calling him "a most gentlemanly and unassuming athlete". Tisdall's last-minute decision to compete in the decathlon some four days later was equally a source of infinite pleasure to O'Connor, even though he only stood the slimmest chance of finishing on the podium.

> I was always proud to hear the announcement during these two trying days repeatedly call out the name of Tisdall, Tisdall of Ireland about to run or about to jump, was sung out dozens of times. The phrase sent a thrill through everyone who had a strain of Irish blood in his veins. [12]

For the first time, thanks to two extraordinary athletes, the Irish nation finally made a real impact at a modern Olympic Games. O'Connor, of course, knew of the many Irish athletes, including himself, who had won honours for Ireland in the past. This was undoubtedly Ireland's finest hour since the formation of the Irish Free State. This time there was to be no denying Ireland its victory and as the Irish tricolour was raised to celebrate the Irishmen's victories, *Amhrán na bhFiann*, the Irish national anthem, echoed throughout the stadium. In just over an hour, Tisdall and O'Callaghan had taken two of the 21 gold medals available in track and field at LA — the same tally Great Britain took home.

CB

EVEN BEFORE THE COMPETITIONS had commenced, the Irish contingent received a deluge of invitations from film stars and the Irish-American community.

> Despite the fact that it must have been a matter of common property that competitors were undergoing a strenuous course of training, invitations to banquets and entertainment parties were continually pouring in from well-known Irish residents of Los Angeles and the surrounding suburbs. Perhaps the most delightful of these invitations were those which took the form of placing their private beaches along the seaside at the disposal of the visitors by several residents. Those beach strips were most enchanting in their loveliness and general layout but there was not one of them to compare with our own beautiful strand at Tramore.[13]

O'Connor believed that "no country in the world was so much honoured in the warmth of the welcome extended to its athletic representatives as was Ireland, this amazing demonstration of appreciation and affection thanks to the large proportion of Irish exiles or descendants of Irish exiles who found a home in LA city". He also observed that "these Irishmen seem to have made good, for large numbers of them hold leading positions there". This fact was underlined when the whole Irish team was invited to visit Fox film studios and special buses were laid on by the studio to bring them out there. This was one of the undoubted highlights of the trip and once again they were greeted by many Irishmen and women who had prospered in Hollywood. At Fox there were strong Irish and Waterford connections, one of the studio's presidents being the nephew of Dr Sheehan, a former Bishop of Waterford and Lismore. Strolling through film sets and mixing with film stars, starlets and extras, the Irishmen met George O'Brien and Maureen O'Sullivan who were supposedly shooting a picture in which 1,894 people were employed. The studio sets covered some 150 acres and, to O'Connor's amazement, had buildings representative of every nationality. During the visit, the Irish contingent was photographed with many leading Hollywood stars. It was possibly during this fantastic outing to Fox film studios that Pat O'Callaghan first came to the attention of studio bosses who were looking for a new lead actor to play Tarzan. Impressed by the Cork man's burly frame and impressive stature, they managed to convince O'Callaghan to take a screen test. Later he would be offered a chance to stay on in Hollywood and try his hand at acting. O'Callaghan, who was already a practising doctor, turned down the offer. Interestingly, Johnny Weissmuller, a former Olympic swimming champion, landed the role of Tarzan alongside the Irish-American star Maureen O'Sullivan.

Some days after his famous victory in the 440m hurdles and much to his delight, Bob Tisdall was invited to a lavish party given by Douglas Fairbanks. With his mission on the sports field accomplished, Tisdall could now relax and, borrowing a motor car from a friend, he began driving through Hollywood in the hope of finding Fairbanks's mansion. After parking outside what he believed to be the right house, he knocked on the front door, only to be confronted by a rather surly butler who informed him that he was at Charlie Chaplin's residence. After making his apologies and now armed with the right directions, the Irish champion eventually found his way to the party at "Pick Fair", Hollywood's equivalent of Buckingham Palace. Once there, he met the hostess Mary Pickford and sat beside the aviator Amelia Earhart at dinner. As the evening progressed, Tisdall discovered that Fairbanks had won $1,000 in a bet thanks to his victory in the hurdles. Apparently, Fairbanks and Will Rogers had been wandering about the Olympic village, looking for some tips on who were the likely favourites. Someone had suggested the Irishman and when Tisdall romped home to Olympic gold, he unexpectedly made friends in high places.[14]

While the Irish athletes stayed on in Hollywood, soaking up the limelight and celebrity lifestyle before leaving for home, Peter O'Connor, along with Percy and Rody Kirwan, took the opportunity to do some sightseeing. Thanks to a Cork Athletic Association at San Rafael, planes were laid on for them. Never having flown before, O'Connor relished the experience, claiming that "it was the pleasantest sensation I ever experienced. No motor car, train or majestic liner could be steadier in its motion. There was almost a complete absence of vibration." Everywhere they went, once again old friends greeted them. They met Nick Barron in San Francisco, a former Irish long-distance runner and now a chief of police in Chicago. In Seattle, they spent some time with Con Walsh, a former hammer-throwing champion and now an inspector of police. The most extraordinary sight they witnessed was in San Rafael, however, where they attended a picnic and watched a hurling match between Cork and Kerry, rounded off by a "rollicking real Irish Dance". Over 30,000 people turned up that day at San Rafael and Peter O'Connor and Rody Kirwan wondered whether they "were in California and not in Ireland so thoroughly was the atmosphere created".[15]

ロ

AFTER THE SUCCESS ON THE SPORTS FIELD and lapping up the festive atmosphere at the Games, a great challenge lay ahead for Irish officials within the corridors of power that ruled international athletics. This final part of the LA story would be played out behind closed doors and concerned the Irish delegation's attempts to resolve the issue of Irish representation and ensure that the 32 counties of Ireland would appear at future Olympics under one flag and one athletics body. It was apt that O'Connor, whose flag protest had caused such a controversy at the Athens Games in 1906, was one of O'Duffy's key advisors and party to the International Amateur Athletic Federation (IAAF) conference that took place a few days after the Games closed. The Irish dispute had been referred to the Congress by the Council of the IAAF in May 1931 after the NACA protested against the English AAA's involvement in athletics in Northern Ireland. When the issue was brought up, O'Duffy argued that there had been no change in the political situation in Ireland since 1924, thereby inferring that the AAA's interference in Ulster was unjustified, since "decisions of Congress should not be subject to change unless circumstances have changed since previous decisions were taken". The President accepted O'Duffy's point of order and said the matter should now be dealt with by the Congress. Just when it seemed that the issue might be resolved internationally rather than domestically, O'Duffy suddenly found himself outmanoeuvred when the Italian delegate proposed, and the Polish delegate seconded, the motion that the matter should not be further discussed. Much to O'Duffy's surprise, the President of the Congress allowed the motion, though it went against his earlier ruling. A vote was taken and, of the 18 delegates who voted, only six supported the Irish request to debate the issue. The motion to discontinue the discussion now passed, the matter was deemed closed and the Congress proceeded to the next items on the agenda.

The thorny issue that the NACA had desperately hoped to see settled in their favour had not even been broached. The Irishmen had secured the support of the majority of the delegates but with the issue now postponed, an English delegate gloated to O'Callaghan, "you had the dagos and the majority but we will get you in the committee".[16] O'Duffy interpreted the curtailed debate as signifying that the status quo remained. This proved to be an optimistic reading of the situation. With no decision taken at international level and no official reaction to the AAA's interest in athletics in Northern Ireland, the issue was unresolved. At the time, the consequence of this meeting remained unclear, but it would soon become apparent that this was a pivotal moment for Irish athletics. The issue of representation would come to the fore before long and regrettably would result in no Irish participation at the next Olympic Games in Berlin. An important opportunity had been lost and, though it may have seemed otherwise, the NACA's grip on athletics in Northern Ireland was seriously weakened.

Though Irish officials failed to carry the day in the diplomatic arena, the Los Angeles Games were an undoubted success for the Irish team. While none of the boxers took a medal and Eamon Fitzgerald had been unlucky to finish fourth in the triple jump, a mere inch outside the bronze medal, the successes of O'Callaghan and Tisdall had placed Irish athletics in the spotlight. According to Peter O'Connor, the success of the trip, from inception to conclusion, was thanks to O'Duffy, and he was glowing in his praise for the NACA president.

> The main credit for this happy state of affairs is due to General O'Duffy, who is a gentleman of extraordinary enterprise and organising ability, and the various receptions and entertainments organised for the Irish party in Los Angeles and other American cities may be attributed to his remarkable personality, which won for him everywhere the esteem and respect of the representatives of all countries with whom he came into contact. If it had not been for the efforts of General O'Duffy in launching forth the great athletic movement of the past few years, there might not have been any competitors either for Amsterdam in 1928 or for Olympia in 1932. . . . The performance of the Irish contingent on this occasion, and the great social success of General O'Duffy, has helped to give Ireland a place on the map, which it never has held before, not only in the athletic but in the political world.[17]

The whole Los Angeles experience would remain one of the most memorable in O'Connor's life. For a man who had grown up in a small fishing town and spent his youth surrounded by boats, he could never have imagined that at the age of almost 60 he would have the chance to rise to such dizzy heights and travel in an aeroplane. But it was the victories of Tisdall and O'Callaghan that he would remember best, as well as the Irish anthem that twice resounded throughout a packed Coliseum stadium. Unlike Athens in 1906, no protests were necessary. The Irish tricolour simply took its place with the flags of other nations. The significance of this emotive moment was not lost on O'Connor.

When the Irish contingent finally left LA on 15 August they went directly to New York without stopping off as they had on the outward journey. The worst leg of this incredibly long rail journey was the crossing of the dusty Arizona desert in scorching heat. According to Bob Tisdall, in a moment of extreme thirst, O'Duffy, desperate to get at a bottle of whiskey that had been stowed away in a locked case, used a pistol to blow off the lock. O'Duffy's status as Garda Commissioner had probably helped him to get the whiskey past the customs and also allowed him to carry a pistol. In this time of prohibition, the organisers of the Los Angeles Games had given dispensations to certain European teams, such as the Italians, to whom red wine was an integral part of a champion athlete's diet. No dispensations had, however, been made for whiskey, although it may indeed have had medicinal purposes!

Four days later, the Irish contingent arrived in New York and following a "wonderful send off" they departed America, homeward bound on the *Majestic*, then reputedly the largest liner in the world.

ଔ

AFTER THE NEWS OF THE VICTORIES of Tisdall and O'Callaghan had reached Irish shores, extensive preparations were made to welcome the conquering heroes home. On their arrival in Dun Laoghaire, government cars transported them to the RDS, where an impressive parade had assembled. Led by the Number One Army Band, veteran athletes, including O'Connor, the Garda Motor Cycle Corps, army athletes, boxers, athletes and over 100 Gardaí marched towards the city centre. At the Mansion House, O'Duffy, O'Callaghan and Tisdall were met by Lord Mayor Alfie Byrne, who pronounced with great optimism that "the impetus given to amateur sport in Ireland will have a far-reaching effect on the future physical development of our youth and assist in no small measure in the onward march of the nation". It was a heady speech that tapped into the delirium and hysteria which the two gold medals had brought about. From the Mansion House, the party continued to the Gresham Hotel on O'Connell Street where, once outside the hotel, O'Duffy, O'Callaghan and Tisdall stood on a motor car and took the salute of the passing parade. Upwards of 250,000 people are thought to have thronged the streets in celebration. At the Gresham, athletes, officials and dignitaries sat down to a sumptuous banquet. After the meal, President Eamon de Valera stood to address the gathering.

> In this country we have a long and inspiring record of achievements in the field of athletics. It is a matter of pride for them to find that long tradition so admirably preserved by their Olympic success. Everyone must have felt proud that it was still possible for Ireland to get men of the type of O'Connor, Kiely, Ryan, McGrath, Sheridan — to name but a few.[18]

In the aftermath of the great homecoming celebrations, it seemed that all was once again well in Irish athletics. The achievements of O'Callaghan and Tisdall had fired the imaginations of Irish people now brimming with enthusiasm for track and field. The groundwork had been laid for a renaissance in athletics and the proactive leadership of O'Duffy seemed to promise that the Los Angeles successes could be the beginning of a new golden era in Irish sport. Not for the first time, however, hopes of a revival would be dealt a cruel blow. Irish athletics seemed destined to always be affected by political events and not long after the successful LA trip, the NACA lost its flamboyant and impulsive President.

In January of 1933, after just one year in power, Eamon de Valera took his political opponents by surprise by calling a snap election. This bold strategic move paid dividends: his party, Fianna Fáil, made significant gains, increasing its electoral share to 49 per cent with 77 seats compared to Cosgrave's pro-Treaty Cumann na nGaedheal party, which won only 48.[19] De Valera would interpret his party's victory as a mandate from the people to continue dismantling the 1922 Treaty with Britain. Within a month, de Valera dismissed Eoin O'Duffy from his post as Garda Commissioner, although he did offer him another post. O'Duffy, who had been an integral part of Irish political life since the formation of the Free State, chose to decline, preferring instead to turn his attention to national politics. Five months later, he became head of the Army Comrades Association, or ACA, whose members were mostly ex-soldiers of the Free State Army. The group, which soon became popularly known as the Blueshirts, had clashed with the IRA frequently during the recent election campaign and were increasingly being considered as the militant wing of Cumann na nGaedheal. Under O'Duffy's leadership, the ACA was now renamed the National Guard and the blueshirt uniforms were made compulsory. In a radical agenda similar to the fascist regime in Italy, O'Duffy denounced political parties and proposed remodelling the Dáil so that deputies would be elected to represent vocational groups rather than territorial constituencies.[20]

When O'Duffy became the Director General of the National Guard, the Limerick NACA county board passed a motion calling on him to resign. After consultation with "Council members and athletes" O'Duffy stood down from his Presidency, stating that "anything flavouring of politics should be taboo to the NACA". The two-and-a-half years during which O'Duffy headed up Irish athletics had been incredibly successful. His motivational skills and passion for sport had effected a long-awaited renaissance in the fortunes of Irish track and field. It would be hard to find someone who could follow in O'Duffy's footsteps and one suspects it was with heavy hearts that O'Connor and Kiely witnessed the General's withdrawal from Irish sport to concentrate on national politics. This time, there would be no public appeals or newspaper interviews calling for O'Duffy to stay. His resignation, though regrettable, was inevitable.

At this time, tensions and cracks were once again beginning to show in Irish society. Since de Valera first refused to pay the land annuities due to Britain under the 1922 Treaty, many cattle farmers had suffered huge losses and the ongoing "Economic War" with Britain saw many flock to O'Duffy's Blueshirts. As events on a national level once again gathered pace, Irish athletics gradually began to lose the significant position it had lately occupied in the public consciousness. Had O'Duffy accepted his dismissal as Garda Commissioner more gracefully and taken up another post, his connection with Irish sport and athletics itself might have continued to prosper. Smarting from his dismissal, and with his importance in Irish public life diminished, O'Duffy sought a way to challenge de Valera's administration. The skills he used to such great effect during his presidency of the NACA would prove less useful in the field of national politics and his volatility soon led him into trouble.

After the Blueshirts were declared an illegal organisation in 1934, O'Duffy went on to form a new political party, merging Cumann na nGaedheal and the National Guard. The new party was the United Ireland Party, now known as Fine Gael, and was effectively a coalition between Cumann na nGaedheal and the smaller parties in the Dáil, with the exception of Labour. His presidency did not survive the first party conference, however, after he openly encouraged farmers to withhold the payment of rates and following recent speeches where he had suggested an invasion of Northern Ireland to drive the British out. By 1936, when the Berlin Olympics took place in the absence of an Irish team, O'Duffy was busy forming a brigade to go and fight for Franco in Spain. Though Duffy's Irish brigade had a negligible impact on events in the Spanish Civil War, it is principally for this somewhat disastrous and farcical expedition that he is chiefly remembered.

Yet before O'Duffy was drawn into the mire of Irish national politics in the 1930s, and before he became enamoured with corporatism and fascism, he was undoubtedly a key figure within Irish sporting life. One can only wonder what direction Irish athletics might have taken had O'Duffy decided to leave the stuff of politics to others and dedicated his energy and enthusiasm to Irish sport.

బ

FOLLOWING THE LOS ANGELES TRIP, Peter O'Connor celebrated his sixtieth birthday that October and just weeks later received an unexpected and belated birthday present. On 8 December 1932, he was one of two men elected to the vice-presidency of the Incorporated Law Society. The Incorporated Law Society of Ireland was and remains a prestigious body, incorporated by a Royal Charter in 1852. The Law Society's responsibilities include providing for the apprenticeship of solicitors and their education, training and examinations. The Society also carries out important disciplinary functions, investigating the conduct of solicitors and also operating as a representative body for solicitors. When O'Connor was elected vice-president, the council comprised 31 ordinary members, who were voted in by the members of the society for one-year terms. Being made Vice-President of such an important body at the age of 60 was a milestone in O'Connor's life. It signified the pinnacle of achievement in his professional career, his election a tacit recognition from his peers that he had now scaled the heights of the legal profession.

During the Economic War, life in Ireland became particularly difficult. Huge tariffs imposed on exports of cattle by the British government crippled many farmers and had a knock-on effect on the economy at large. These hardships were also felt in the offices of Peter O'Connor & Son and at one point O'Connor had to let go some of his staff. Much of the firm's business was in the agriculture sector and many of its clients became bankrupt or teetered on the brink of ruin. As a result, O'Connor quite naturally disapproved strongly of the Economic War and was much opposed to the government.

> Owing to President de Valera acting so dishonestly in refusing to pay the British government the Land Commission annuities of £4,000,000 per year which was agreed to be paid on the signing of the treaty in 1921, for moneys advanced to enable the tenant farmers of Ireland to buy out their holdings, every head of cattle now exported to England is subject to a tariff of £6 per head and Great Britain in this way is now getting back more than £4,000,000 per year, but the farmers are the great

> sufferers, as the price they get for their cattle does not allow
> them any profit and they are in a desperate financial position.
> As a result the business of a solicitor, and also of shopkeepers,
> which chiefly depends on the prosperity of the farmer, is seri-
> ously affected.[21]

As always, O'Connor's philosophy was shaped by his deeply
pragmatic outlook on life. To his mind, de Valera's determination
to dismantle the Treaty was simply wrong economically and also
from a moral standpoint. O'Connor certainly did not believe that
de Valera had been given a mandate to dismantle what the Irish
people had approved in a referendum. Quite what O'Connor,
who was a committed pacifist, made of O'Duffy's Blueshirt
movement is not known, although he most likely sympathised
with the stand the cattle farmers were taking against de Valera's
government.

> Our present government is out to burst all capitalists, who
> through thrift, sobriety and enterprise have built up a good
> business, and accumulated sufficient wealth to provide for
> their old age, but de Valera realizing that all such capitalists
> are politically opposed to his mad methods of government
> here and his refusal to pay the Land Commission annuities to
> Great Britain, a most dishonest action, is out to ruin them. [22]

In 1936, when he attended a sports meeting in Clonmel at which
de Valera was present, he led a procession of veteran athletes with
his famous flag from Athens raised high. As the army of veteran
athletes passed by the Irish President,[23] most looked to de Valera
in salute. O'Connor, however, walked straight on, his face immu-
table and gaze fixed directly in front of him.

14

Berlin, 1936: An Irishman's Perspective of Hitler's Olympics

IN LIGHT OF IRELAND'S ASTOUNDING successes at the Los Angeles Olympics in 1932, it was disappointing and somewhat surprising that Ireland was not represented at the Berlin Games in 1936. Though the likes of O'Callaghan and Tisdall had been all-conquering on the field in Los Angeles, General Eoin O'Duffy and the NACA delegates, including O'Connor, had failed to carry the day in the diplomatic arena. The English AAA seized the initiative in February of 1933 when it changed its name to the International Board of the AAA, the Scottish AAA and the Northern Irish AAA. To the amazement of the NACA, the IAAF decided to recognise the newly named body. Just four months later, O'Duffy resigned his presidency and the NACA found itself further weakened. The situation went from bad to worse at the next IAAF conference in August 1934, as a ruling was passed which stated that "only one association could represent a nation" and crucially that "the jurisdiction of members of the IAAF is limited by the political boundaries of the country or nation they represent". The motion, which was passed despite strong opposition from Irish delegates, meant that for the NACA to be a recognised member of the IAAF, they had to give up any ambitions of an all-Ireland body. The NACA rejected the IAAF's ruling and the problem remained unresolved as the Berlin Games approached. Numerous meetings were held to address the issue but no significant progress was made.

The problem was complex and essentially political in nature. In an interview during a trip to the US in 1935, O'Connor explained the dilemma facing Irish sport in layman's terms:

> Politics ruined whatever chances there were of having Irish representation in Berlin. The Irish Athletic Association [NACA] insists on having Ireland as a whole represented. The Olympic Council refers to Ireland as the "Free State" with Ulster athletes competing for Britain. Under these circumstances it is hardly possible that we will have a team at the 1936 Olympiad and it's a great pity. . . . We held a convention in Dublin not so long ago to devise a way of getting around this political question. We finally struck on a plan which many of us thought would prove agreeable to both North and South. You see the whole argument was about the flag. The Ulster crowd wanted the Union Jack and, needless to add, the Free State delegates wanted no part of that emblem. So a suggestion came that an athletic flag emblematic of the four provinces be substituted and although this gesture was well received nothing came of the meeting. I am hoping that the various athletic bodies get together and find a way whereby Ireland will have a team in Berlin. We have some good talent at home and with proper attention a strong athletic squad could be whipped into superb condition.[1]

Unfortunately, the reasonable suggestion of competing under a token flag, which did not explicitly represent either the Irish Free State or Great Britain, was not taken up with any particular enthusiasm by either side. One suspects that the only possible way an Irish team could have gone to Berlin was if the NACA relented on its demand to represent the interests of athletes from both north and south of the border, as it had done before the formation of the Irish Free State. The obvious drawback to such a compromise, however, was that Ulster athletes would only be able to represent Great Britain and compete under the Union Jack. Such a concession would have upset the many nationalists and republicans who still held out the hope of a 32-county Ireland, and was clearly too bitter a pill for the fledgling Irish state to swallow. There would be no compromise, as O'Connor lamented to Arthur Duffey and James B. Connolly, when the three old friends met up in Boston. "It is almost like two countries now in Ireland and they cannot agree . . . we want Ireland to be treated as a regular nation, until we are we will not be competitors."[2]

What most distressed O'Connor about Ireland's absence from the impending Olympiad was the fact that Irish athletics itself would be the first to suffer. After the hysteria of 1932 and the great homecoming celebrations of the Irish team, there was a notable failure to capitalise on the resurgence of interest in athletics. By late 1935, it was clear that no Irish team would travel to Berlin and that the interest in athletics was beginning to wane. Without the possibility of more Olympic medals and tales of heroism in far-off exotic places, Irish athletics was faced with a return to the doldrums and an uncertain future. In an emotional outburst tinged with nostalgia and nationalist fervour, O'Connor encapsulates what Ireland could be missing out on by not sending a team to Berlin:

> I am firmly convinced that athletes do more for a nation than thousands of politicians. At Los Angeles in 1932 I was thrilled and so was every Irishman who was present at that mighty gathering when the loud speakers roared out "O'Callaghan, Ireland, first in the hammer event", "Tisdall, Ireland, first in the hurdles" and so on when Tisdall again competed in the decathlon. Here were tens of thousands of spectators cheering every mention of little Ireland, and those cheers brought tears of joy to many a Celt. And then when the Irish Tricolour ascended the flagpole in that sun-kissed stadium it was something worth going 6,000 miles to see.[3]

O'Connor had experienced first-hand the power of sport and athletics as a positive unifying force, capable of bringing glory to even the youngest and smallest of nations. He was therefore loathe to see the Irish Free State turn down the opportunity to win further laurels and decline a place amongst the other nations of the world on the sports field. There was simply no compromise that could satisfy all parties and consequently no way round the impasse. Despite understanding the situation better than most, O'Connor felt that politics was having a detrimental effect on sport in Ireland, but he would soon realise that the problems that Ireland were facing on a domestic level were slight in comparison to the political machinations afoot in the international athletic arena. The Olympics and its noble ideals were about to be over-shadowed by the figure of Adolf Hitler and his sinister notions of Aryan supremacy.

૮ઢ

SINCE THE REVIVAL OF THE OLYMPICS in 1896, the Games had evolved markedly and grown in political as well as cultural im-portance. In the course of time, host countries and their respective governments had begun to view the Games as an important showcase event, an opportunity to encourage tourism and raise the profile of their countries. The Berlin Games in 1936, however, would be a watershed in that evolution.

In contrast to previous Olympics, visitor numbers to Berlin from overseas were down. In countries such as America and Brit-ain there was considerable debate as to whether teams should be sent at all. The anti-Jewish policies of the Nazi government dis-couraged many of the world's leading athletes from competing. Since Hitler's rise to power in 1933, he had begun to target the German Jewish community, a fact that had not escaped the atten-tion of the international press. Despite loud protestations on both sides of the Atlantic, the American and British teams finally de-cided to compete. Though there would be few Jews present in Berlin to challenge Hitler's notions of Aryan supremacy, it would take an American from Ohio State University to shatter Hitler's public relations exercise. The man in question was Jesse Owens and his performance at the Games was to be perhaps the most dramatic at any Games, then or since.

Even though no Irish athletes would compete at the Berlin Games, Peter O'Connor, Percy Kirwan and Dr Pat O'Callaghan figured amongst a small number of Irish people who made the trip. Of all the Irish observers present, O'Connor left the only comprehensive eyewitness account of Hitler's Games from an Irish perspective. O'Connor was always keen to relate the experiences of his travels to anyone who was interested, so when approached by the *Waterford Star* on his return from Germany, he gladly consented to share his thoughts about Berlin.

The two veteran Irish athletes, O'Connor and Kirwan, caught the only steamer available from London to Ostend and then travelled by train to Berlin. The craft was packed to the brim with passengers, carrying hundreds more than her 2,500 capacity was meant to hold. At the end of the long journey, the visitors to Germany's capital received an almost royal welcome. The weary travellers must have been delighted at the warm reception when their train pulled into Berlin, but they were also puzzled. The initial impression of the host nation was quite at odds with the image portrayed in the international press of an oppressive regime bent on conquest. Indeed, according to O'Connor, the whole city had an air of festivity about it, the buildings being "lavishly festooned . . . with flags, banners evergreens and gay bunting". He marvelled at the beautiful thoroughfares of the city flanked by trees in their full summer leaf, with lawns and grass verges meticulously tended. O'Connor and his companions had arrived in Berlin on 1 August and, whatever the internal politics of Germany at the time, there was no doubting the Germans' enthusiasm for the Games:

> Each successive batch or group of visitors was heartily welcomed with warmth and cordiality, and though we were minus a knowledge of the language, we nevertheless knew by instinct what was meant. That was very easy. The meaning of the people was unmistakable. There is no doubt at all that the German people decided to give the Games and those who patronized them their most loyal and unqualified greetings and support.[4]

As all hotels in Berlin had been booked for months in advance by the German military, who were either residing in or visiting the capital, the Waterford men had to be accommodated with German families, an interesting cultural experience that provided some amusing moments:

> I had to reside with a private family, although I had tried to get hotel accommodation as far back as February. Neither the owner nor his wife or children could speak English, so I was compelled to resort to the use of a German dictionary, which was a very inadequate medium for the interchange of expression. Breakfast was the only meal I ate in the house during the day, but I had the greatest trouble in making the people I was staying with understand the kind of food I wanted. The dictionary let me down and pantomime signs were just as ineffective. When I asked for the usual bacon and eggs, etc. the bacon was served up minced. But I got over this trouble by drawing a rasher on a piece of paper and my tick tack signs with my hands to the form in which I wanted the bacon given me, were effective, though somewhat ludicrous.[5]

O'Connor was no less appreciative of the spectacular Olympic stadium which had been constructed specially for the Games. Though its monumental proportions were clearly an expression of the aggressive fascist ideology of the Nazi regime, the stadium itself was a delight for spectators and participants. Built between 1934 and 1936, some 42 million reichmarks had been spent on its construction. The German architect Werner March had paid particular attention when constructing the stadium to the needs of spectators; consequently all were guaranteed an excellent view of the events:

> From the opening day until the running of the great Marathon race there was not a seat vacant in this vast arena. The Stadium had a seating accommodation of 100,000, but on no day during the progress of competitions were there less than 25,000 spectators who were content with standing room only. The Berlin Stadium was the finest I have ever seen. In my opinion it was better than that at Los Angeles, excellent in every way though the latter was. At the time of the Los Angeles Games the Stadium there was then regarded as the very best that could be erected for its purpose, but from the point of

view of vision it was not so well adapted as that at Berlin. The latter covered a much wider area, with the result that spectators could see the finish of each event from any point of the great enclosure without having to rise from his seat. The reverse was the fact at Los Angeles and much inconvenience was due to this cause in the American venue.[6]

The stadium was an architectural masterpiece and avant-garde for its day. Despite its sinister history, the stadium still remains an important tourist attraction, having survived not only the test of time but the destruction of Berlin during World War II and the city's subsequent occupation. Indeed, it is considered a stroke of luck that British forces seized the stadium and Reich sports field at the onset of the Cold War, because their presence and care ensured the survival of this historic Olympic venue. Undoubtedly the ideological abuse of the stadium by the Nazis tarnished its reputation, yet it remains a shrine to Olympic history and in particular to the great Jesse Owens.

In spite of the royal welcome, the superb organisation of the Games and the world-class stadium, O'Connor could not help feeling somewhat ill-at-ease observing the huge military presence all around him. What most disturbed him was the manner in which almost all sections of German society, women and children included, seemed to be galvanised for military action. As a father of nine children, the Hitler Youth made a particularly strong impression on him:

> Everywhere the presence of the military and police element was distinctly felt, at least by me. I remarked that practically fifty per cent of the spectators in the Stadium were connected with the Army or the Police force, whilst Boy Scouts and Girl Guides with palpably military bearing and displaying undoubted military precision were to be seen all round one. All the adults and boys and girls are, as I was told, trained in gymnastics and physical drill from childhood upwards.[7]

O'Connor had experienced many sensations in the course of his lifetime and witnessed varying levels of hysteria and emotion first-hand, from the sheer elixir of an adoring, appreciative crowd, to the anger and confusion of an American public whose President had just been assassinated. In contrast to such extremes, the sheer uniformity and military bearing of the German people perplexed him greatly. Very much a self-made man and master of his own actions, it is possible O'Connor found such collective, uniform behaviour unsettling. In particular, he afterwards highlighted a synchronised athletic display by some 10,000 Germans gymnasts, all under the age of 25, in the Berlin Polo grounds, whose "movements were carried out with such precision and dexterity as to give the impression of automatons pulled by one string". O'Connor's initial awe at witnessing the spectacle was soon tempered by a distrust concerning the motives of the political machine behind such an immaculately choreographed exercise. His observations were ominously prescient in light of future events and left an indelible impression on him. Another sign of the time that did not impress him greatly was the German people's habit of saluting their leader at every given opportunity:

> When several national anthems were played one after the other and as every spectator stood during that time at the Nazi salute, with the arms rigidly outstretched . . . the constrained attitude for lengthy periods was somewhat fatiguing. Nevertheless the sights I witnessed at these times were such as will never be forgotten.[8]

Such earnest displays of prowess and collective will left visitors in no doubt as to the seriousness with which the German people and their athletes had prepared for the Games. The host nation was expected to dominate most events. However, notwithstanding the Third Reich's most earnest efforts, a new force was about to make itself felt in international sport. Adolf Hitler's attempts to manipulate and orchestrate the Olympic festival to promote his racist and anti-Semitic beliefs were undermined as the African-American athlete Jesse Owens threw a spanner in the works. On the second day of competition, Owens scored a sensation, taking gold in the 100 metres in a time of 10.3 seconds, equalling the world and Olympic records. The home crowd went wild, 100,000 Germans bursting into spontaneous applause, suggesting that many amongst the home crowd did not subscribe to Hitler's notions of Aryan superiority. It was on the third day of competition, however, that the most memorable and significant moment of the Berlin Games took place in the long jump competition.

As a result of Ireland's failure to field a team in Berlin, O'Connor was not invited to officiate at the Games, as he had been in 1932. At Los Angeles as judge of the long jump, he had been able to savour once again the atmosphere of Olympic competition first-hand. The long jump event at Berlin was to prove far more eventful.

During the trials for the long jump, Jesse Owens found himself in danger of not qualifying when his first two jumps were declared invalid. Following the American custom, Owens took a warm-up run, running straight through the jumping pit, but was amazed to see a red flag raised. In a second genuine attempt, he seemed to hit the take-off board accurately but once again the dreaded red flag appeared.[9] To fail a third time would mean elimination from the competition. It was dramatic stuff, which must have reminded O'Connor of his own trials in the final of the hop, step and jump in Athens, when, like Owens, everything hung on his final jump. As Owens began to ready himself for his final crucial qualifying jump, the German long jumper, Lutz Long, approached him and proceeded to engage him in conversation. Long was leading the competition at the time due to his qualifying jump and was already through to the next phase. Tall, blond and blue-eyed, Long was the embodiment of Hitler's Aryan ideals. Though he spoke only broken English, and Owens no German whatsoever, the two seemed to have an instant rapport and it became clear to all watching that Long was trying to steady Owens's nerves. After chatting for some minutes Owens returned to the jumping pit, geared himself up and easily qualified for the final. Long's selfless gesture was greeted with a clamour of approval by the German home crowd, who were by this time under the spell of Owens's phenomenal athleticism. When the American went on

to win the long jump final, Long was among the first to congratulate him, once again under the watchful gaze of the Führer, who
was none too pleased. Long's actions and the subsequent delight
of the Berlin crowd demonstrated that the Olympic spirit could
eclipse racist sentiment. It was the defining moment of the Berlin
Games, when sport and sportsmanship triumphed over politics
and ideology. As Long sacrificed his chance of a gold medal, so
too went Germany's best opportunity to take gold in a track
event. Though Germany would win more golds than any other
nation in the Games, its successes would be chiefly in swimming
and gymnastics. Germany only won five gold medals in the
Olympic Stadium itself, all in field events: in the men's shot-put,
javelin and discus, and in the women's discus and javelin. There
would be no home wins in the traditional Olympic track events.
This is reputed to have surprised and annoyed Hitler a great deal.
The fact that an African-American was the sensation of the
Games, winning four gold medals, and had displayed an athleticism superior to anything seen before must have rubbed salt in
the Führer's wounds. Thanks to Jesse Owens, Hitler's massive
propaganda exercise had backfired.

∞

THE FOLLOWING DAY, 6 AUGUST, Peter O'Connor and Percy Kirwan made their way to the Olympic village, a 45-minute bus journey from the stadium. Like the rest of the world, they wanted to
meet Jesse Owens, who had only the day before picked up his
third gold medal in the 200 metres (he would take his fourth gold
as part of the American relay team). The trip meant that they
would miss the finals of the javelin, the 110-metre hurdles and the
triple jump. The chance to meet the man who in three short days
had become the most talked about athlete in the world was clearly
too great a temptation to resist. Unfortunately, luck was not on
their side because Owens had just left to watch the day's action in
the stadium after spending the morning relaxing in the Olympic
village.[10] Thus the two eager Irish veteran athletes missed meeting

Owens by a matter of minutes. Despite their disappointment, they had a chance to see the Berlin Olympic village, with its white stucco walls and red-tiled roofs, specially built to house athletes and cater to their every need. At the LA Olympics, O'Connor as an official judge at the Games had been accommodated at the first Olympic village, and mixed freely with athletes, officials and organisers. In contrast to the relaxed atmosphere at LA, there was a significant military presence and tight security at the Berlin Olympic village, though he noted that the facilities were undeniably first class.

O'Connor had always had the greatest of respect and admiration for African-American athletes and his scrapbooks are littered with picture portraits and autographs of athletes such as Gourdin and Owens. The Irish had shown a particular predilection for jumping from the 1880s until O'Connor's retirement in 1906, and had held the world record for roughly 40 years — O'Connor's own world record standing for over twenty years. Irish domination had ended when the African-American Harvard athlete Ned Gourdin sailed past the magical barrier of 25 feet in 1921. In the 15 years since Gourdin had broken O'Connor's long-standing record, every successive world record holder and Olympic gold medallist was of African-American origin. These finely tuned athletes had proven to be the natural successors to the Irish jumping legends. The manner in which African-American athletes such as Owens and boxers such as Joe Louis were beginning to dominate world sport had a striking parallel in the Irish domination of track and field and boxing in late Victorian times — which probably did not escape O'Connor. His generation of Irish athletic champions had been as concerned with raising the profile of their race as well as demonstrating their individual supremacy. The sporting success of the likes of Martin Sheridan and John Flanagan on US teams at the earlier Olympics had proven highly effective in combating anti-Irish prejudices and the belief that the Irish as an ethnic group were intent on resisting Americanisation. The likes of Sheridan and Flanagan had demonstrated that Irishmen could preserve their European heritage while also embracing American values and customs. Now it was the turn of African-American athletes to raise the profile of their race. As Owens stole the show at Berlin, Joe Louis was deep in training preparing for a return fight against Max Schmeling, the German boxer who had stolen his world heavyweight title. Within months, Louis would regain his crown and his success would be portrayed as a victory for democracy over fascism, the American way of life over that of Nazi Germany.[11] The successes of Owens and Louis and their sudden transformation into All-American sporting heroes would have a profound effect on American society and do much to strengthen the arguments for civil rights activists combating racism and an end to segregation. Just as Irishmen had won respect for their nation across the world, now African-Americans were doing the same for their people.

On leaving Berlin, O'Connor and Percy Kirwan stopped off in London where, on 15 August, they had another chance to see the American Olympic track team in action against a selection of British and Canadian athletes in White City Stadium. Owens only ran the third leg of a relay race that day, in what was to be an inconspicuous final appearance as an amateur athlete. Following their triumphs at Berlin, Owens and his teammates were forced by the American Athletics Union to appear at fundraising exhibitions across Europe, despite the fact that they were all fatigued and drained both emotionally and physically. By the time Owens arrived in London, he had reluctantly performed at two German athletic meetings, first in Cologne and then in Bochum. Given no chance to rest or recuperate, and with barely enough money to buy food or refreshments, the American team was now performing indifferently. By now, Owens was desperate to go home. Since his successes in Berlin, he had received by telegraph a constant stream of lucrative offers from American businesses, promoters and showmen promising huge financial sums. The temptation to accept some of these offers was hard to resist. To do so would, however, mean turning his back forever on the world of amateur sport.

While Jesse Owens sat around his London hotel deliberating what course he should follow, Peter O'Connor finally caught up with him. Having narrowly missed him at the Olympic village in Berlin, he and Percy Kirwan were clearly determined that lightning would not strike twice. In what was perhaps the most difficult and challenging time in his life thus far, Owens, always amenable and generous with his time, spent some 40 minutes chatting to the two Irishmen.

Sadly, no written record remains of their conversation, but Danny McGrath, who travelled to the 1948 Olympics in London with O'Connor, is certain they talked animatedly about long jumping. Owens's jumping had invoked comparisons with the revolutionary style that O'Connor popularised in the wake of his 1901 world record. When he visited America in 1901, numerous athletics coaches and newspaper journalists analysed and studied his unique mid-air scissors kick movement in detail. Thus Owens may have known of O'Connor by name. It is quite possible that Owens's first coach and mentor, the Irish-American Charles Riley, had told him something of him. Whatever the case, O'Connor and Kirwan were delighted to meet Owens and had their picture taken with him. Quite what he made of the two well-spoken veteran Irish jumpers is not known. The following day, after his refusal to continue the American Olympic team's barnstorming tour of Europe, some hours before the official closing of the Berlin Games, Jesse Owens was suspended by the American Amateur Union from competing in all amateur competition in the US and his scintillating career as an amateur came to an abrupt halt.

15

The Final Years

AFTER HITLER'S INVASION OF POLAND in 1939, Europe played host to the worst conflict the world has ever known. Thanks to its neutrality, Eamon de Valera's fledgling state was not dragged into the conflict. Indeed, Ireland enjoyed a period of relative stability, after the hardships of the Economic War in the previous decade. O'Connor was disappointed that the Tokyo Olympics was cancelled, because he had been looking forward to making the trip to the Land of the Rising Sun. By now an inveterate traveller, the trip to Japan would have been the longest he had ever undertaken. While the Allies battled for supremacy against fascist Germany and Italy, life at Peter O'Connor & Son went on as usual and now approaching his seventh decade, O'Connor had a lot to look back on with pride.

By 1940, two of his sons had entered the priesthood. Eddie had been ordained as a Jesuit in 1935 and was now in Rome, where he would remain for the course of the Second World War, his distant voice occasionally crackling across the airwaves as he broadcast on Vatican Radio. Walter was also about to be ordained as a Jesuit. His youngest and favourite son, Arthur, had started out as a bank clerk and was quickly progressing up through the ranks of the banking world, carving out his own career for himself. Two of his daughters, Mary and Kathleen, had entered convent life and become teachers. Joan and Madge, the two remaining daughters, had just finished school and helped out in the office and at home.

Only Jimmie, his second eldest son, had given O'Connor cause for concern, taking twelve years to qualify as a solicitor, which he finally did in 1937. Since 1930, his younger brother Peter had been working in the office at a nominal salary. Peter's timely arrival had enabled O'Connor to dispense with a managing assistant, whom he had been paying £6 per week. Having a qualified son in the office also meant that O'Connor could spend less time in the District Court and concentrate on building up his portfolio of clients. By the time Jimmie eventually qualified, his younger brother was already effectively heir to the office, since the practice could only realistically support two solicitors. Jimmie undoubtedly felt hard done by, being excluded from the office by his younger brother, and this eventually led to a serious falling-out with his father.

In 1940, Jimmie convinced his brother Walter that their father had deliberately scuppered Jimmie's chances of attaining the prestigious position of probate registrar in Dublin, though only candidates with five years' experience as solicitors could be considered for the position. Walter, who was both deeply religious and conscientious, wrote to his father expressing sincere concerns about his "spiritual welfare should — God forbid — death overtake him in his present state of mind". Though O'Connor no doubt appreciated his son's heartfelt sentiments for the welfare of his soul, he was stunned when he learned what lengths Walter had gone to in order to ensure his salvation. Anxious to act as peacemaker, Walter had organised and convened a special conference in Dublin involving "four prudent men", with whom he "discussed the whole case in question omitting no relevant details". The star-studded cast which Walter had assembled were none other than the Rector of Clongowes College, Fr F. McGrath SJ; the Rector of Milltown Park, Fr S. McMahon, who had practised as a barrister before becoming a Jesuit; the Irish Attorney General of the time, Patrick Lynch SC; and Norman Judd, O'Connor's amiable and gregarious Dublin cousin.[1] O'Connor was none too impressed that such a group of eminent men, including the most respected legal mind in the country, had spent an entire afternoon sitting around a table discussing his personal family affairs as well as how he should conduct his business, not to mention the welfare of his soul. Understandably irate, O'Connor made Jimmie *persona non grata* at Upton and it was only several years later that father and son were reconciled, principally thanks to Norman Judd's subtle skills of diplomacy and generosity in helping Jimmie get his own partnership in a legal practice.[2]

∝

AFTER THE END OF WORLD WAR II, the world and Europe in particular began to piece itself back together, both emotionally and physically, trying to heal the wounds of a sustained period of bloody conflict. In the summer of 1948, Peter O'Connor travelled to his last Olympic celebration. After a gap of 12 years, athletes gathered from across the globe to take part in the "London Games of New Hope". Ireland had remained neutral during the War and during that time O'Connor did not venture abroad. Europe was at war, there was rationing at home and it was considered too dangerous to go to America in this period due to the constant threat of German U-boats. O'Connor's last foreign trip had been to the Berlin Olympics, where he had seen and experienced Nazi Germany first-hand.[3] Now three years after the allies had proven victorious and the Third Reich was no more, O'Connor returned to a London that had been battered and bruised by the German Blitz. As always, O'Connor was accompanied on the trip by his trusty friends from Kilmacthomas, Percy and Rody Kirwan. The trio were also joined this time by a much younger man, Danny McGrath from Cappoquin, who was one of Ireland's pre-eminent athletes and rising stars during the war years. Throughout the Games, Danny and Peter sat side-by-side and never missed a day's action from 30 July to 6 August. The most outstanding athlete of the Games was Fanny Blankhurst Cohen, who won four gold medals at the age of 32, and Emil Zátopek who won the marathon. This was Ireland's first showing at an Olympics since 1932, as no team was sent to Berlin in 1936. The four Irishmen were disappointed that the Irish failed to make an impression in London, as great hope had been invested in John Jo Barry in the 5,000 metres and Jimmy Reardon in the 400 metres, neither proving successful. It was a far cry from Irish successes at Los Angeles in 1932, but O'Connor, the Kirwan brothers and Danny McGrath all agreed that Ireland's participation at this Games, thanks to the efforts of Billy Morton, was none-theless a step in the right direction.

After O'Connor's trip to London in 1948, Maggie's general health began to deteriorate significantly. On 19 January 1951, after a prolonged illness, Maggie, Peter O'Connor's wife of 47 years, passed away. Maggie had given Peter nine healthy children and provided him with a comfortable home for almost half a century. O'Connor deeply felt the loss of his "dear wife" and companion. In his final years Peter O'Connor continued to live at Upton with his daughter Madge and Eileen their housekeeper. The corridors of the large Georgian mansion that had once reverberated to the sounds of active family life now fell silent. All of his children, ex-cept for Madge, had long since flown the coop. Peter and Arthur were both happily married and Jimmie also got married in 1953. Eddie, his eldest, was now at Milltown Jesuit College in Dublin and Walter was working in the missions in Africa. His youngest, Joan, had married in 1949, her marriage the last happy family oc-casion when all of the nine and their parents were reunited.

In these final years, Peter O'Connor kept the same routine that he had throughout his life. He would rise at seven, cross the road to early morning mass at De La Salle College and Eileen always had his breakfast ready on his return. A creature of habit, he in-variably ate two boiled eggs and some brown bread for breakfast. Then, after a quiet pull of his pipe in his favourite armchair by the fire in the drawing room, he would make his way from Newtown into Waterford city by foot, to visit his practice in O'Connell Street.

As Peter O'Connor turned 80, his son Peter effectively took on the running of the office. Nonetheless, O'Connor still liked to keep an eye on things, and offer advice and direction when it was re-quired. He still indulged his penchant for calligraphy, taking par-ticular pleasure in inscribing legal documents in decorative calligraphic script. His mornings were spent in his office on the second floor, meeting old clients, perusing legal documents and writing to friends and family. Ms Courtney, his principal assistant since the 1920s, always ensured the day's mail was ready for him on his arrival and that the gas fire had been lit in his room. The partner's desk at which he sat was always submerged under a sea of documents of all types and sizes. Close to hand, there was a small Canterbury or swivel bookcase that contained his favourite books. Little had changed since the time of Dunford. A large Victorian bookcase stood opposite O'Connor's desk, at the far end of the room and contained his much-treasured collection of the *Irish Law Times*. Despite the novelty of electricity, the room was only dimly lit and old gas fittings were still in place in the ceiling. Three large portraits of the patriots, Thomas Francis Meagher, Robert Emmet and Daniel O'Connell, hung in his office. All of the walls in his office were adorned with photographs and memorabilia from his sporting years. Clients would often pause to gaze upon the many sporting legends portrayed and events depicted on these walls and O'Connor would always be at the ready to tell an anecdote or two or shed light on his travels and experiences. At 12.30 each day, he would take his leave of the office and board the bus home. His movements were regular like clockwork, as one of his grandchildren Hilary remembers, and if any of his grandchildren were lucky enough to meet their granddad on his way home at lunchtime, he would always pay their one pence fare and present a nice shiny sixpence as a parting gift.

When an opportunity of fine to middling weather presented itself, Peter O'Connor was to be found at the end of the garden at Upton, sitting on an old garden seat in the sunlight sheltered by a straw hat. There he would hold court, puffing his pipe, in the company of his last dog Wally, a wheaten terrier. He was very protective of his garden's produce, his prized pears, apples and tomatoes, and always kept a lookout for any local schoolboys intent on pilfering his stock. In later years, he even built up one of the walls in his garden so his apples would not accidentally or otherwise fall into a neighbouring garden. In latter years, O'Connor employed a well-known local gardener, Mr Lanigan, to undertake the upkeep of the garden. Many years before, Peter O'Connor had kept fantailed pigeons in the loft of the old stables at Upton. The pigeons were now long gone but a pet canary called Dick, whose cage hung in the dining room by the bay windows, remained. Since the

1920s, the O'Connor family had kept bees and still retained two hives, though his son Peter now looked after them.

After Maggie died, O'Connor became very attached to his dog Wally and his son Peter used regularly to take him rabbit-hunting in Faithlegg. On one occasion, during a hunting expedition, another of his grandchildren, Rosemary, recalled Wally getting into serious difficulties at Faithlegg in the River Suir and her father, Peter O'Connor junior, being ordered to jump in to the river to rescue the terrier. This incident brought these expeditions to an abrupt halt. Wally was the last in a long line of Irish terriers whom Peter O'Connor owned in his lifetime. At one time or another, O'Connor kept Irish red terriers, soft-coated wheaten terriers, Kerry Blues and Glen of Imaal terriers. He was also reputed to have been the first in Ireland with a Staffordshire bull terrier. Many of his sporting contemporaries and legal peers shared his interest in terrier trials, notably the sports pundit "Carbery", P.D. Mehigan, who hunted with Kerry Blues.[4] Wally's near-drowning at Faithlegg now closed this chapter of his life.

In 1952 the Helsinki Games were due to take place and Peter was as adamant as ever that he wanted to attend another Olympics. His family knew he wasn't quite fit enough to go, so in the end reason triumphed over passion and he had to content himself with second-hand reports from Percy and Rody on their return. O'Connor's attendance and involvement in Olympics and athletics was at an end.

In his final years, O'Connor trusted to routine and conserved his energies but was a genial and generous host to all who came to visit him, especially Arthur his favourite son, his wife Kathleen and their four young daughters. Almost to the very end, Peter O'Connor was blessed with good health, his only complaint mild arthritis. In the summer of 1957, while he was in the garden at Upton, he uncharacteristically lost his balance, slipped and fell. After that he was confined to bed and, after a short illness, he died at Upton on 9 November 1957. Peter O'Connor was buried alongside his beloved wife Maggie in Ballygunner cemetery, Waterford.

છ

WITH PETER O'CONNOR'S PASSING the final connection with a glorious era of Irish sporting achievement was severed. The generation of athletes to which he belonged had taken up the mantle laid down by the likes of Maurice and Pat Davin, with a hunger for success that has yet to be matched by successive generations of Irish athletes. Early Irish Olympians such as Tom Kiely, Pat and Con Leahy, John Flanagan, Martin Sheridan and Peter O'Connor, to name but a few, did much to raise the profile of the Irish race at a time when Ireland's independence from Britain had yet to be won. Despite their superlative achievements, many of these athletes are now largely forgotten, their names gradually having slipped from the national consciousness, casualties of modern Irish history. In their time, however, the impact of O'Connor's generation was immense, as one commentator in 1932 noted:

> Ireland's great athletes have kept their country on the map; by their example they perpetuated that natural desire for physical development which is the safeguard of the virility of the race. Lacking athletic expression, this great quality of the Irish race, the bone and sinew, would indeed be in danger of death by atrophy.[5]

This observation is a fitting epitaph for Ireland's many early Olympians and world champions and provides much food for thought as the Athens Olympics of 2004 approaches. Ninety-eight years on from the successes of Peter O'Connor, Con Leahy and Martin Sheridan at the 1906 Intercalated Games in Athens, Irish athletes will once again return to Greece. How they will fare remains to be seen, but one thing is certain: they will have a hard act to follow.

Notes

The full publication details of all sources cited can be found in the Bibliography.

Chapter 1

[1] As one of the last of her kind, the schooner *Nellie Bywater* subsequently appeared in several films, most notably in *The Elusive Pimpernel*, starring David Niven, before foundering in a storm in the Caribbean in 1952.

[2] Morgan.

[3] Cleary, 57.

[4] Ibid, 59.

[5] The Connors/O'Connors were long-term tenants and leaseholders of the Wicklow town commissioner, as evidenced by a map of the Corporation lands of 13 January 1869, which details the land leased to Edward O'Connor, Peter's uncle, in the Barony of Arklow.

[6] The 1820s were difficult years for Irish agriculture, with the potato crop failing in successive years, a portent of the terrible disaster that would strike Ireland in the 1840s. Since only 56.1 per cent of the land in Wicklow could be cultivated, fishing was the other main source of employment in the county. This may explain Arthur O'Connor's choice of career as a shipwright. See Hannigan, "Wicklow Before and After the Famine", *Wicklow History and Society*, 789–823.

[7] See Rees, "Maritime Wicklow", footnote no. 38.

[8] In the early sixteenth century Andrew Judd became a merchant trader of the Staplers' Guild and Skinners' Guild. In 1550 as master of the Skinners' Guild he was chosen to be Lord Mayor of London and was knighted by Edward VI. Sir Andrew led an interesting and eventful life, marrying three times and becoming extremely wealthy owing to his extensive business interests. He was also a founder of Tunbridge Wells school and a merchant of Muscovy. In political matters,

he displayed astute judgement, taking the side of Mary and Philip during the Wyatt rebellion, for which he earned their gratitude in person when he met Philip in Calais at the headquarters of the Staplers' Guild.

[9] Cleary, 61.

[10] Carbery, 89.

[11] Rees, 63–4.

[12] Hannigan, "The National Schools in Wicklow Town (1832–1919)", 43.

[13] O'Connor family papers.

[14] *Wicklow People*, 25 December 1909.

[15] Ibid.

[16] Mulhall, 108.

[17] Carbery, 89.

[18] For the next five years the farm was kept going by two Wicklow cousins of the O'Connor family, the Maguires and the Sinnotts, until in 1897 the two families fell out over the ownership of the property. Both the families felt they held a title to the estate and began quarrelling as to who should possess it. As in many family feuds involving property, a reconciliation or a compromise proved impossible and the matter was referred to the courts. Following a court case in 1898, the property was valued at about £210 pounds. Since neither side was willing to compromise, the judge directed that the farm should be sold to J. Walsh of Wicklow for the sum of £130. In 1905 the land was sold to Wicklow Golf Course which remains on the site to this day, the 8th green of the golf course marking the spot where the O'Connor family homestead once stood.

Chapter 2

[1] Viliers-Tuthill, *Beyond the Twelve Bens*, 69-78.

[2] Carbery.

[3] Carbery, 89–90.

[4] Ibid.

[5] Ibid.

[6] O'Maolfabhail, 127–28.

Chapter 3

[1] Hunt in *Mullingar History*, 6–8.

[2] Ibid., 31–2.

[3] *Westmeath Examiner*, 21 April 2001.

[4] *Sport*, 5 November 1898.

[5] *Midland Reporter*, 25 August 1898.

[6] *Westmeath Examiner*, 21 April 2001.

[7] *Sport*, 16 November 1898.

[8] Ibid.

Chapter 4

[1] Fewer, 60.

[2] *Sport*, 28 June 1902.

[3] *Sport*, 22 July 1899.

[4] Fabricius.

[5] Wilcox.

[6] *Daily Telegraph*, 6 July 1900.

[7] *Waterford News*, 14 July 1905.

[8] *Wicklow People*, 16 June 1900.

[9] *Scottish Sport*, June 15 1900.

[10] Ibid.

[11] Ibid.

[12] Ibid.

[13] *Wicklow People*, 16 June 1900.

[14] *Scottish Sport*, 7 July 1900.

[15] *Sport*, 7 July 1900.

Chapter 5

[1] *Daily Telegraph*, 6 July 1900.

[2] *Sport*, 28 July 1900.

[3] Ibid.

[4] Ibid.

[5] *Freeman's Journal*, 13 July 1900.

[6] *Waterford News*, 15 July 1904.

[7] Unidentified English newspaper extract in O'Connor's scrapbook.

[8] Lucas, 362.

[9] Cox.

[10] "Scratchman" was a colloquial term; the scratchman conceded some inches to his adversaries based on an official handicap system.

[11] Unidentified newspaper excerpt in O'Connor scrapbook.

[12] Unidentified excerpt from O'Connor scrapbook, see also *Waterford News*, 24 August 1900.

[13] *The Irish Times*, 30 August 1900.

[14] *The Irish Times*, 31 October 1900.

[15] *Waterford News*, 28 March 1901.

Chapter 6

[1] *Waterford News*, 19 April 1901.

[2] *Sport*, 28 June 1902.

[3] *Sport*, 1 July 1901.

[4] *Sport*, 1 June 1901.

[5] O'Connor scrapbook.

[6] *Waterford News*, 7 June 1901.

[7] *Sport*, 1 June 1901.

[8] *Waterford News*, 24 May 1901.

[9] *Waterford News*, 28 June 1901.

[10] Ibid.

[11] Coleman, *Glasgow Exhibition 1901*.

[12] Scottish newspaper extract in O'Connor scrapbook.

[13] O'Connor scrapbook.

[14] Ibid.

[15] *Waterford News*, 5 July 1901.

[16] *Glasgow Evening Despatch*.

[17] O'Connor scrapbook.

[18] *Sport*, 6 July 1901.

[19] Ibid.

[20] Unidentified newspaper extract from O'Connor scrapbook.

[21] *Waterford News*, 14 September 1900.

[22] *Waterford News*, 5 July 1901.

[23] *Waterford News*, 12 July 1901.

[24] Ibid.

[25] Henry, 16–17.

[26] Unidentified extract from O'Connor scrapbook.

[27] Ibid.

[28] Ibid.

[29] Deakin talking to Lovesey in 1969 from AAFLA archive.

[30] Letter contained in O'Connor scrapbook.

[31] Excerpt from "The Irish-American", published in *Sport*, 28 July 1901.

[32] *Waterford News*, 2 August 1901.

[33] See Perry.

Chapter 7

[1] *Waterford News*, 5 July 1901.

[2] Schaefer, 3.

[3] De Búrca, 32–33.

[4] Letter to Redmond published in the *Waterford News*, 24 August 1901, and contained in O'Connor scrapbook.

5 Undated *New York Journal* excerpt contained in scrapbook, and reprinted in *Sport* 21 September 1901.

6 Bayor, 290.

7 *Waterford News*, 16 August 1901.

8 O'Connor scrapbook.

9 Ibid.

10 *Waterford News*, 4 October 1901.

11 *Sport*, 21 September 1901.

12 Letter from O'Connor to Redmond of 9 September 1901, O'Connor scrapbook.

13 *Sport*, 28 September 1901.

14 O'Connor scrapbook.

15 *Sport*, 28 September 1901.

16 *Waterford News*, 11 October 1901.

17 O'Connor scrapbook.

18 Ibid.

Chapter 8

1 The anonymous letter published in the *Waterford News*, 6 December 1902, appears in print form in O'Connor's second scrapbook. O'Connor was very careful in cataloguing in chronological order and dating every letter or article that he had published in newspapers, so it is reasonable to assume he wrote this letter. In addition, almost every document in his first two scrapbooks was written by him or relates to him directly.

2 Mulhall, 46.

3 *Irish Daily Independent*, 9 June 1902; *Waterford News*, 6 June 1902.

4 *Waterford News*, 5 September 1902.

5 Ibid.

6 Ibid.

7 *Sport*, 24 January 1903.

8 Unidentified English newspaper extract of 17 January 1903 in O'Connor scrapbook.

9 *Sport*, 19 July 1902.

[10] Excerpt from *Ireland's Saturday Night* of 19 July 1902; reprinted in *Waterford News* 15 July 1904.

[11] *Waterford News*, 5 September 1902.

[12] Wallechinsky, xxi.

[13] Lucas, 363.

[14] *Waterford News*, 15 July 1904.

[15] O'Connor scrapbook.

[16] *Waterford News*, 14 July 1904.

[17] De Búrca, 66.

[18] Puirséal, 138.

[19] National Archive, File ED9 18398.

[20] Ibid.

[21] De Búrca, 80.

Chapter 9

[1] Mallon, 2.

[2] Lennartz, 8–9.

[3] Mallon, 3.

[4] According to the renowned German Olympic Sports Historian Carl Diem; see Hill, *Olympic Politics*.

[5] According to Morley, the "Erin go Bragh" flag first came to prominence during the 1798 rebellion and was later used by the United Irishmen, Daniel O'Connell and the Fenians. Significantly in relation to O'Connor, the flag was adopted by supporters of Home Rule from the time of Parnell until the collapse of the Irish Parliamentary Party in 1918. Morley contends that the British government's use of the flag in recruitment campaigns during the First World War may have contributed to its subsequent disappearance from the spectrum of Irish life.

[6] Letter from O'Connor to Seamas O'Ceallaigh, in GAA museum, Croke Park.

[7] Hammack, Ch. 6.

[8] Sweeney.

[9] Thanks to Con Power for sharing this story which he heard from Maurice Leahy, Con Leahy's brother.

[10] *The Irish Field*, 24 February 1906.

[11] O'Connor scrapbook.

[12] Untitled excerpt in O'Connor scrapbook, dated 22 April 1906.

[13] Sullivan, 5.

[14] Ibid.

[15] Lennartz, 13.

[16] O'Connor scrapbook.

[17] *Waterford Chronicle*, 25 April 1906.

[18] *The Limerick Leader*, 25 August 1956.

[19] Ibid.

[20] Ibid.

[21] Ibid.

[22] Ó Ceallaigh letter, GAA museum Croke Park.

[23] Mallon, 161.

[24] Mallon, 47–48.

[25] Ibid.

[26] Connolly, 452.

[27] Lennartz, 17.

[28] *The Limerick Leader*, 25 August 1956.

[29] Sullivan, 81.

[30] Ó Ceallaigh letter, GAA museum, Croke Park.

[31] Mallon, 45.

[32] Henry, 21–2.

[33] *The Limerick Leader*, April 1956.

[34] Sullivan, 77.

[35] Ibid. 95.

[36] Mallon, 38.

[37] Lucas.

[38] Connolly, 452.

Chapter 10

[1] Undated excerpt from English newspaper in O'Connor scrapbook.

[2] Ibid.

[3] From an article by Ronald A. Smith contained in *Problems in American Sport History*, 121-128.

[4] Coincidentally, between 1887 and 1889, Lord Alverstone was the barrister who acted for the *Times of London* following allegations printed in the paper that Charles Stewart Parnell had supported a small subversive IRB faction known as the Invincibles who assassinated the Irish Chief Secretary Lord Cavendish and his assistant, T.H. Burke, in the Phoenix Park in Dublin in 1882. A commission was set up to investigate the claim but the letters were eventually proved to be forgeries and the *Times*'s case collapsed, Parnell being cleared to great acclaim.

Chapter 11

[1] *Irish Daily Independent*, 10 December 1909.

[2] *Irish Daily Independent*, 13 December 1909.

[3] O'Connor scrapbook.

[4] Ibid.

[5] Ibid.

Chapter 12

[1] Sadleir letter, O'Connor family papers.

[2] Looking at the Sadleir family history, it becomes clear why Annie May was determined to have a trustworthy and capable man looking after her business affairs. A relation of hers, John Sadleir MP, a financial speculator, caused one of the biggest scandals of the Victorian age, making the Sadleir name synonymous with financial dishonesty and incompetency. After his disastrous financial losses became public in 1856, John Sadleir committed suicide on Hampstead Heath in London. Nonetheless, his deeds and his reputation lived on through characters such as Merdle in Charles Dickens's *Little Dorrit* as well as in the works of less enduring Victorian writers such as Charles Lever, Joseph Hatton and Mary Elizabeth Bradden (O'Shea, 498–9). It is little wonder Miss Sadleir was determined to deal only with O'Connor, because he had clearly earned her trust.

[3] Power, 245.

[4] Newspaper excerpt dated 24 January 1924 in O'Connor scrapbook.

[5] See *The Irish Law Times*, Vol. 65, p. 108.

Chapter 13

[1] Griffin, 104.

[2] Guiney, 78.

[3] Griffin, 104–5.

[4] Griffin, 107.

[5] *Irish Independent*, 8 March 1932.

[6] Ibid.

[7] *Waterford Star*, 2 September 1932.

[8] Ibid.

[9] Ibid.

[10] Ibid.

[11] Letter from Peter O'Connor to Denis Power, courtesy of Con Power.

[12] *Waterford Star*, 10 September 1932.

[13] *Waterford Star*, 2 September 1932.

[14] One of the memorable stories recounted by Bob Tisdall in Thames Television's excellent documentary, "A Golden Hour".

[15] *Waterford Star*, 10 September 1932.

[16] Griffin, 129.

[17] *Waterford Star*, 10 September 1932.

[18] Griffin, 113.

[19] Collins, 358.

[20] Ibid., 359.

[21] Sadleir letter, O'Connor family papers.

[22] Ibid.

[23] The official title of the Irish head of government at the time was President of the Executive Council of the Irish Free State, changing to Taoiseach in December 1937, following the introduction of the Constitution.

Chapter 14

[1] Interview with Liam O'Shea in *New York Advocate* in 1935.

[2] *Boston Post*, 11 September 1935.

[3] *New York Advocate*, 1935.

[4] *Waterford Star*, 21 August 1936.

[5] Ibid.

[6] Ibid.

[7] Ibid.

[8] Ibid.

[9] Baker, 96.

[10] See Baker, *Jesse Owens: An American Life*, for a comprehensive and concise account of Owens' time in Berlin.

[11] See McRae's excellent *In Black and White* for a full exposition of this theme.

Chapter 15

[1] Walter's letter and the ensuing correspondence between various parties is contained in the O'Connor family papers.

[2] In January 1945 when a half partnership in a solicitor's office in Tullamore costing £1,500 was advertised, Norman wrote to O'Connor undertaking to back Jimmie to the tune of £500 to get him settled for life, "to be repaid whenever Jimmie is able to do it — in other words on the old 'Kathleen Mavourneen' system." O'Connor could not but respond to this gesture from his cousin and felt obliged to match his generosity. Though the bid for the Tullamore practice failed, just one year later in 1946, Jimmie managed to obtain a very promising and suitable position in Thurles. In 1948, after some eight years of estrangement and a lengthy written apology, Jimmie was once again admitted to Upton for Christmas dinner.

[3] In January of 1945, O'Connor was interviewed on Irish radio and shared his first-hand experiences of Berlin in 1936.

[4] Mercedes O'Flaherty.

[5] *Irish Independent*, 9 March 1932.

Bibliography

Select Sports Bibliography

Baker, William J., *Jesse Owens: An American Life*, New York: Macmillan, 1986.

Carbery (P.D. Mehigan), "Seventy Years of Irish Athletics", Dublin: Carbery, 1945.

Connolly, James B. "The Capitalization of Amateur Athletics", *Metropolitan Magazine*, July 1910.

Cox, Jay. "The Original Orange Olympic Champ", Syracuse University Magazine (2000), http://sumagazine.syr.edu/summer00.

Davin, Pat, *Recollections of a Veteran Irish Athlete*, Dublin: Iuverna Press, 1939.

De Búrca, Marcus, *The GAA. A History*, Dublin: Gill & Macmillan, 2000.

Dyreson, Mark, "America's Athletic Missionaries: Political Performance, Olympic Spectacle and the Quest for an American National Culture, 1896-1912", *Olympika: The International Journal of Olympic Studies*, Vol. I, 1992.

Fabricius, Ed., "Pennsylvania Athletics: A Tradition of Excellence", http://pennathletics.ocsn.com.

A Golden Hour (Documentary), Narr. Liam Nolan, Writ. Patrick Collins, Thames Television.

Griffin, Padraig, *The Politics of Irish Athletics 1850–1990*, Leitrim: Marathon, 1990.

Guiney, David, *Gold Silver Bronze*, Dublin: Sportsworld.

Henry, Noel, *Irish Marathon Legends*, Dublin: Irish Runner, 1992.

Horbe, Peter, *Sport und Irische Geschicte. Eine analyse vershiden sozio-politische aspekte des Sports*, Koln, 1973.

Lennartz, Karl, "The 2nd International Olympic Games in Athens 1906", *Journal of Olympic History*, March 2002.

Lucas, John, "The Hegemonic Rule of the American Amateur Athletic Union 1888–1914: James Edward Sullivan as Prime Mover", *The International Journal of the History of Sport*, Vol. 11, No. 3, December 1994.

Mallon, Bill, *The 1906 Olympic Games*, Jefferson: MacFarland, 1999.

Mallon, Bill and Ian Buchanan, *Quest for Gold. The Encyclopedia of American Olympians*, New York: Leisure Press, 1984.

Mandle, W.F., *The Gaelic Athletic Association & Irish Nationalist Politics 1884–1924*, Dublin: Gill & Macmillan, 1987.

McRae, Donald, *In Black and White. The Untold Story of Joe Louis and Jesse Owens*, Bath: Scribner, 2002.

Molloy, Maura, *One Tailteann Week: A Chronicle of the Games in Ancient Days*, Dundalk: Dundalgan Press, 1928.

O'Ceallaigh, Séamus, *The Story of the GAA*, Limerick: GAA, 1977.

O'Maolfabhail, Art, *Camán 2,000 Years of Hurling in Ireland*, Dundalk: Dundalgan Press, 1973.

O'Riain, Seamas, *Maurice Davin (1842-1927) First President of the GAA*, Dublin: Geography, 1992.

Pope, S.W., "Amateurism and American Sports Culture: The invention of an Athletic Tradition in the United States, 1870-1900", *The International Journal of the History of Sport*, Vol. 13, No. 3, December 1996.

Puirséal, Padraig, *The GAA in its Time*, Dublin: Purcell, 1982.

Riess, Steven A. (ed.), *Major Problems in American Sport History*, New York: Houghton Mifflin, 1997.

Schaefer, John, "The Irish American Athletic Club: Redefining Americanism at the 1908 Olympic Games", *Archives of Irish America*, NYU.

Sullivan, James E. (ed.), *Spalding's Athletic Library: The Olympic Games at Athens 1906*, New York: American Sports Publishing, 1906.

Wallechinsky, David, *The Complete Book of the Olympics*, London: Aurum Press, 2000.

Ware, Séamus, *Laochra na hEireann agus na Cluichí Olimpeacha 1896–1996*, Baile Átha Cliath: Coiscéim, 1996.

Wilcox, Ralph C., "The English as Poor Losers and Other Thoughts on the Modernization of Sport: The Literary Works of James Brendan Connolly", *The British Society of Sports History*.

General Bibliography

Bayor, R. and T. Meagher (eds.), *The New York Irish*, Baltimore: Johns Hopkins UP, 1996.

Cleary, Jimmy, "Wicklow Harbour", *Wicklow Historical Society Journal*, Vol. 1, No. 3, July 1990.

Colclough, Bernard and Walter O'Neill, *Waterford & Thereabouts*, Waterford, 1993.

Coleman Julie, *Glasgow International Exhibition 1901, Official Guide and Daily Programmes*, University of Glasgow, Mu25-a.29 http://special.lib.gla.ac.uk/exhibns/month/oct1999.

Collins, M.E., *History in the Making. Ireland 1868–1966*, Dublin: Educational Company of Ireland, 1993.

Cronin, Mike, *The Blueshirts and Irish Politics*, Dublin: Four Courts Press, 1997.

Dowling, Daniel, *Waterford Streets: Past and Present*, Waterford: Waterford Corporation, 1998.

England, Capt. Richard, *Schoonerman*, London: Hollis & Carter, 1981.

Farrell, Mary (ed.), *Mullingar: Essays on the History of a Midlands Town in the 19th Century*, Mullingar: Westmeath Public Library, 2002.

Fennelly, Rev. Sean, *The Life & Times of Dr Thomas Fennelly, Archbishop of Cashel & Emly*, Journal of Lough Gur & District Historical Society, 2000.

Fewer, T.N., *Waterford People: A Biographical Dictionary*, Waterford: Ballylough, 1998.

Hammack, David C., *Power and Society. Greater New York at the Turn of the Century*, New York: Russell Sage, 1973.

Hannigan, Ken, "The National Schools in Wicklow Town (1832–1919)", *Wicklow Historical Society Journal*, Vol. 1, No. 2, June 1989.

Hannigan Ken, and William Nolan (eds.), *Wicklow History and Society*, Dublin: Geography, 1994.

Herlihy, Jim, *The Royal Irish Constabulary*, Dublin: Four Courts Press, 1997.

Kee, Robert, *Ireland: A History*, London: Abacus, 2003.

Kiberd, Declan, *Inventing Ireland: The Literature of the Modern Nation*, London: Vintage, 1996.

Lalor, Brian (ed.), *The Encyclopedia of Ireland*, Dublin: Gill & Macmillan, 2003.

MacAuley, Ambrose, *The Holy See, British Policy and the Plan of Campaign in Ireland 1885–93*, Dublin: Four Courts Press, 2002.

McEneaney, Eamonn, *Discover Waterford*, Dublin: O'Brien Press, 2001.

McGarry, Fearghal, "General O'Duffy, the National Corporate Party and the Irish Brigade", in Augusteijn, Joost (ed.) *Ireland in the 1930s*, Dublin: Four Courts Press, 1999.

Morgan, Trevor, "The Cumberland Connection: Hugh Jones, Shipbuilder, Millom", *Maritime Wales*, Vol. 7, Wales: Gwynedd Archives Service.

Morley, Vincent, *Flags of Ireland*, http://www.connect.ie/users/morley/flags.htm

Mulhall, Daniel, *A New Day Dawning: A Portrait of Ireland in 1900*, Cork: Collins Press, 1999.

O'Shea, James, *Prince of Swindlers: John Sadleir MP 1813–1856*, Dublin: Geography, 1999.

Perry, Leanne, *Spring Heeled Jack: Fiction Based on Fact*, http://www.casebook.org/dissertations/ripperoo-spring.html.

Power, Patrick C., *History of Waterford City and County*, Dungarvan: de Paor, 1998.

Rees, Alwyn and Brinley Rees, *Celtic Heritage. Ancient Tradition in Ireland and Wales*, London: Thames and Hudson, 1998.

Rees, Jim, "Maritime Wicklow (Part 1)", *Wicklow Historical Society Journal*, Vol. 2, No. 5, July 1999.

Sweeney, Tony, *The Aga Khan and His Family*, http://www.agakhanstuds.com/history.

Vere-Hodge, H.S., *Sir Andrew Judde*, Tonbridge school.

Villiers-Tuthill, Kathleen, *Beyond the Twelve Bens. A History of Clifden and District 1860–1923*, Galway: Connemara Girl, 2000.

Villiers-Tuthill, Kathleen, *History of Kylemore Castle & Abbey*, Galway: Kylemore Abbey, 2002.

Primary Newspaper Sources

The Freeman's Journal

The Irish Field

The Irish Independent

The Irish Times

The Limerick Leader

The London Daily Telegraph

Scottish Sport

Sport

The Times (London)

The Wicklow People

The Waterford Chronicle

The Waterford News

The Waterford Star

Acknowledgements

In writing any book, there are invariably many people to thank as the ink begins to dry and the dust finally settles. I have endeavoured to acknowledge all those who have contributed to this book and I apologise in advance if I have accidentally omitted anyone. First and foremost, this book could not have been undertaken without the generous and constant support of my parents Tom and Rosemary. Their enthusiasm, patience and assistance was particularly invaluable in helping trace Peter O'Connor's ancestry and carry out painstaking searches for deeds, birth certificates and other essential data. Other family members and relations also made significant contributions, none more so than the late Kathleen O'Connor (the wife of Arthur O'Connor) who sadly passed away before this book was completed. Felicity O'Connor and Hilary Powell contributed several photos. A posthumous thanks also to the late Noel Judd of Glenageary for sharing his detailed knowledge of the Judd family ancestry. This book has not just been written for those who love sport, but also for the extended O'Connor family, many of whom have unknowingly contributed to the story of Peter O'Connor. I hope they enjoy discovering his life story as much as I have.

I would particularly like to thank the following: Dr Karl Lennartz and the staff at the Cologne Sport Hochshule for their hospitality and access to their marvelous archives and library; Liam Ó Donnchú and the staff at Lár na Páirce in Thurles for access to their Peter O'Connor Archive; Patricia Burdick of the Colby College Special Collections, Maine, US for help in tracing a rare James B.

Connolly article; Tom Hunt of Mullingar who was extremely help-
ful in helping to piece together O'Connor's time in his town; Ken
Hannigan of the National Archive who drew my attention to the
fascinating correspondence that passed between Peter O'Connor
and Matthew Murtagh in 1905; His Majesty King Constantine who
gave permission to reproduce a photograph taken by his uncle
Prince George in 1906; Bob Tisdall who generously shared some of
his memories of the 1932 Los Angeles Olympics over the phone
from Australia. Were it not for the encouragement of Dr Ron Cal-
lan of UCD telling me to go away and write, this book might never
have materialised.

Many others made contributions to this book which I greatly
appreciate: in Waterford city and county, Bernard Colclough, Mrs
Eilean O'Neill (née Gough), Tom Kiersey Solr., Maurice Keller
Solr., Mrs Anne Coghlan, Mrs Casey, Eamonn McEneaney (Waterford Treasures), the De La Salle Brothers (Newtown), Danny
McGrath (Cappoquin), Richard Raher (Tramore), Danny and
Louie Kirwan (Kilmacthomas) and Niall Quigley Solr. (Carrick-
on-Suir). In Wicklow, Claire and Ann Maguire, Bridget Flannery
and Brendan Flynn of Wicklow Golf Club. Thanks also to Tom
Connolly (Clifden), James Healy and Tom Kenny (Galway), Con
Power (Mallow) and Elizabeth Clifford of the Lough Gur Historical Society. In Dublin, many thanks to Mercedes O'Flaherty for
her expertise in all things canine, Gerry Murtagh and Anne
Hickey for reading some early transcripts and offering much useful and constructive advice; and the members of the Hibernian
Athletic Historical Association for their role in organising the cen-
tenary celebration of O'Connor's world record in 2001. I wish to
thank the following institutions and their staff: in Dublin, the National Library, the National Archive, University College Dublin
Library, Deansgrange Library, The Law Society of Ireland (Blackhall Place), The Croke Park Museum, The Church Representative
Body Records (Churchtown), The Religious Society of Friends,
Swanbrook House (keepers of Quaker records), The Register of
Deeds, Henrietta St and Joyce House, Westland Roe; the public
libraries of Waterford City, Wicklow Town and Limerick City; the

British Newspaper Library at Colindale, The Guildhall, London, The Barrow-in-Furness Archive in Cumberland, Random House, Fox Studios and Ian Stringfellow of Top Flite UK. Every effort has been made to establish copyright for the photographs contained in this book. Equally, I have endeavoured to be as accurate as possible in documenting this relatively unknown period in Irish sporting history. I have tried as much as possible to cite all my sources and avoid errors. If any minor errors or omissions remain, I will be happy to rectify them in future editions.

A special thanks to my agent Jonathan Williams for introducing me to the exceptional team of David Givens and Brian Langan at The Liffey Press. Edmund Ross and Claire Durkin, artists and photographers, showed great expertise in the restoration of many of the rare photographs in this book. Elizabeth MacAuley, my copy editor, gave close and insightful readings of the text and she and her husband Ian were a pleasure to work with. In the three years it took to bring this book to its completion, many friends provided plenty of encouragement, support and welcome distraction. In Dublin, Rob Murtagh, Paul Lowry, Mark Heidenfeld, Frank and (the late) Barry Cunnane, Alan White, Alex Baburin and Gavin Wall, in Munich Erik Schmittel, e in Italia i miei cari amici padovani Carlo Rossi, Narciso Marigo, Federico Manca, Erald Dervishi ed il professore Alessandro Bordin. Grazie a tutti per la vostra amicizia e se vedemmo in giro prestin!

About the Author

Photo: Gerry Graham

Mark Quinn, born in Dublin, read English and Italian and subsequently graduated with an MA in Modern American Literature from University College Dublin. He currently works as a National Tour Guide and is also an International Master of Chess, having represented Ireland at four Chess Olympiads, in Russia, Armenia, Turkey and Slovenia. As the great-grandson of Peter O'Connor, he had access to previously undisclosed family papers, photographs and memorabilia in writing this biography.

Index